FROM HURONIA TO WENDAKES

New Directions in Native American Studies
Colin G. Calloway and K. Tsianina Lomawaima, General Editors

From Huronia to Wendakes

ADVERSITY, MIGRATIONS, AND RESILIENCE, 1650–1900

Edited by

THOMAS PEACE AND KATHRYN MAGEE LABELLE

Foreword by

CHIEF JANITH ENGLISH, WYANDOT NATION OF KANSAS

UNIVERSITY OF OKLAHOMA PRESS : NORMAN

Library of Congress Cataloging-in-Publication Data

Names: Peace, Thomas, 1980– editor. | Labelle, Kathryn Magee, 1983– editor.
Title: From Huronia to Wendakes : adversity, migrations, and resilience, 1650–1900 /
    edited by Thomas Peace and Kathryn Magee Labelle ; foreword by Janith English,
    Wyandot Nation of Kansas.
Description: First edition. | Norman, OK : University of Oklahoma Press, [2016] |
    Includes index.
Identifiers: LCCN 2016004748 | ISBN 978-0-8061-5535-7 (hardcover : alk. Paper)
Subjects: LCSH: Wyandot Indians—History. | Wyandot Indians—Government
    relations.
Classification: LCC E99.H9 F76 2016 | DDC 973.04/97555—dc23
LC record available at https://lccn.loc.gov/2016004748

From Huronia to Wendakes: Adversity, Migrations, and Resilience, 1650–1900 is Volume 15 in the
New Directions in Native American Studies series.

The paper in this book meets the guidelines for permanence and durability of the Committee on
Production Guidelines for Book Longevity of the Council on Library Resources, Inc. ∞

1   2   3   4   5   6   7   8   9   10

Contents

Illustrations

Figures

Maps

Foreword

REFLECTIONS FROM CHIEF JANITH ENGLISH,
WYANDOT NATION OF KANSAS

To the amazing scholars who have felt such a strong connection with Our Ancestors that they dedicated the time and scholarship necessary to offer new perspectives honoring the history and culture of the Wendat People: may your work be read by many; and may it inspire others to build on a foundation of understanding and respect for the processes that lead to disruption and renewal. It is our hope that the experiences of Our Ancestors might help identify wise and respectful responses to the constant changes taking place throughout the world today. Our people are grateful for your contributions to the understanding of our past and our hope for the future.

As this project developed, the authors addressed some of my concerns related to the retelling of the complex stories of culturally diverse Indigenous Nations. The static memorization of facts, linear thought, lack of multidisciplinary input, and, most of all, failure to consider the historical context of events have led in the past to an educational climate in which scholars jealously guarded their precious thoughts and conclusions like an eagle defends its nest. Collegiality was the exception rather than the norm, and the survival-oriented "publish or perish" seemed to be the mantra of academics. However, this book has shattered the paradigm of dedication to praxis rather than process.

The story of the centuries-long challenge for the survival of the people of the international Wendat Confederacy is a challenging and intricate one. To tell it requires a lens wide enough to include the perspective of people dedicated to raising children who appreciate interconnectedness and interdependence over power and control. Their stories will appear, like the unpredictable meanderings of the rivers, ever changing. We hope that these stories will be meaningful for diverse people facing contemporary challenges in today's world.

The authors' willingness to listen respectfully to the Wendat people stimulated a curiosity to know more about our Our People. Even more importantly, their work on this project has facilitated healing through the respectful climate of sharing ancient stories of unmet expectations. The level of academic achievement and self-knowledge displayed by this team of authors left no trace of the aloof condescension sometimes displayed toward Indigenous people. Their approach provided an outlet for delightful and stimulating interchange. Though some of our oral history might be occasionally sprinkled with a pinch of misinformation after centuries of retelling, it was always welcomed and thoughtfully received. Most importantly, the work constantly took seemingly puzzling and isolated facts and illuminated them in a broader context. As always, these discoveries have energized and stimulated our people to collect and share the widely scattered information that may lead to a more comprehensive understanding of our culture and heritage.

When I worked in behavioral health nursing, I tried to always remember the old saying, "Never make a person bleed until you can make the commitment to stand beside him and help him heal." We hope that the retelling of painful events and difficult processes described in this book might result in further examination of the multigenerational grief and depression that often accompany the people of diaspora. The authors have demonstrated the willingness and ability to treat our painful subjects with sensitivity and grace. If I were to pick one word to describe the essence of this project, it would be respect. For that, we extend our gratitude. The authors already have our trust.

Acknowledgments

The plans for this project were initially hatched on a clear summer's day in Ottawa in 2007. We had just sunk our teeth into our dissertation research at Library and Archives Canada (LAC). Kathryn had begun to reevaluate seventeenth-century Wendat history with an eye toward understanding the Wendat dispersal in the 1640s and 1650s, while Tom had embarked on a regional and comparative study of Mi'kmaw and Wendat experiences of the British conquest of New France. We had gathered to discuss our experiences as relatively new scholars of Wendat history.

In the intervening years, these seeds have sprouted, both in our work as individuals and by sharing and learning from colleagues, friends, and present-day members of Wendat, Wyandot, and Wyandotte Nations. There are many people without whom this book would have never materialized. In addition to the chapter contributors, members of the present-day Wendat, Wyandot, and Wyandotte Nations have been integral to this process. Chief Janith English and John Nichols (Wyandot Nation of Kansas); Jonathan Lainey and Linda Sioui (Nation huronne-wendat); Sallie Cotter Andrews and Beverlee Pettit (Wyandot Nation of Oklahoma); and Judith Kukowski (Wyandot of Anderdon Nation) have volunteered their time and insight, for which we are forever grateful. In addition, the editors would like to give special thanks to Carolyn Podruchny for her continuous support and enthusiasm. Carolyn has deeply shaped both of our scholarship and is considered a close mentor and friend. In fact, it was Carolyn's abiding interest in our research that led to our meeting at LAC in 2007.

This project could not have come together without significant institutional support. To this end Colin Calloway, Colin Coates, and Sabrina Kehoe were instrumental in securing funding opportunities for the authors to collaborate. We are grateful for institutional assistance from the Social Sciences and Humanities Research Council, whose postdoctoral fellowships gave us the time to put this project together. The University of Saskatchewan's Interdisciplinary Center for Culture and Creativity (ICCC) fellowship enabled us to edit the book together, writing the introduction and conclusion. Finally, we would like to thank the staff at the University of Oklahoma Press, specifically Tom Jonas, Thomas Krause, Lori Rider, Sarah Smith, and Alessandra Jacobi Tamulevich, as well as the series editors Colin G. Calloway and K. Tsianiana Lomawaima, for all of the hard work they have put into making this book a physical reality.

Tom would like to thank his family: Susan and Adrienne for their love, support, and especially their flexibility as this project moved through its final stages, and Oliver, who arrived as we put the finishing touches on this manuscript. Similarly, Kathryn would like to thank her husband, Maurice Labelle Jr., her two sons, Ézekiel and Enaïs, and her adopted Wendat and Wyandot family for all their encouragement throughout this project.

Thomas Peace
Kathryn Magee Labelle

FROM HURONIA TO WENDAKES

Introduction

Kathryn Magee Labelle and Thomas Peace

Wendake. Simply defined it means "where the Wendats live."[1] Over the past four centuries, this word has referred to many places, spread over hundreds of miles. Before the arrival of Europeans, the ancestors of the Wendats lived along the northern shores of the lower Great Lakes and the Saint Lawrence River. By the fifteenth century these peoples had organized their villages into a confederacy. Wendat Confederates lived in the area known today as central Ontario, between the southern shores of Georgian Bay and Lake Simcoe. During the time period in which this book begins—the late 1640s—the Wendats had begun to move away from this geographic space. Some went east and others west to create a number of new Wendakes. Not all of these Wendakes lasted, and some, through devices such as the Christmastime hymn "The Huron Carol" or the 1980s novel and 1990s film *Black Robe,* have been appropriated and contested. Importantly, though, today Wendake continues in the Canadian provinces of Quebec and Ontario and the American states of Michigan, Oklahoma, and Kansas. For all of these societies, however, historic Wendake Ehen, known more commonly to non-Wendats as Huronia, continues to resonate on the shores of Georgian Bay as a place of cultural and historic importance.[2]

The peoples of Wendake Ehen (the seventeenth-century Wendat Confederacy) comprised four tribes: the Attignaouantan ("bear"), Attingneenongnahac ("cord"), Arendaronnon ("rock"), and Tahontaenrat ("deer").[3] Cutting across the tribal divisions were eight clans: Turtle, Wolf, Bear, Beaver, Deer, Hawk, Fox, and Sturgeon or Loon.[4] The clans structured Wendat political

3

and social life, linking clan segments from different villages and across tribal lines.[5] The eighteen to twenty-five enclosed villages that made up Wendake Ehen each had a population of about 1,000 people.[6] According to archaeologist Gary Warrick, between 28,000 and 30,000 people called this place home.[7]

The Wendats of Wendake Ehen were well situated at the center of at least four important trading networks.[8] Wendat villages were accessible from Lake Ontario via the Humber River, from the Ottawa Valley via the Mattawa and French Rivers, and from the north and west via Lake Huron. Wendats took advantage of this central space, developing a robust reputation as linchpin diplomats and traders within the region. Of particular note was the Anishinaabe-Wendat alliance—a coalition between the Wendat Confederacy and their Anishinaabe neighbors (the Nippising, Ottawa, Ojibwe, and Algonkin). Although trade in Wendat corn and Anishinaabe wild game formed the core of this relationship, by the time of European contact the coalition had evolved into a dynamic and powerful political machine.

With the arrival of French explorers and settlers, the Wendats continued their role as middlemen and cultural brokers within the region. These activities were based out of the place called Quebec by Europeans but known to the Wendats as the confluence of the Oria'enrak and Lada8anna Rivers (known today as the Saint Charles and Saint Lawrence Rivers).[9] The relationship between the two peoples grew rapidly in its early years, but it was not until after the French returned in the early 1630s—after being expelled from the Lada8anna Valley by the English Kirke brothers in 1629—that French and Wendat interaction began to have serious consequences. The biggest difference when the French returned was that Jesuits had replaced Recollet missionaries. The Jesuits were an important force among the Wendats, serving as both religious and economic intermediaries in Wendake Ehen and also at Lorette and Detroit during the eighteenth century. These missionaries sought to convert Wendat souls and lubricate the expanding trade in furs. Within two decades their presence in Wendat society created divisions within the Confederacy. When these growing political and religious differences combined with intensifying warfare and a series of lethal epidemics and droughts, the Wendat population was drastically reduced.

The Wendats responded to these influences by leaving their villages and moving away from Wendake Ehen. In 1649 the Haudenosaunees executed a series of successful military campaigns against the Wendats, leading the Confederacy to reevaluate the security of its villages. After several councils and much discussion, the Wendat Confederates agreed to leave the Wendake mainland and relocate to Gahoendoe Island, approximately a day's paddle from their villages and three miles from the mainland. This was only a temporary solution, however. Haudenosaunee attacks still threatened the islanders, and drought created starvation and desperate circumstances. Once again the Wendats held councils and confirmed a strategy of relocation. Although some ventured out independently, joining Anishinaabe and Haudenosaunee communities, the majority of surviving Wendats took two paths. One group traveled east to Quebec. Over the course of the next fifty years they settled in several locations, finally establishing themselves in 1697 at Jeune-Lorette. The second group traveled west toward Michilimackinac, a nascent fur trade post located at the confluence of Lakes Huron, Michigan, and Superior. Like their eastern counterparts, they occupied several village sites on the shores of all three lakes before establishing themselves at Michilimackinac in 1671. They stayed there for three decades before deciding to relocate to Detroit in 1701. Some Wendats remained in the Detroit area after this migration, while others continued to move and began to identify themselves as Wyandot by the mid-eighteenth century. They voluntarily established themselves at Upper Sandusky, Ohio, in the 1730s but were forced to relocate to Kansas City, Kansas, in 1843 and Wyandotte, Oklahoma, in 1867. Today, Wendat societies continue to thrive in both Canada and the United States. They are the Nation huronne-wendat, whose members live in the present-day province of Quebec; the Wyandot of Anderdon Nation, whose members live on either side of the Detroit River in Michigan and Ontario; the Wyandot Nation of Kansas in the present-day state of Kansas; and the Wyandotte Nation of Oklahoma in the present-day state of Oklahoma. In 1999 the chiefs of all four nations signed a declaration reinstating a modern confederacy agreement.

The three and a half centuries of migration, resilience, and survival in the face of this separation are important components to understanding Wendat history. Much like the history of the Shawnees, Anishinaabeg, and Dakotas, this cycle of migration and resettlement situates Wendat histories as intrinsically transnational and deeply linked to the North American experience. Similar to these other groups, Wendat peoples moved across the continent, adapting to new circumstances and new peoples in ways that reflected their past. Rather than seeing these migrations as signs of defeat and destruction, new research on the Wendats and other Indigenous societies demonstrates how Indigenous peoples have used migration as a form of cultural resistance and adaption in the wake of colonial encounters.[10]

. . .

The story of the Wendats after their dispersal is a popular one—a result, we suspect, of the ubiquity of the destruction narrative. The Hurons (to use the French term that dominates descriptions of these people in the colonial literature and much of the historiography) play a prominent role in North American popular culture, particularly in literature. Their depiction in stories such as *The Last of the Mohicans, Black Robe,* and *The Orenda* are not benign. The treatment of the Wendats by novelists has improved over time: Joseph Boyden's recent novel *The Orenda* is hardly comparable to James Fenimore Cooper's mid-nineteenth-century "classic" *Last of the Mohicans.* But the predicted fate of the Hurons remains the same: they are a people destined for destruction. A Huron identity, these stories suggest, is something that could only exist in the past.[11]

Though these authors emphasize Wendat demise in the mid-seventeenth century, this narrative trope is a core component of a broader set of early to mid-nineteenth-century cultural practices that aimed to remove Indigenous peoples and cultures from North American life. These narratives work toward what Ojibwe historian Jean O'Brien describes as the process through which settler societies "convinced themselves that Indians . . . had become extinct even though they remained as Indian people—and do so to this day."[12] Cherokee novelist Thomas King uses the evocative phrase "Dead Indians" to refer to this ongoing process.[13] Relevant nineteenth-century examples of such Dead Indians can be found in Cooper's *Last of the Mohicans,* or, more directly related to this book, in Antoine Plamondon's well-known 1838 portrait of the Wendat artist Zacharie Vincent, *Le Dernier Huron* (The Last Huron), which likewise inspired François Xavier Garneau's well-known nineteenth-century poem by the same name.[14] The historiographical trajectory of Wendat pasts cannot be disconnected from this broader social and political phenomenon, which sought to create dead and vanishing Indians while simultaneously recrafting what are increasingly considered "the false histories of European discovery" to favor the achievements of Euro-American settler societies.[15] Of course, as the pages that follow amply illustrate, neither Zacharie Vincent nor any of his contemporaries were in fact the last of the Wendats. Nor did they want to be. While Cooper and Plamondon (and plenty of historians) were busy trying to write and paint the Wendats out of existence,

Vincent and many other Wendats, such as Peter Dooyentate Clarke, a nineteenth-century cultural keeper from the Wyandot of Anderdon Nation, were actively asserting their Wendat identities.[16] Collectively, our research has tried to bring some of these postmigration stories into broader historiographical and public discussions about North America's pasts.

· · ·

Despite the popular narratives of Wendat removal, destruction, and assimilation, Wendat peoples have in fact held prominent roles during key moments in North American history. Wendats actively shaped North American colonial history from the first meetings with Europeans to conflicts such as the Seven Years' War, the American Revolution, the War of 1812, and the American Civil War. Scholars have acknowledged the Wendats' influence, weaving them into larger narratives of European-Native encounters, colonialism, and conquest.[17] Work on the Wendats has furthered our understanding of their specific belief systems, language, economies, migrations, diplomacy, and politics.[18] Indeed, coinciding with a revisioning of Indigenous history and the rise of social history in the 1960s, seventeenth-century Wendats took on critical importance for scholarly case studies examining gender roles, agency, and ethnohistorical methods. Notwithstanding the importance of these key and often groundbreaking contributions, few scholars have taken up the task of building on these works, extending the study of these people into the eighteenth and nineteenth centuries.[19] Scholarship on the Wendats, therefore, though not necessarily sharing nineteenth-century racist sentiments, has furthered the impression of Wendat destruction in the seventeenth century.

At its heart, *From Huronia to Wendakes* responds to this historiographical context. This book brings together the work of emerging scholars studying Wendat communities in the post-1650 era. Each chapter is based on graduate school projects—PhD dissertations—produced within the last decade, exemplifying some of the most recent scholarship in the field. Taken collectively and alongside the important work being conducted within present-day Wendat communities, our doctoral studies suggest that it is time to expand Wendat scholarship from the earlier works on Huronia to studies that more deeply consider a multitude of Wendakes. In contrast to past scholars of the Wendats, we have sought to provide a collaborative narrative that, by remaining attentive to place, balances the colonial biases of the primary sources with the experiences of Indigenous nations.

Our interpretations are the results of the historical context in which we live and work. Since the 1960s, developments in the history of Indigenous peoples in North America have paralleled broader social and political change. The groundbreaking work of Elizabeth Tooker, Conrad Heidenreich, Bruce Trigger, and others in the 1960s and 1970s followed the civil rights era, the American Indian Movement, and, in Canada, the release and reaction to the 1969 White Paper on the abolition of the Indian Act. These milestones in North American history triggered significant changes in Canadian and American jurisprudence regarding Indigenous peoples. The Supreme Court of Canada decided a series of court cases beginning with *Calder v. Attorney General of British Columbia* in 1973 and continuing with the 2014 ruling in *Tsilhqot'in Nation v. British Columbia*, which over time have acknowledged, recognized, and refined legal definitions of Aboriginal title and rights. In the United States during the 1970s and early 1980s, the Alaska Native Claims Settlement Act, Rhode Island Claims Settlement, and Maine Indian Claims Settlement Acts developed from similar legal arguments about Indigenous rights, spearheading related pieces of legislation. For US scholars this legal context facilitated the creation of the 1990 Native American Graves Protection and Repatriation Act (NAGPRA), a piece of legislation that has helped shape the evolution of historiographical ethics related to the study of Indigenous peoples. In Canada, the overlap between politics, historiography, and the law has led to the important findings and recommendations of the Royal Commission on Aboriginal Peoples in 1996, and more recently the Truth and Reconciliation Commission of Canada, both of which provide a foundation for a new relationship between the Canadian state, Canadians, and First Nations.

Both politically and historiographically, the 1990s were a pivotal decade for the Wendats. In 1990 the Supreme Court of Canada ruled in favor of the Nation huronne-wendat in *R. v. Sioui*. This case paralleled the pivotal work of Georges Sioui, who, in his book *Pour une autohistoire amérindienne,* called for the production of Indigenous history by Indigenous historians, a perspective strongly held by the council at Wendake. Further, he outlined the importance of the "Great Circle of Life" to the Wendat people and their quest to maintain relationships with all living things. Cultural pride and a desire to revise previous interpretations about the decimation of his ancestors drove Sioui to present and publish subsequent histories for not only his and the other Wendat nations, but also the public at large. Since then, other Wendat, Wyandot, Wyandotte scholars working in academia, such as Clifford Trafzer, Jonathan Lainey, and Linda Sioui, have made similar contributions to our understanding of Wendat societies and histories.[20] Taken together, and alongside broader Indigenous activism across North America, these trends represent part of a Wendat renewal. In 1999 Wendat nations from Quebec, Ontario, Michigan, Kansas, and Oklahoma came together in south-central Ontario to bury the bones of their ancestors and restore the Wendat Confederacy. It is in this historical context that our research began, inspiring projects focused on survival rather than demise.

Though we think our work makes an important intervention in the historiographical canon related to Wendat pasts, our ideas have likewise been deeply shaped by important developments in the fields of Indigenous studies and history. As academia has slowly responded to Indigenous critiques related to scholarly practices, and as Indigenous scholars have increasingly shaped the scholarly agenda, Native North American history has begun to incorporate new themes revolving around questions of identity, transnationalism, environment, and communities (among many others). Methodological approaches have also expanded, acknowledging ethnohistorical inquiry as a basic part of research on Indigenous communities and giving more weight to oral history and, more importantly, autohistory.[21] Building on the important works of scholars who study Native diasporas and migration, such as Kathleen Duval, Stephen Warren, Michael Witgen, Gregory Smithers, and Brooke Newman, our collection offers another example of how Indigenous history can be approached from within its own historical and cultural context, not that imposed by the definitions of imperial officials who claimed Indigenous spaces through their writing and map-making.[22] Indigenous worldviews and community-based perspectives are at the heart of these interpretations, as is the idea that "movement and dispersal were integral components to their culture."[23] Our book gives credence to these current developments, with the hope that the chapters that follow will encourage similar methodologies and questions.

• • •

Taken together, each chapter in this book works toward several common goals. First, we seek to explore themes of migration, diaspora, and cultural change in a transnational environment. Indigenous peoples across North America participated in social, political, and economic networks that often excluded European newcomers and were therefore unrecorded. As we develop better understandings of these poorly documented contexts through listening to Indigenous oral traditions and historians, as well as listening more attentively and critically to traditional archaeological and written sources, our view of North America's past shifts to better capture the experiences of the people living at the time. Consequently, we hope that the following chapters can be applied to reorient school curriculums and postsecondary lectures concerning Indigenous, Canadian, and American history, providing educators with tangible examples of Indigenous survival and rejuvenation that are often overlooked in current classroom lessons and textbooks.

In addition to these historiographical aspirations, we aim for a methodological intervention in terms of Wendat studies. Historical research is often an independent task. But to understand the Wendats after 1650—a people whose communities are spread over hundreds of miles and fall within diverse political jurisdictions and contexts—collaborative research is absolutely necessary. We have done this in two ways. First, our group of diverse scholars, who until now have worked independently from each other on Wendat, Wyandot, and Wyandotte histories, have built a collaborative research network, broadening our understanding of Indigenous history between the seventeenth and nineteenth centuries and fostering opportunities for future academic collaboration. Second, we have approached and worked with seven representatives of the emerging modern Wendat Confederacy to gain insight and guidance from tribal historians, archivists, elders, and members of the involved nations. Although in most cases we worked through the structures of tribal governments in approaching representatives to read and comment on our work, when this was impossible due to already stretched resources, we asked friends and colleagues from these nations to serve in this role. In all cases, their comments mark neither the official opinion of tribal governments nor their sanction; rather, taken together, these chapters and the community's commentary on them seek to bridge a gap between academic and Wendat, Wyandot, and Wyandotte knowledge about the past. In taking this approach, this book has helped build relationships among the authors and members of the communities we have studied and written about. We hope that this book will lay a path to a new scholarly beginning, supporting and encouraging collaborative projects and promoting similarly spirited research practices among Canadian, American, and Indigenous historians in the future.[24]

Delivered in a narrative style, the chapters that follow encapsulate both the connections and diversity of these dispersed people. The book expands the historiography of the Wendats beyond 1650, helping us understand how individual communities survived in the years following their dispersal from their homeland. In the first chapter Kathryn Magee Labelle looks at the relocation of six thousand Wendat refugees to Gahoendoe Island in 1650. Labelle emphasizes the influence of women in Wendat decision making whenever Haudenosaunee attacks forced the communities to move. She argues that rather than being forcibly removed and uncontrollably dispersed, the Wendats carefully deliberated over their future using customary decision-making practices. Although they ultimately had to abandon their homeland, this decision was just as much about crop failure caused by drought as any of the additional factors that put pressure on their society.

Andrew Sturtevant's research in chapter 2 continues to trace the western Wendat communities as they migrated down to Detroit at the turn of the eighteenth century and then to Sandusky in the 1730s. Rather than seeing the foundation of Sandusky as evidence of discord and division within Wendat society, Sturtevant suggests that the creation of new settlements was part of an overarching Wendat strategy to create a new landscape that radiated from the central community at Detroit into the Ohio Valley. This strategy allowed the Wendats to both take advantage of new resources and expand their influence. Instead of a story of Wendat division and dysfunction, therefore, the purported "defection" of a portion of the Wendat community is seen rather as testimony to the enduring and exclusive ethnic identity linking the Wendats together.

In chapter 3 Thomas Peace draws similar conclusions of cultural resilience and innovation in the east by following the lives of two Wendat men from Jeune-Lorette, André Otehiondi and Louis Vincent Sawatanen. Peace examines Wendat strategies for ensuring the survival of a community surrounded by French villagers and less than ten miles from the center of France's imperial administration. He focuses on the long-distance political, economic, and social networks individual Wendats developed with neighboring Indigenous and non-Indigenous communities, as well as the more local adaptations the community made to ensure they maintained a prominent place in the colonial world developing around them. Capitalizing on their close proximity to Quebec, the Wendats carefully chose how they would interact with outsiders. Adopting this strategy gave the Wendats at Lorette greater political weight than their small population—of only about 150 people—would have otherwise allowed.

In chapter 4 Michael Cox builds on the themes of Wendat interaction with colonial forces and extends them to his work on the Sandusky Wyandot. Focusing specifically on the introduction of Protestantism in this community,

Cox demonstrates how these people embraced syncretic religious practices that balanced Protestant theology with more traditional Wendat and Catholic religious practices. Although the community did not universally embrace Protestantism, Cox emphasizes the important groundwork this period played in cultivating a place for Protestantism within Wyandot society.

Chapter 5 is similarly focused, but instead of addressing religion, Brian Gettler demonstrates the extent to which Jeune-Lorette came to be integrated in both local and international commercial networks. He charts how, over the course of the nineteenth and early twentieth centuries, the Wendats at Jeune-Lorette developed a thriving heterogeneous economy. In contrast to the handful of studies that have analyzed the community's economy during this period, Gettler addresses not only the production of moccasins and snowshoes, still signature Wendat commodities today, but also the role community-based consumption and finance played in Jeune-Lorette's economic development.

Finally, in chapter 6 Annette de Stecher provides a nuanced study of the Lord Elgin trays. These birch bark trays were made in Jeune-Lorette to commemorate a meeting between Wendat leaders and the Canadian governor general. De Stecher provides a nuanced interpretation of the interwoven nature of Wendat material culture and colonialism. She argues that the public performance of ceremonial events based in Indigenous diplomatic traditions was a means by which the Wendats maintained their identity as a nation with distinct political structure and authority and asserted both their physical presence in the region and their role in Indigenous and settler community networks. These two moose hair–embroidered bark trays acquired by Governor General Lord Elgin and his wife, examples of Jeune-Lorette's successful artisan industry, demonstrate the diplomatic role such artwork also played.

The book's conclusion reflects on the process of engaging with members of the Wendat, Wyandot, and Wyandotte Nations as we transformed our doctoral research into these chapters. The commentaries, cited extensively in the conclusion and reproduced in full on the website *Active History,* are not representative of these nations as a whole but rather reflect the perspectives of respected members of their communities.[25] Their feedback goes beyond the scope of any one essay. These responses, written by Wendat experts on their own history, provide keen insight and expand on many of the themes developed by the authors. They look to future projects and initiatives that can further Wendat culture and heritage for generations to come. We hope that this section of the book will help set an agenda for future community-based research on Wendat history.

Wendat, Wyandot, and Wyandotte history, like all histories and people, is fluid and ever changing. Interpretations of the 1960s and 1980s are not the same as those of the present day, just as the nineteenth-century Wendats are not the same as their seventeenth-century ancestors. With this in mind, the intent of this book is to develop and explore new questions that tell the story of how the communities that once made up the Wendat Confederacy evolved and changed over the centuries that followed their dispersal from Wendake Ehen.

NOTES

1. "Wendake" is primarily used as a noun to refer to the Wendat homeland on the shores of Georgian Bay or to their present-day community, which is often referred to in this book by its earlier name: Jeune-Lorette, Quebec. Here we use the word loosely, drawing on its broader meaning: "where the Wendat live." See Jean Poirier, *La Toponymie des Hurons-Wendats* (Québec: Commission de Toponymie du Québec, 2001), 43.

2. We are grateful to Linda Sioui for teaching us this terminology.

3. There may have also been a fifth group, the Ataronchronon ("marsh"), but their relationship to the confederacy is uncertain. Bruce Trigger suggests that they may have been part of the Attignaouantan. See Bruce Trigger, *The Children of Aataentsic: A History of the Huron People to 1660* (Montreal: McGill–Queen's University Press, 1976), vol. 1: 30.

4. Conrad Heidenreich, "Huron," in *The Handbook of North American Indians,* vol. 15, ed. Bruce Trigger (Washington, DC: Smithsonian Institute, 1978), 371.

5. Trigger, *Children of Aataentsic,* 1:54–55.

6. Heidenreich, "Huron," 288; Trigger, *Children of Aataentsic,* 1:32.

7. Gary Warrick, *A Population History of the Huron-Petun, A.D. 500–1650* (Cambridge: Cambridge University Press, 2008), 153.

8. Trigger, *Children of Aataentsic,* 1:208–14, 236–45.

9. Unless otherwise noted, this toponomy comes from Poirier, *Toponymie des Hurons-Wendats.* See 28 and 29 for Lada8anna and 31 and 32 for Oria'enrak.

10. See, for example, Stephen Warren, *The Worlds the Shawnees Made: Migration and Violence in Early America* (Chapel Hill: University of North Carolina Press, 2014); Michael Witgen, *Infinity of Nations: How the Native New World Shaped Early North America* (Philadelphia: University of Pennsylvania Press, 2013).

11. James Fenimore Cooper, *The Last of the Mohicans* (Philadelphia: H. C. Carey and I. Lea, 1826); Brian Moore, *Black Robe* (New York: Dutton, 1985); Joseph Boyden, *Orenda* (Toronto: Penguin Canada, 2013).

12. Jean O'Brien, *Firsting and Lasting: Writing Indians Out of Existence in New England* (Minneapolis: University of Minnesota Press, 2010), xii.

13. Thomas King, *The Inconvenient Indian: A Curious Account of Native People in North America* (Toronto: Anchor Canada, 2012), 53–54.

14. François-Xavier Garneau, "Le dernier huron," in *Traverse les vents* (1840), Archives du Conseil de la Nation huronne-wendat (ACNHW), Collection François Vincent, cartable C-J.

15. The terminology in this sentence is borrowed from King, *Inconvenient Indian*, and Witgen, *Infinity of Nations*.

16. Peter Dooyentate Clarke, *Origin and Traditional History of the Wyandotts and Sketches of Other Indian Tribes of North America, True Traditional Stories of Tecumseh and His League in the Years 1811 and 1812* (Toronto: Hunter, Rose, 1870). For a good summary of Zacharie Vincent's life and art, see Louise Vigneault and Isabelle Masse, "Les autoreprésentations de l'artiste huron-wendat Zacharie Vincent (1815–1886): Icons d'une gloire politique et spirituelle," *Journal of Canadian Art History* 32, no. 2 (2011): 41–73. Louise Vigneault has also published an online book, *Zacharie Vincent: Life and Work*, through the University of Toronto's Art Canada Institute. It is available at http://www.aci-iac.ca/zacharie-vincent (accessed August 2015).

17. Daniel Richter, *Facing East from Indian Country: A Native History of Early America* (Cambridge, Mass.: Harvard University Press, 2003); Ian Steele, *Warpaths: The Invasion of North America* (New York: Oxford University Press, 1994); George T. Hunt, *The Wars of the Iroquois: A Study in Intertribal Trade Relations* (Madison: University of Wisconsin Press, 1940); Colin G. Calloway, *One Vast Winter Count: The Native American West before Lewis and Clark* (Lincoln: University of Nebraska Press, 2003); Alan Taylor, *The Divided Ground: Indians, Settlers and the Northern Borderland of the American Revolution* (New York: Knopf, 2006); Richard White, *The Middle Ground: Indians, Empires, and Republics in the Great Lakes Region, 1650–1815* (Cambridge, Mass.: Harvard University Press, 2003); Gilles Havard, *The Great Peace of Montreal of 1701: French-Native Diplomacy in the Seventeenth Century*, trans. Phyllis Arnoff and Howard Scott (Montreal and Kingston: McGill–Queen's University Press, 2001); Denys Delâge, *Le pays renversé: Amérindiens et Européens en Amérique du nord-est, 1600–1664* (Montreal: Boréal Express, 1985).

18. Elizabeth Tooker, *An Ethnography of the Huron Indians, 1615–1649* (Syracuse, N.Y.: Syracuse University Press, 1964); Bruce Trigger, *The Huron: Farmers of the North* (New York: Holt, Rinehart and Winston, 1969); Trigger, *Children of Aataentsic*; Conrad Heidenreich, *Huronia: A History and Geography of the Huron Indians, 1600–1650* (Toronto: McClelland and Stewart, 1971); Roger Carpenter, *The Renewed, the Destroyed, the Remade: The Three Thought Worlds of the Iroquois and the Huron, 1609–1650* (East Lansing: Michigan State University Press, 2004); Warrick, *Population History of the Huron-Petun*; Georges E. Sioui, *Huron-Wendat: The Heritage of the Circle* (Vancouver: University of British Columbia Press, 1999); Karen Anderson, *Chain Her by One Foot: The Subjugation of Native Women in Seventeenth-Century New France* (New York: Routledge, 1991); John L. Steckley, *Words of the Huron* (Waterloo: University of Wilfrid Laurier Press, 2007); Michael M. Pomedli, *Ethnophilosophical and Ethnolinguistic Perspectives on the Huron Indian Soul* (Lewiston, N.Y.:

Edwin Mellen, 1991); Arthur Edwards Jones, *"8ouendake Ehen" or Old Huronia* (Toronto: Fifth Report of the Bureau of Archives for the Province of Ontario, 1908).

19. Exceptions are Denis Vaugeois, ed., *Les Hurons de Lorette* (Quebec City: Les éditions du Septentrion, 1996); special volume on Wendake, *Recherches Amérindiennes au Québec* 30, no. 3 (2000); Alain Beaulieu, Stéphanie Béreau, and Jean Tanguay, *Les Wendats du Québec: Territoire, économie et identité, 1650–1930* (Quebec: Les Éditions GID, 2013).

20. Jonathan Lainey, *La "monnaie des sauvages": Les colliers de wampum d'hier à aujourd'hui* (Quebec City: Les éditions du Septentrion, 2004); Linda Sioui, *La réaffirmation de l'identité wendate/wyandotte à l'heure de la mondialisation* (Quebec: Les Éditions Hannenorak, 2012).

21. For articles discussing ethnohistory, see James Axtell, "The Ethnohistory of Early America: A Review Essay," *William and Mary Quarterly,* 3rd ser., 35, no. 1 (January 1978): 110–44; James Axtell, "Some Thoughts on the Ethnohistory of Missions," *Ethnohistory* 29, no. 1 (Winter 1982): 35–41; Henry S. Spalding, "The Ethnologic Value of the Jesuit Relations," *American Journal of Sociology* 34, no. 5 (March 1929): 882–89; William Fenton, "Review: Huronia: An Essay in Proper Ethnohistory," *American Anthropologist* 80, no. 4 (December 1978): 923–35; John R. Wunder, "Native American History, Ethnohistory, and Context," *Ethnohistory* 54, no. 4 (Fall 2007): 591–604; Daniel Richter, "Whose Indian History?" *William and Mary Quarterly,* 3rd ser., 50, no. 2 (April 1993): 379–93; Eric Hinderaker and Rebecca Horn, "Territorial Crossings: Histories and Historiographies of the Early Americas," *William and Mary Quarterly,* 3rd ser., 67, no. 3 (July 2010): 395–432; Anna J. Willow, "Cultivating Common Ground: Cultural Revitalization in Anishinaabe and Anthropological Discourse," *American Indian Quarterly* 34, no. 1 (Winter 2010): 33–60. For information on the use of Native American oral tradition, see Julie Cruikshank, *The Social Life of Stories: Narrative and Knowledge in the Yukon Territory* (Lincoln: University of Nebraska Press, 1998). For a discussion of autohistory, see Georges E. Sioui, *For an Amerindian Autohistory* (Montreal: McGill–Queen's University Press, 1992).

22. Kathleen Duval, *The Native Ground Indians and Colonists in the Heart of the Continent* (Philadelphia: University of Pennsylvania Press, 2006); Witgen, *Infinity of Nations;* Gregory Smithers and Brooke Newman, *Native Diasporas: Indigenous Identities and Settler Colonialism in the Americas* (Lincoln: University of Nebraska Press, 2014); Warren, *Worlds the Shawnees Made.*

23. Warren, *Worlds the Shawnees Made,* 24.

24. It should be noted that researchers are increasingly expected to consult and work with Indigenous communities from the very beginning of their projects.

25. Wendat responses to this book can be viewed at http://activehistory.ca/from-huronia-to-wendakes-wendat-responses/.

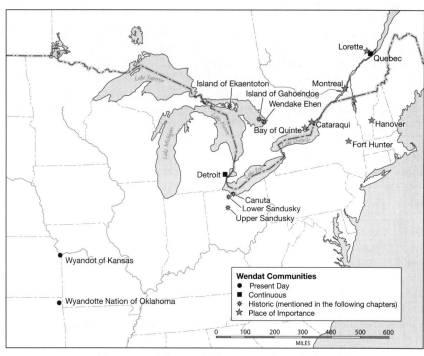

Map 0.1. Four Centuries of Wendakes. Map by Tom Jonas. Copyright © 2016 University of Oklahoma Press.

CHAPTER 1

"Like Wolves from the Woods"

GAHOENDOE ISLAND AND EARLY WENDAT
DISPERSAL STRATEGIES

Kathryn Magee Labelle

In the summer of 1648 the Wendat Confederacy faced a seemingly hopeless situation. Within less than a year the Haudenosaunees ("People of
the Longhouse") waged a series of raids to pillage several major villages,
leaving Wendats engulfed in a crisis of death and destruction.[1] Jesuit missionaries living within Wendake recorded the events with grief and despair. "The
country of the Hurons," they observed, "is seen to be in desolation; fifteen
villages have been abandoned, the people of each scattering where they could,—
in the woods and forests, on the lakes and rivers, and among the islands
most unknown to the enemy."[2] This language of "desolation," emphasizing
the "scattering" of traumatized Wendats, has fed historical interpretations of
this period in Wendat history for generations.

Scholars have both informed and perpetuated this tradition by continuing to promote a narrative of victimhood that pins the Wendats between
the "evil" Haudenosaunees, who pushed them to evacuate their homes "like
wolves from the woods,"[3] and the insightful Jesuits, who herded them like
sheep to relocation settlements.[4] With this narrative in mind, the Wendats
are often depicted as passive victims rather than independent instigators of
innovative relocation strategies. This is not to say that the Haudenosaunees
and Jesuits are irrelevant to the story, nor to assert that the Wendats were not
victims. Rather, it recognizes that there has been an overemphasis on these

aspects of their history. Scenes of Wendats scattering dominate the narrative and overshadow the Wendats' simultaneous attempts to maintain order and create solutions.

In April 1649 six thousand Wendat survivors convened at the mission of Sainte Marie (after successfully defending the mission from another Haudenosaunee attack) to discuss the most effective way to secure a plan for their future.[5] After hours of deliberation, the majority resolved to move to the island of Gahoendoe, located roughly three miles from the northernmost part of Wendake and the southern tip of Georgian Bay.[6] This was one of the Wendats' first major attempts at relocation, yet its importance in the process of dispersal has received little attention.[7] For the most part, the Gahoendoe experience has been used to reinforce the narrative of Wendat victimhood, marginalizing the significance of this migration by depicting it as a complete failure and a brief stopover in the much longer and geographically distant migrations later in the seventeenth century.

Consequently, this chapter seeks to unpack the Gahoendoe experience and reevaluate the established narrative of victimhood by highlighting moments of Wendat perseverance and agency in the immediate aftermath of the Haudenosaunee conquest. To refocus our attention, the chapter looks at the decision-making process that preceded the move *to* Gahoendoe in 1649, as well as the circumstances that pushed the Wendats to reconsider their choice a year later. How did Wendats negotiate their removal? What criteria informed these decisions?

Seventeenth-century Native North Americans functioned within a unique system of power structured by waterways.[8] By 1649 the Wendats had a well-established alliance with their Anishinaabe and French neighbors. Linked together by the French, Mattawa, Ottawa, and Saint Lawrence Rivers, these societies shared a complex network based on kinship and trade. The Wendats served as "middlemen" in this system, acquiring furs from the Anishinaabeg in exchange for corn, then providing the French with furs in exchange for European goods.[9]

Can the move to Gahoendoe be seen as a Wendat attempt to maintain their status as middlemen and cultural brokers in their Anishinaabe-French alliance? By understanding the island relocation as a continuation of Wendat ideas of place and power, can Gahoendoe be interpreted as an integral part of a calculated plan to overcome the military defeat by the Iroquois and keep a foothold in the geopolitical world of the Northeast? If so, does this interpretation complicate the established reference to chaotic "scattering," offering a more nuanced description of a complicated strategy characterized by deliberate decision making and action? Overall, this chapter uses the Gahoendoe experience to unpin the Wendats from their customary position as Haudenosaunee foes (wolves) and Jesuit followers (sheep), creating a new narrative focused on Wendat agency and perseverance.

CRISIS MANAGEMENT AND CUSTOMARY PROTOCOL

In order to fully understand the motivations and process that led Wendats to support a relocation strategy, we must return to the spring meeting at Sainte Marie in 1649. It was there that six thousand Wendats met to evaluate the severity of their situation. The Wendats considered the repercussions of consecutive Haudenosaunee attacks: many of their villages were already destroyed, and the conflict was unlikely to end soon. The human loss was also significant. In addition to the many men, women, and children taken as captives, the Wendats lost approximately 630 to 880 warriors.[10] The loss of so many young men weakened the Wendats' ability to fend off future invasions, not to mention the destabilized psychological state of victims' families and loved ones. The nature of the Haudenosaunee retreat further debilitated the Wendat survivors. With their fields destroyed, the Wendats were faced with the horrific circumstance of being unable to grow crops for the coming year. The Haudenosaunees not only took the Wendats' remaining provisions for the winter months but also their corn seeds. Even their untouched fields could not be sown.[11] In the end, the attacks created a situation where the future of the Wendats was almost certainly one of eventual demise if they remained within the borders of Wendake mainland. The group decided that creating a plan of evacuation and relocation was the next and most needed strategy.

Wendats followed traditional protocol in order to facilitate their migration. Leaders conducted councils to identify potential strategies of relocation. One of the first issues they dealt with was whether to remain together or split into smaller groups. The Wendat Confederates had lived for centuries within a relatively confined territory in close proximity to one another. To depart from this familiar custom would have been to restructure their entire approach to village life. Still, some argued that smaller groups, the size of small bands and families, would allow for easier mobility and the potential to hide from the enemy.[12]

Another suggestion was to have entire villages reestablish themselves or create new villages. This approach appealed to those that wanted to maintain their village identity, as well as a higher level of security and resources.[13] Most believed, however, that this strategy still left them too vulnerable, because the new villages might not be able to defend and sustain themselves independently.[14] Thus, after weighing the odds and options, the majority of Wendats concluded that they would remain together and relocate to an island. Such a move, they felt, would provide protection and power to ensure their survival.[15]

THE ISLAND STRATEGY

At first, the island of Ekaentoton[16] seemed like a promising option. Located in the northern part of Lake Huron and approximately 108 nautical miles from Sainte Marie,[17] this island was 1,068 square miles with 108 freshwater lakes.[18] It was already inhabited by the Anishinaabe nations of the area, and a Jesuit mission had recently been established there as well. During the deliberations at Sainte Marie, the Jesuits tried to persuade the Wendats to make the move. The land, they argued, was said to be good and the fishing excellent. Most likely, of course, the presence of other missionaries on the island also encouraged the Jesuits to support a move there. The Wendats considered the Jesuit proposal but remained hesitant because of the location's long frost season.[19]

The Wendats also had to weigh the geopolitical ramifications of moving to Ekaentoton. By joining the Anishinaabeg, the Wendats would have been required to relinquish their position as middlemen within the French-Wendat-Anishinaabe fur trade. If the Wendats relocated to an Anishinaabe settlement, the French would have direct access to the Anishinaabeg and would not need to go through the Wendats for furs. Further, Ekaentoton was in Anishinaabe territory, outside the spatial power of Wendake. By relocating to this island the Wendats risked losing prestige and power within trade networks, which depended heavily on their geographic location.

These factors led the Wendats to reject the Jesuit proposal of Ekaentoton in 1649 and convinced them to look closer to home. Located approximately twenty-three nautical miles northwest of Sainte Marie, the island of Gahoendoe was one of the largest islands within Wendake.[20] Its 13,413 acres provided ample space for agriculture, and the fishing was plentiful.[21] The island also had an established and thriving Wendat village.[22]

Security was another factor in the Wendats' decision to move to Gahoendoe Island, which was easily defendable. Because it lay only three miles from the mainland, the Wendats had the advantage of being able to see any impending attacks from the island's eastern shore (the western shore had no significant land mass in proximity). The location also facilitated future opportunities to return to the mainland and recruit allies from other Wendat villages.

The relationship between the occupied space at Gahoendoe and maintenance of power within the geopolitical and economic Wendat world also mattered. Wendake was the heart of commercial activity for the Saint Lawrence fur trade. This island was, therefore, not only within the influence of Wendat territorial authority but also an established stopover for the Anishinaabeg and Wendats. It was here that Algonquin boats would unload furs and conduct trade with their Wendat allies.[23] Partially because of this trade, Gahoendoe was a strategic location at the confluence of Anishinaabe and Wendat spheres of influence. Its former role as a meeting ground would be strengthened if the Wendat community took the island as the central seat of their Confederacy. Despite the frequency of warfare with the Haudenosaunees, trade between the Anishinaabeg, Wendats, and French continued throughout 1648 and 1649, with an accumulation of more than five thousand livres in beaver furs.[24] Thus, the Wendats perceived Gahoendoe as an option that would provide not only subsistence and physical safety but also a viable location for maintaining their traditional role as middlemen and securing Wendat hegemony in the fur trade. With these factors in mind, the majority of the Wendats agreed to move to Gahoendoe.

THE RATIFICATION PROCESS

Before this move could take place, however, the decision had to be ratified by the community as a whole. Deliberations took place on several levels, beginning with the Women's Council. Although the Jesuits did not record the details of these meetings, the resulting wampum belt—made by the women themselves—and the messages delivered by the headmen at subsequent village and confederacy councils on their behalf make it clear that women continued to congregate and initiate decisions for their communities.[25] The Wendats followed traditional protocol despite the urgency and seriousness of the situation. Women's councils informed civil leaders of their decisions, and civil leaders publicized the decisions that were then voted on and ratified through consensus.[26] The decision to leave the mainland was not made in a state of panic and haste.

As a final step in solidifying their impending departure, the women sent twelve of the most prominent headmen to invite the Jesuits to join them in their migration to Gahoendoe. This invitation was made for two reasons. First, the Jesuits played a crucial role as liaisons to the French fur traders and colonial officials. By keeping the missionaries in close proximity, the Wendats ensured that their relationship with the French would continue. Second, the Jesuits also controlled access to a number of items the Wendats hoped to use. Guns, for example, promised a potential advantage in the event of future Haudenosaunee invasions.

Further, because the Wendats were able to fend off the Haudenosaunees at Sainte Marie, the Jesuits there were one of the few groups able to maintain decent amounts of livestock and agricultural provisions, which could help support their population. In their storage, the missionaries had at least ten fowls, two pigs, two bulls, four cows, and a substantial amount of corn (which had been provided by the Wendats in the last harvest).[27] These goods would have provided much-needed support in the first phase of relocation.

The official invitation to the Jesuits followed Wendat diplomatic protocol. The headmen called a council during which they proceeded to speak about the Wendat decision and the reasons why they wished the Jesuits to accompany them. Their appeal was provocative and deliberate, playing on the missionaries' religious goals of conversion and their concern for women and children. Although the group already included some Christian converts, the headmen suggested that they would encourage the refugees on Gahoendoe to convert and increase the number of Wendats willing to partake in baptism. In addition, they pointed to the weakened state of their people and their inability to properly defend themselves without French help. The headmen then called attention specifically to the struggling widows and children, urging the missionaries to have compassion. Next, the headmen presented the Jesuits with ten wampum belts representing "the voice of the women and children." According to one headman, the message of these symbolic gifts was both to have compassion for the widows and their children and "to revive in [the Jesuits] the zeal and the name of Father Echon (the name which the Hurons have always given to Father Jean de Brébeuf); . . . that [the Wendats] hoped that his example would touch [the Jesuits], and that [their] hearts could not refuse to die with them, since they wished to live as Christians." In other words, the women desired that the Jesuits support the Wendats' decision to move to Gahoendoe, in light of the high number of struggling widows and orphaned children, who, in return for assistance, would accept Christianity and serve as a willing population for future conversions. It was this last presentation to the council that helped convince the Jesuits. According to the missionaries it was "the disposition of their souls, and the reasons which nature could supply them—[that] conquered us." Shortly after, the Jesuits agreed to relocate to Gahoendoe.[28]

The negotiations that led to the Wendat migration to Gahoendoe resulted from calculated planning and strategic decision making. Although the options were limited, Gahoendoe represented the best opportunity for survival. Much of the scholarship discussing this point in Wendat history tends to overemphasize the role of the Jesuits in these deliberations. The actual circumstances, however, depict a different situation. The move to Gahoendoe was clearly a Wendat decision. The Jesuits had wanted to go to Ekaentoton, an idea that was rejected by the Wendats. Further, the Jesuit decision to accompany the Wendats to Gahoendoe was made in response to invitations instigated by Wendat women.

THE RELOCATION

The initial stages of the relocation were a success. Roughly eight thousand Wendats (86 percent of the total population) took part.[29] Wendat nations and villages combined in this mass relocation effort.[30] The loss of so many warriors in the spring of 1649 has led scholars to suggest that the majority of the population was made up of women.[31] The Haudenosaunee wars had taken hundreds of able-bodied Wendat men, with the Jesuits contending that there were "hundreds and hundreds of widows who had lost entire households."[32] That said, if the overall population before 1649 was around ten thousand and 86 percent moved to Gahoendoe after the dispersal, it is unlikely that the Wendat predispersal population was as unbalanced as scholars have suggested. This is not to make light of the loss of hundreds, perhaps more than a thousand warriors, but in the context of the entire population, it is hard to believe that nearly 90 percent of the survivors were women. There is no doubt, however, that the sixty Europeans who took up residency on the island were all men. This group consisted of thirteen priests, including Fathers Pierre-Joseph-Marie Chaumonot and Paul Ragueneau; four assistants; twenty-two *donnés* (secular employees who served the Jesuits); eleven domestics; six soldiers; and four boys.[33]

REBUILDING WENDAT SOCIETY

Once on the island, the Wendats made concerted efforts to organize their new home in ways that matched the villages they had left but also reflected their new circumstances and wartime conditions. Building around the long-houses that had been built before their arrival, Wendat refugees established two large villages as well as several outlaying longhouses located in more remote areas.[34]

These settlements represent innovative planning. The village that archae-ologists now call the Charity Site was built on the shore of present-day Doug-las Lake. Most people lived in longhouses that were shorter and narrower than those found on the Wendake mainland, and they were also built closer together. The number of people living in a longhouse did not change; archae-ologists agree that the houses were still able to hold sixty to eighty people.[35] Rather, the new design was most likely an attempt to optimize the amount of space on the island. Back on the mainland, villages usually relocated every eight to ten years in order to rotate the soil of their fields. The limited amount of land on an island required space preservation in order to ensure that land would be available in the future. The close proximity of the houses to one another may have also been a defensive strategy: closer, tight-knit villages were easier to defend in the face of Haudenosaunee attack.

The Charity Site had at least one cleared field that was planted by June 1649.[36] As fields were an integral part of Wendat subsistence culture, it was paramount that all the villages had enough cultivated land to produce the food needed to sustain their population. The prospects for agriculture were good. William Fenton stipulates that an Iroquoian population of twenty thousand people can subsist on seven thousand acres of land.[37] Taking into consideration the size of Gahoendoe (13,413 acres) and the population of the Wendats (eight thousand), there would have been ample space for cultivation of crops, at least for their first decade on the island.

The second large settlement, named Sainte Marie II by the French and lo-cated only a few hundred meters from the southern shore of Gahoendoe, was within plain sight of mainland Wendake. The Jesuit mission was con-structed in close proximity. In addition to at least one hundred longhouses built in the same fashion as the Charity Site, this settlement—because of the proximity of the Jesuits—included European-style fortifications. Under the guidance of several skilled soldiers, the Europeans immediately built two forts: one around the mission and the other around the Wendat village of Sainte

Marie II.[38] Assistance from the Wendats and the realization that the ground naturally provided stone and mortar without any digging simplified the building project. According to Father Ragueneau, the fortification was an improvement over the wooden palisade constructed at Sainte Marie I on the mainland. The structure encompassing the mission followed seventeenth-century military rules and was approximately 120 feet square with bastions at each four corners.[39] For the most part, the Jesuits felt that the stone would be impenetrable by Haudenosaunee weapons and impervious to fire. In addition, the stone walls surrounding the settlements were thought to be high enough that the enemy would not be able to scale them and strong enough to withstand a battering ram. Because of their firearms, French soldiers were later posted at the bastions for twenty-four-hour protection. This arrangement was completed by the end of the summer. With these additions to their village, most Wendats felt secure on the island, feeling that the location and buildings allowed for optimal defense against a Haudenosaunee attack from the mainland.[40]

Overall, the construction of Wendat villages on Gahoendoe reflected both customary practices and alternative innovations. It required a large amount of labor and dedication from every migrant, each contributing to the building of residences, palisades, and fields. The French responded to Wendat desires for security by applying their experience with cement and stone fortifications. After two months of occupation, the Jesuits believed themselves "to be in a complete state of defense, so that the enemy, despite all he can do, [was] little dreaded by [them]."[41] Thus far, the decision to relocate to Gahoendoe was a success. It provided the potential for maintaining the Wendat Confederacy and supporting the subsistence needs of its people. The French and Anishinaabe alliances would remain strong, along with Wendat trade and diplomatic initiatives. Further, anxiety over Haudenosaunee attacks could be alleviated by a newfound security in a denser and more centralized community.

THE POINT OF NO RETURN

The Wendats barely had time to benefit from their successful relocation. They soon faced a new crisis, only a few months after establishing themselves on the island: the weather had turned against them. As early as June 1649, the Wendats expressed to the Jesuits their anxiety over the lack of rain and its potential effect on the harvest.[42] Indeed, the droughts of 1649–50 caused widespread crop failure, culminating in a food shortage that proved to be a more disastrous threat to the Confederacy than the possibility of Haudenosaunee attack.

As with their response to Haudenosaunee warfare and disease, the Wendats were resilient in the face of their declining yields. Alternative foods were the first line of defense. Despite their distaste for labor-intensive acorns, these nuts became their most important source of nutrition. Groups were sent out to collect acorns in the late months of summer and autumn in order to acquire provisions for the winter. In addition, a bitter root called otsa was often collected. Those that did not have the luxury of these items relied on wild garlic, which they would bake under ashes or boil in water. Some Wendats began to strip the trees of their bark and boil it. This created a bitter broth that they would drink in order to give their bodies the impression of being full.[43] The lack of animal bones and minimal remains of corn and acorns in archaeological surveys are a testament to the dire situation.[44]

Eventually the hunger became a pandemic and famine plagued the entire population. For those without enough food or the ability to obtain more, bartering for supplies became an alternative. Some sold their material possessions in exchange for meals of acorns or broth. They frequently traded clothing for food and were even desperate enough to take the clothes off of deceased bodies. This became such a common practice that one dying man pleaded with his companions to "bury me now, at once; for my life is over and thou seest plainly that I am numbered among the dead. Now, what I fear is this, that, if I should die before being buried, other poor people as destitute as I am, may rob me of these rags that cover my nakedness."[45]

Another option was to seek out the Jesuit reserves. The readily accessible supplies stored at the mission enticed many Wendats to meet the priests and request aid. The Jesuits decided who was eligible to acquire the food, and not surprisingly, Christian converts were the only ones given rations. In order to implement distributions in a controlled fashion, the Jesuits introduced small pieces of copper stamped with a sign recognizably designed for the acquisition of food. They then instructed coin holders to line up at midday. Favorites received Indian meal boiled in water, while others could obtain acorns or smoked fish.[46] This strategy resulted in increased Wendat conversions and an overrepresentation of Christian survivors as they gained strength through Jesuit support.

As the spring drew near, those who were able to survive the winter made attempts to venture off the island in search of a wider supply of food, usually acorns that were more easily collected on the melting mountaintops of the mainland. They also wanted to check fishing grounds that were now exposed to the southern sun. These trips were extremely risky and not taken lightly. In early March 1650 a large group of men, women, and children attempted to cross to the mainland. They had split up into smaller bands in order to make it harder for the Haudenosaunees to attack. Only minutes after their departure from the island, the ice began to crack and several members of the group drowned. Others remained paralyzed on the surface, unable to move for fear of falling through. They were equally aware that the amount of noise created by the catastrophe could alert the Haudenosaunees on the mainland to their presence. Survivors were forced to remain on the ice overnight until a Wendat rescue party deemed it safe to make the crossing the next day.[47]

As the famine hit its height in the winter of 1649, the Wendats were pushed to the brink of extinction. At this point (rather than before they moved to the island) people began to transgress social norms, implementing survival tactics that would never have been condoned in a healthy Wendat society. At first, they ate the excrement of animals and human beings, but soon they began digging up the corpses of animals and eating the boiled fur and bones. This was not enough to sustain the starving population, however, forcing many to turn to cannibalism. This practice was forbidden within Wendat society, except as part of prisoner of war ceremonies, and even then only warriors were sanctioned to eat the flesh of their enemies. The Wendats driven to eat their relatives and friends did so as a horrific and reluctant last resort. Indeed, the situation was such that brothers were seen eating brothers, mothers eating their children, and children their parents. The Jesuits observed, "everywhere corpses have been dug out of the graves, and, now carried away by hunger, the people have repeatedly offered, as food, those who were lately the dear pledges of love."[48]

In the end, the combined efforts to attain food through alternative supplies, bartering, Jesuit provisions, escape to the mainland, and cannibalism were not enough to save the majority of the population. In circumstances comparable to the epidemics of the 1630s, families and loved ones watched each other die with very little opportunity to save them. Many parents did not have the strength or resources to help their children, let alone themselves. One young mother, for instance, was found dead with her two infant children continuing to suck at her breasts. Shortly after, the children also died. In another case, a mother visited the Jesuits with her four children. Despite the children's repeated requests for their mother's milk, her body could no longer provide the nourishment they required. The mother caressed her children, weeping at her feet, until they each died one by one. To make matters worse, the dying mother no longer had the energy to bury her family and left the children to the Jesuits, who promised to take care of the bodies.[49]

Jesuit baptismal records serve as an additional source for understanding the devastating nature of this famine. Nearly three thousand baptisms took place between March 1649 and March 1650.[50] This figure indicates the number of deaths, or at least those who were expecting to die and had accepted baptism.[51] Traditionalists (Wendats who did not become Christians) were of course not part of this number but must have been similarly affected by the famine, suggesting that the Jesuit records are a low count of the total Wendats touched by the crisis. Thus, although the Jesuits asserted that "hundreds and hundreds died" on Gahoendoe, in reality it was most likely thousands.[52]

NEW STRATEGIES: DIASPORA

The food crisis pushed the Wendats to reconsider their move to Gahoendoe and shaped their entire experience on the island. Instead of a place of refuge, it became a death trap. With the coming of spring, Haudenosaunee war parties became more active on the mainland, creating increased anxiety within an already distraught population. On March 25, 1650, a group of Wendats were attacked while they attempted to harvest fish from the mainland coast. The Wendats dispersed in all directions, leaving distances of fifteen miles between each group. This strategy did not dissuade the Haudenosaunees, however, and the entire company was lost except for one man who managed to escape and return to the island to share the details of the attack. In early April two other bands headed by the Wendat leaders Andotitak and Thawenda were defeated. This battle was brief and took place about thirty miles in the interior. Roughly eight days later, the island Wendats received news that two large Haudenosaunee war parties were on their way to Gahoendoe with the intention of attacking the Wendats and destroying their fields.[53]

The culmination of the winter famine and the present and impending Haudenosaunee attacks resulted in a quest for new survival strategies. If the Haudenosaunees were to land on the island, the surviving Wendats were too weak to orchestrate any kind of formidable opposition. Moreover, the depopulation of the island community and the weakened state of the remaining

Wendats made it difficult to plant the crops needed in order to survive any further occupation of the island. These factors combined to persuade the Wendats to begin making serious plans for evacuation.

The decision was made in a night council. During these deliberations, different destinations for relocation were discussed. In the beginning the majority felt it wise to split up entirely, grouping into small bands and hiding in the parts of Wendake unfamiliar to the Haudenosaunees. Others suggested that some move south to the Susquehannocks and their Swedish allies or to the west with the Anishinaabeg, while some entertained the thought of meeting with the Haudenosaunees and merging with them. Still others suggested that they might move closer to French settlements for protection. In the end, they agreed on a strategy of calculated dispersal.[54] The majority of migrants left immediately, taking different routes to distant locations.

A small contingent stayed behind to harvest the crops already sown before leaving the island themselves. It was also decided at the night council that women, children, and the older individuals of the community that could not make the journey off the island would stay behind. As a final conclusion to these negotiations, two headmen were sent to the Jesuit mission to deliver the news. They explained their desperate situation in the following way: "My brother, thine eyes deceive thee when thou lookest on us; thou believest that thou seest living men while we are but specters, the souls of the departed. The ground thou treadest on is about to open under us, to swollow [sic] us, together with thyself, that we may be in the place where we ought to be, among the dead." Shortly thereafter, the Wendats evacuated Gahoendoe. The surviving Wendats took only what they could carry, leaving almost everything behind.[55]

CONCLUSION

The Wendats chose Gahoendoe Island because of its combined advantages for defense, ability to maintain trade relationships, and opportunities for fishing and agriculture. The geopolitical power provided by the location of the island and its historical significance for the Wendats were also important factors influencing their decision to move. They optimized spatial power by occupying a relatively small site within their geographic sphere of influence. Haudenosaunee raids, although always a threat, never had much success during the year at Gahoendoe, thanks to the island's protection from stone walls, cement fortifications, and French soldiers and firearms. Approaching enemies were also noticed long before they made their final landing on Gahoendoe. In regards to trade, nothing suggests that Gahoendoe would not have served its purpose as a meeting ground for exchange between the Anishinaabeg, Wendats, and French. Before word of the evacuation had reached the French settlements east of Wendake, for instance, a fur brigade had already departed with Gahoendoe as their final trade destination.[56] For all intents and purposes, these factors remained fundamental to the Wendats' decision to migrate away from their mainland villages. Had it not been for the drought and subsequent food crisis, the plan might have been a success.

The drought of 1649–50 was the most decisive issue shaping the Wendats' decision to leave Wendake Ehen. The climatic situation, combined with the limited territory on the island, damaged the prospects of any substantial food supply for the Wendat population. Consequently the island was no longer secure. People were weak and dying, and by 1650 the community began to collapse both physically and socially, transgressing cultural norms to the point of cannibalism. Unlike their mainland counterparts, such as the Haudenosaunee or Anishinaabe nations, the Wendats were trapped within the confines of the island's perimeter. On the mainland, when agriculture failed, communities could resort to hunting and gathering, venturing out farther and farther from their villages in order to meet the needs of their people. On the island this was no longer an option, and hunting was only a temporary solution. In the same way, the supply of roots and acorns was limited to what the island had already produced that year. In the end, Gahoendoe could not support such a large human population.

The decision to leave Wendake Ehen was most certainly made out of desperation and in reaction to a seemingly hopeless situation. Councils were held to consider strategies of relocation. In the end, the collective resolution to evacuate Gahoendoe was a calculated attempt to reorganize the Wendat Confederacy to generate situations of continued survival, not inevitable defeat. The exodus of Wendake was the beginning of a new tactic focused on dispersal and migration. Thus, although the epidemics of the 1630s and the Haudenosaunee attacks of the 1640s were crucial in the Wendats' final decision to leave, it was the food crisis and the often overlooked Gahoendoe experience that pushed them to restrategize, reshaping their community into a diasporic entity, which led to a new reconfiguration of the Wendat world.[57]

NOTES

This chapter is based on my PhD dissertation, "Dispersed, but Not Destroyed: Leadership, Women, and Power within the Wendat Diaspora, 1600–1701," Ohio State University, 2011, and the subsequent book *Dispersed but Not Destroyed* (2013, University of British Columbia Press), revised and reprinted with permission of the publisher. All rights reserved. This new interpretation of the Gahoendoe experience is the result of invaluable feedback from the University of Saskatchewan History Research Series. In particular I would like to thank J. R. Miller, Valerie Korinek, Simonne Horowitz, Robert Englebert, Maurice Labelle, and Matthew Neufeld for their diligent reading and insightful suggestions.

1. It was also during this conflict that the Jesuit missionaries Fathers Brébeuf and Lalemant were captured. They were later tortured and put to death by the Iroquois. Reuben Gold Thwaites, ed., *The Jesuit Relations and Allied Documents: Travels and Explorations of the Jesuit Missionaries in New France, 1610–1791* (Cleveland: Burrows, 1896–1901) (hereafter cited as *JR*), vol. 34: 87–99, 125–27, 137; Roger Carpenter, *The Renewed, the Destroyed, the Remade: The Three Thought Worlds of the Iroquois and the Huron, 1609–1650* (East Lansing: Michigan State University Press, 2004), 126.

2. *JR* 34:197.

3. Ibid., 35:189.

4. Bruce Trigger, *The Children of Aataentsic: A History of the Huron People to 1660* (Montreal: McGill–Queen's University Press, 1987), 722; *JR* 35:177.

5. *JR* 34:199.

6. Known today as Christian Island.

7. Bruce Trigger dedicates a small section to Gahoendoe (*Children of Aataentsic*, 767–82), and Roger Carpenter delivers a brief synopsis of this period (*Renewed*, 127–29).

8. Here "spaces of power" refers to Elizabeth Mancke's definition "as a system of social power, whether economic, political, cultural or military, that we can describe functionally and spatially." See Elizabeth Mancke, "Spaces of Power in the Early Modern Northeast," in *New England and the Maritime Provinces: Connections and Comparisons* (Montreal: McGill–Queen's University Press, 2005), 32. In addition to my own work, Thomas Peace uses and develops this concept extensively in his dissertation. See Thomas Peace, "Two Conquests: Aboriginal Experiences of the Fall of New France and Acadia" (PhD diss., York University, 2011), 11–18.

9. Claude-Charles Bacqueville de la Potherie, *Histoire de l'Amerique septienale* (Paris: Chez Brocas, 1753), vol. 2: 51; *JR* 21:239.

10. Jose Antonio Brandão, *Your Fyre Shall Burn No More: Iroquois Policy toward New France and Its Native Allies to 1701* (Lincoln: University of Nebraska Press, 1997), 204.

11. Carpenter, *Renewed*, 126. These numbers do not include the thousands of Wendats who decided to relocate voluntarily to Iroquois country.

12. *JR* 34:197, 204.

13. Ibid., 34:203.

14. The truth of this lies in the fate of a group of Wendats who decided to try this strategy, building a village that the Jesuits would call Saint Charles. They struggled with severe bouts of starvation and abandoned their village in less than a year to re-join the rest of the Wendats. *JR* 35:177; Letter XII (May 14, 1721) in Pierre de Charlevoix, *Journal of a Voyage to North America* (London: R. and J. Dodsley, 1761), vol. 1: 309.

15. *JR* 34:197.

16. Today this island is known as Manitoulin Island.

17. According to the Jesuits it is 140 miles (60 leagues). *JR* 34:205.

18. Labelle, *Dispersed but Not Destroyed,* 52.

19. *JR* 34:205, 207, 203–9; Trigger, *Children of Aataentsic,* 771; Carpenter, *Renewed,* 127.

20. *JR* 35:25.

21. William Fenton has calculated that 7,000 acres were needed to sustain a pop-ulation of 20,000 Nadouek people. Considering that the Wendat population was at most 10,000 people by 1640, the 13,413 acres of Gahoendoe should have been able to support the entire population. Fenton's analysis is described in Bruce Trigger's *The Huron: Farmers of the North* (New York: Holt, Rinehart and Winston, 1969), 28. The Jesuits record the good fishing attributed to the island. *JR* 34:199.

22. *JR* 34:203, 197, 203–5; 35:83.

23. Ibid., 35:205.

24. Ibid., 34:59–61.

25. Ibid., 34:209. Although the production of wampum belts was not necessarily a gendered task, some evidence suggests that women may have had a principal role in creating the belts within some Native societies. In this case, however, the Jesuits explicitly stated that the ten belts were made by the women "who made us a present of the little which was left to them in their misery." For more on gender roles and the production of wampum belts, see Jonathan C. Lainey, *La "monnaie des sauvages": Les colliers de wampum d'hier à aujourd'hui* (Quebec City: Les éditions du Septentrion, 2004), 30–31.

26. *JR* 34:209.

27. Ibid., 35:25.

28. Ibid., 34: 209–11.

29. These numbers differ considerably from most interpretations. At the time of Bruce Trigger's publications in the 1970s and 1980s, *JR* provided the most informa-tion on population statistics, and Trigger asserts that the Jesuits' numbers were an exaggeration. In these accounts, we find that three hundred families were already residing on the island before June. Another report indicates that there were more than one hundred "cabins" by 1650. If one Wendat family comprised approximately five to eight people, then at minimum there were 1,500 people living on Gahoendoe before the major migration in the spring of 1649. In addition, one cabin, or long-house, housed roughly sixty to eighty people. Thus, one hundred cabins can be translated into a minimum population of six thousand. Combined, these numbers indicate that the entire Wendat population of Gahoendoe was most likely close to eight thousand. Despite Trigger's skepticism, archaeological data supports these

estimates. Early in the 1990s Northeastern Archaeological Associates was awarded a contract to excavate what is now known as the Charity Site but was originally one of the largest Wendat settlements on Gahoendoe in the seventeenth century. The data collected at this site, and several others from the surrounding area, revealed that well over one thousand people were living within one settlement and confirmed at least one site with more than one hundred longhouses. Taking these numbers into consideration, as well as the loss of more than seven hundred warriors in the spring campaign against the Iroquois, the Wendat community on Gahoendoe represented at least 86 percent of the entire Wendat population. Gary Warrick has since published similar estimates, with an average Wendat population of 8,700. Trigger, *Children of Aataentsic*, 772; Trigger, *Huron*, 13; *JR* 35:87; Ontario Association of Professional Archaeologists (OAPA), "The Charity Site," http://www.apaontario.ca/r_charity01.html (link now expired, copy of document in possession of the author); L. J. Jackson, R. Rose, A. Ariss, and C. Theriault, "The Winter of Discontent: The Charity Site, 1991," *Arch Notes* 6 (November/December 1992): 5–9; Gary Warrick, *A Population History of the Huron-Petun, A.D. 500–1650* (Cambridge: Cambridge University Press, 2008), 237–38.

30. *JR* 34:209.

31. Trigger, *Children of Aataentsic*, 772.

32. *JR* 34:217.

33. Ibid., 35:23.

34. Ibid., 35:87.

35. OAPA, "Charity Site."

36. *JR* 35:83.

37. It is not clear to what type of soil Fenton refers. One can surmise that his theory is focused on tillable land with agricultural potential. Trigger, *Huron*, 28. See also Conrad Heidenreich, *Huronia: A History and Geography of the Huron Indians, 1600–1650* (Toronto: McClelland and Stewart, 1971), 158–59.

38. *JR* 35:25, 85.

39. Martin Felix, "Plan of the Remains of Sainte-Marie II on Christian Island (1855)," in Trigger, *Children of Aataentsic*, 773; *JR* 35:85.

40. Ibid., 35:27, 85; 40:47; 34:225.

41. Ibid., 34:225.

42. Ibid., 35:85.

43. Ibid., 34:215; 35:175.

44. OAPA, "Charity Site."

45. *JR* 35:93, 95.

46. Ibid., 35:99.

47. Ibid., 35:183–85.

48. Ibid., 35:21; 13:77; 17:65.

49. Ibid., 35:91–93.

50. Ibid., 34:227; 35:23, 75.

51. Jesuits later equate the number of baptisms (3,000) to the number of deaths. Ibid., 35:199.

52. Ibid., 40:49.
53. Ibid., 35:187, 191; 36:119.
54. Ibid., 35: 193, 195–97.
55. Ibid., 36:179, 186–87; 35:191.
56. Ibid., 35:201–3.
57. Ibid., 35:189.

CHAPTER 2

"Over the Lake"

THE WESTERN WENDAKE IN THE AMERICAN REVOLUTION

Andrew Sturtevant

In 1755 and 1756 warriors from the "Wondot Nation of Indians" led the unfortunate Charles Stuart, a colonist captured in western Pennsylvania, on an extended tour of their western Wendat homeland, a cultural and political space that embraced both sides of Lake Erie (see map 2.1). From western Pennsylvania the warriors traveled by horseback to the Shawnee villages on the Scioto River. Soon after passing the last Shawnee town, the party reached a small, seasonally occupied Wendat hunting camp of eight families somewhere in the Scioto watershed. After this camp, the party stopped at two other hunting camps, each spaced about a day's journey apart and each containing a handful of Wendat families. After weeks of traveling, on December 21, 1755, Stuart finally arrived at the "Wondot Town" of Canuta, located at Sandusky Bay on the southern shore of Lake Erie. During his approximately four months in this "Small Indian Town," Stuart learned that Canuta served as the "Head Quarters of the Wondot Hunters." The Detroit Wendats, including his captors, came to Sandusky every fall and then dispersed into hunting camps throughout the region. In late April 1756 the Wendats took Stuart to their home at Detroit. The village there, at the Pointe à Montréal across the Detroit River from the French fort, was the "Chief Wondot Town," inhabited by some 650 inhabitants. The Wendats kept Stuart there until June, when the Jesuit missionary to the Wendats arranged his ransom and Stuart departed for England via Quebec.[1]

The Wendat party's sojourn through the Ohio Valley charts a compelling map of the Wendat homeland and of Wendat social and political relations in the 1750s. In Stuart's telling, the separate Wendat settlements in the Great Lakes—at Detroit, Sandusky, and elsewhere—did not constitute separate and isolated villages but rather parts of a geographically dispersed but socially, economically, and politically integrated Wendat space. Within this world, Wendat people, goods, and information circulated constantly and rapidly— as had Stuart himself—from Detroit, to Sandusky, to the hunting camps, and back again.[2] The Wendats also maintained family ties between the various settlements.[3] In short, as another British captive observed, the "Wyandots at [Sandusky] and those at Detroit [were] connected."[4] In this corner of the Great Lakes, the Wendats had reconstructed a geographically extended homeland, a new Wendake similar to the homeland that had been destroyed in 1649 (see chapter 1). This "geography of solidarity" allowed the Wendats to expand their influence into the Ohio Valley.[5]

Following Stuart's description, this chapter explores the creation and meanings of this reconstituted Wendake. It first argues that despite, and sometimes because of, the disruptions they faced following 1649, the Wendats remained a cultural, social, and political entity throughout the eighteenth century. In this light, their expansion into the Ohio Valley represented not a fission of dissenters from the Wendat community but an expansion of a geographically scattered but politically and socially unified Wendat homeland. This unity—and the geographic strategy it engendered—found impressive expression during the American Revolution. During that conflict, the Wendats took advantage of their homeland to maintain a flexible and pragmatic geopolitical strategy in which the Sandusky leaders Donquat and Orontony closely coordinated with the senior Wendat leaders at Detroit. Cooperating with their fellow Wendats "over the lake" (that is, on either side of Lake Erie), Wendats at Sandusky and Detroit formulated a common strategy in which the Sandusky settlements served as critical intermediaries between Detroit and the Ohio Valley.[6]

The Wendat story is not, as it has often been told, one of diasporic collapse and diffusion, but instead one of cultural resilience etched into an expansive geographic territory. That the Wendats should have maintained and in fact reconfigured these bonds contradicts our usual understanding of diasporic peoples, especially in this region. According to that narrative, the

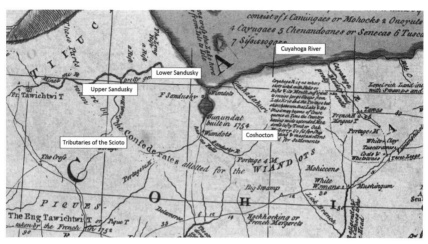

Map 2.1. A New Western Wendake. Detail from Lewis Evans, "Bowles's new pocket map of the following independent states of North America: viz. Virginia, Maryland, Delaware, Pensylvania [sic], New Jersey, New York, Connecticut & Rhode Island: comprehending also the habitations & hunting countries of the confederate Indians" (London, 1784). Lawrence H. Slaughter Collection of English Maps, Charts, Globes, Books and Atlases, New York Public Library, Map Div. 97-6006 (LHS 228), ID no. 434112.

catastrophe of colonialism had effectively destroyed these communities. The "hammer blows" of disease, war, and dislocation had "shattered" Native peoples such as the Wendats into feeble refugees who, out of necessity, clung to their new European allies to retain their lives.[7] And few bore those blows more squarely than the Wendats, whose privileged relationship with the French had exposed them to the ravages of epidemic disease and then dispersal at the hands of their Haudenosaunee foes. As their Jesuit allies pointed out, the Wendats had suffered devastation of biblical proportions.[8] In their long sojourn through the western Great Lakes, the Wendat remnants relied heavily on their Anishinaabe and French allies simply to survive. Finally, the Wendats split along ethnic lines, with some leaving their village at Detroit to form a separate, rival settlement south of Lake Erie. This defection was the ultimate dénouement of a catastrophic process that began when the Wendats first met Champlain.

Read in another way, however, the relocation of some Wendats to Sandusky illustrates not the weakness and ultimate dissolution of the Wendats but their enduring vitality and adaptability.[9] In this reading, the Wendats were certainly shaped, but by no means shattered, by the hammer blows. Forged in the turmoil of their diaspora and tempered by the hardships that followed, the Wendats proved capable of responding and adapting to their changed circumstances. By pragmatically drawing on French culture and innovatively interpreting convention in new environments, the Wendats found new ways to be Wendats by the time they arrived at Detroit in the early eighteenth century.

"ONE BODY": WENDAT CULTURAL AND POLITICAL RESILIENCE

The integrated Wendake that Stuart observed in the 1750s was a manifestation of the powerful cultural, familial, and political ties that knit the Wendats together. Without a strong sense of belonging to the Wendat community and the tangible familial and relational bonds holding them together, the Wendats scarcely could have maintained such a geographically diffused homeland. The weight of distance and diverging interests would have pried the Wendats into so many scattered, disparate communities. That they did not do so attests to a sharply delineated, exclusive, and dynamic Wendat identity, born out of both tradition and innovation. The Wendats had forged an identity based both on tradition and innovation in the years following their flight from Lake Huron (see chapters 1 and 3). This identity—really more of a set of self-perceptions, cultural preferences and priorities, systems of belonging, and concrete relationships—served as a touchstone for the dispersed Wendats and allowed them to remain united, despite their diffusion into a large homeland. This section provides a glimpse into these bonds.

This Wendat identity was constructed from a number of components and tied together by kinship and clan. Particularly, a sense of Iroquoian linguistic and cultural superiority, defined in explicit opposition to alien Algonquian traditions, combined with a long-term commitment to Christianity and a shared narrative of suffering and diaspora, fused the Wendats into a single, integrated community, further strengthened through the practices of clan exogamy. Neither a relic of a bygone era nor an entirely new creation, this Wendat identity was a dynamic and responsive set of cultural traits and allegiances that simultaneously set the Wendats apart from other nations and gave internal coherence to the community. Wendat identity changed over time, but it continued to tie this western Wendake together.

The first constituent of this Wendat identity was a sense of Iroquoian exceptionalism and superiority to their Algonquian-speaking neighbors in the Great Lakes. The constituent people who formed the Wendat community—the Tionontatés, Neutrals, and various Wendats—shared common cultural linguistic and cultural traditions referred to broadly as a Northern Iroquoian cultural pattern.[10] These patterns contrasted sharply with those of the Algonquian-speaking peoples among whom the Wendats lived after 1649—the Odawas, Potawatomies, Ojibwas, and others. Iroquoian and Algonquian tongues belong to different language families and are not mutually intelligible, which encouraged a sense of separateness and inscrutability between the Wendats and their neighbors at Detroit. Moreover, the Wendats and other Iroquoians relied much more heavily on the cultivation of crops than the Algonquians did, which had significant cultural implications from gender expectations to settlement patterns. The Wendats carried this preference for farming to Detroit, where it served to distance them from their Algonquian-speaking neighbors.[11]

This sense of Wendat exceptionalism helps explain the infrequency of marriage—or at least church-sanctioned, recorded marriage—between the Wendats and Algonquian-speaking peoples at Detroit. Even though the Wendats lived within a few miles of the Algonquians' villages at Detroit, there are only three recorded cases of children being born from a Wendat-Odawa union in the parish records, one case of intermarriage with the Algonquian-speaking Potawatomies, and none with the Ojibwas. By contrast, Wendat people had nine children in this period with members of the five Iroquois nations.[12] This evidence suggests, therefore, that part of being Wendat was being Iroquoian, or more accurately, not being "Algonquian." Wendat identity was formed, therefore, oppositionally, by demarcating a Wendat "us" from an Algonquian-speaking "them."[13] This accounts in part for the antagonism between the Wendats and their Algonquian-speaking neighbors, particularly the Odawas.[14]

The Wendats' long-term commitment to Christianity also provided a critical marker of Wendat self-conception while alienating them from their neighbors. Jesuit missionaries had invested considerable energy in converting the Wendats, and many Wendats carried this religious identity with them when they left their homelands. As a result, French observers frequently described the Wendats as the "best Catholics" in the region.[15] More importantly, the Wendats themselves testified to their identity as Christians and Catholics. In the aftermath of Pontiac's War in 1764 the Wendat leader

Otiokouandoron, also known as Babi, professed that "we are Baptized" and vowed to live in "eternal Peace" as Scripture commanded.[16] After their long-term missionary Pierre Potier died in 1781, the Detroit Wendats reported that the "loss . . . has left a general desolation in our villages." Presenting a wampum belt that symbolized their "adoption of the Christian religion," they implored the governor of Canada to send them a new "spiritual conductor" to replace Potier.[17]

In fact, Catholicism became such a critical element of Wendat identity that it served as a marker of political authority among at least some Wendats. Chief Janith English (Wyandot Nation of Kansas) notes that when she was elected chief of the Wyandot Nation of Kansas in 1996, a relative told her that she should wear a crucifix as part of her regalia "because our family has always worn one." Although many of the Wendats would later convert to Methodism or Quakerism (see chapter 4), this tradition demonstrates the importance of Catholicism to eighteenth-century Wendats (not to mention the durability of Wendat culture).[18]

Finally, a shared history of common suffering and mutual support gave these cultural and linguistic commonalities meaning and allowed the Wendats to formulate a shared narrative of what it meant to be Wendat. These people had faced a crisis of biblical dimensions. After having been forced into exodus by the Haudenosaunees, they had wandered through what seemed to them a wilderness of strange peoples and strange lands. They had fought against Native and European enemies. Once they had escaped the wrath of the Iroquois, they provoked the ire of the Sioux. They had also endured a rocky relationship with their Odawa allies. Through it all, they had loved and married one another, quarreled and laughed, and lived day by day in the presence of their fictive and real kin. For a century after the Wendat dispersal, the people who had come to be known as Detroit Wendats had relied on each other, had suffered alongside one another, and had remained united. These experiences and suffering allowed them to forge a narrative, a collective history, of what they had endured and how they had relied on one another. It is no surprise, then, that they identified themselves as part of an incorporated and coherent community.

If a sense of Iroquoian exceptionalism, Christianity, and a shared Wendat story provided the basis of a Wendat identity, the practice of clan exogamy—epitomized by the institution of the longhouse—supplied the practical means and the technology of that unity.[19] The practice of marrying outside of one's clan found its expression in the Wendat institution of the *famille* or *cabanne,* which referred to those related people who lived in the same longhouse. Because of the Wendats' matrilineal, matrilocal, and exogamous customs, these longhouses were, by necessity, integrated units that involved peoples from different clans. Because the Wendats were matrilineal and matrilocal, the women in each longhouse all belonged to the same clan, as did their children. Because of the Wendats' exogamous tradition and matrilocality, the men living in the longhouses belonged to different clans from their wives. Each longhouse, then, contained many related women and children from the same clan and men from different clans. Elders from the Deer and Wolf clan even lived in the same longhouses as those of the Turtle clan.[20] In a very real way, then, the longhouse brought together people from different clans into one integrated domestic space.

These components combined to create a sense of belonging and loyalty to the Wendat community, whether they lived at Detroit or Sandusky. The Wendats were, as the French never tired of pointing out, an extremely proud and haughty people, a fact that little endeared them to their Native neighbors.[21] The Wendats themselves testified to this loyalty as well. In 1707 they rejected an invitation from the Senecas to move to Iroquois territory because they feared that their existence as a distinct people would be subsumed and "the Wendat name [would] become extinct." They again rejected such invitations in 1739 and 1750.[22] Thirty years later, in 1740, when the Wendat leader Sastaretsy requested permission to live close to Montreal, he stipulated that he did not want to be "mingled with other nations."[23] In the aftermath of the crisis that divided the Wendat community in the 1740s and 1750s, they likewise testified to the bonds that held them together. The Wendats noted that their previously intact "body" had been divided but now had been healed once again.[24] This unity allowed them to create a new Wendat homeland—a new Wendake—in the Pays d'en Haut during the eighteenth century.

CREATING A NEW WENDAKE: WENDAT EXPANSION INTO THE OHIO VALLEY

This enduring cohesion sheds light on the Wendats' gradual expansion into the Ohio Valley during the middle decades of the eighteenth century. Scholars have often read this emigration as evidence of the erosion and dissolution of the Wendats. The weight of colonialism had been too much for the western Wendats, and it ultimately snapped the ligaments tying them together. According to this reading, the defection of a Wendat faction to Sandusky in the

1730s represented a profound split between the two camps. While one faction remained at Detroit and continued to support the French, the rebellious Sandusky faction abandoned the French for the British and moved closer to the British colonies. The break, then, was a decisive split within the Wendat polity.[25] Indeed, Henry Hamilton, the British governor of Detroit, suggested that the Sandusky and Detroit Wendats were "Rivals & Jealous, except when a Common Indian Interest engages them to Unanimity."[26] Later the Sandusky Wendat Donquat confessed that the "Wyandots over the lake [at Detroit]" were "nothing to him." He identified only with "those who live in Sandusky."[27]

Hamilton and Donquat notwithstanding, this chapter offers an alternative reading of the Wendat movement to Sandusky. Placing this movement to Sandusky in the context of precontact northern Iroquoian settlement patterns, it suggests that the Wendats moved to the Ohio Valley in order to expand their homeland into a new region, rather than divide the nation in two. Creating a larger homeland—a new Wendake—gave the Wendats access to new resources and allowed them to reposition themselves as diplomatic intermediaries.

This expansion into the region south of Lake Erie began in the mid-1730s, likely to take advantage of the abundant game found there. Heretofore the Wendats had only visited the region in passing, on their way to attack their traditional enemies, the Cherokees and Catawbas. Shortly after a peace accord between those groups and the Wendats removed the threat from the region, Wendat hunters began venturing south of the lake.[28] Some evidence indicates that they may have arrived as early as 1736, when a French census taker recorded that some Iroquoian speakers—most likely Wendats—lived on the south shore of Lake Erie.[29] These may have been the same forty Wendats who had moved south to live with the Shawnees in 1735.[30]

South of the lake the Wendats found an abundance of game. They claimed a hunting territory that stretched from the Maumee River in the west along the southern side of Lake Erie to the Scioto watershed in the east and at least as far south as present-day Coshocton, Ohio.[31] As Charles Stuart observed in 1755, Wendat hunters came from Detroit to the region every October and dispersed into hunting camps spread throughout the region before returning to Detroit in April. Indeed, Stuart even referred to the Wendat village at Sandusky as the "Head Quarters of the Wondot Hunters during the Winter Season."[32] In another example from the same decade, a Detroit Wendat whom the French called Le Glorieux spent the winter at Sandusky.[33] Likewise, James Smith, another British captive, encountered scores of Wendats hunting in the region during the mid- and late 1750s.[34] A Wendat leader confirmed in 1761 that Sandusky was only inhabited by "some hunters, who search for their livelihood there."[35] The Wendat seasonal migration to Sandusky was so great that even the Jesuit missionaries followed their parishioners there during the winter.[36]

While the Wendats had begun hunting in Sandusky in the mid-1730s, they did not intensively occupy the region until after 1738. In that year a conflict with the neighboring Odawas—the Wendats' longtime neighbors and erstwhile allies—forced most of the Wendats to flee to the relative safety of Sandusky in the winter of 1738–39. Although most of the Wendats eventually filtered back to Detroit, some refused to return. Led by the headmen Anguirot and Nicolas Orontony, they formed a village at Sandusky Bay called Etionnontout, also known as Junondat, and these separatists encouraged their fellow Wendats to join them.[37] By 1740 they had begun clearing trees to plant crops.[38] This development marked an important transition for the Wendats at Sandusky. The evidence suggests that heretofore Sandusky had likely been a seasonally occupied hunting ground, but now the settlers lived at Sandusky throughout the year, hunting in the winter and growing crops in the summer. In the mid-1740s Pierre Potier counted twelve Wendat longhouses at Sandusky, although some appeared to be only temporarily occupied.[39]

The decision of some Wendats to settle permanently at Sandusky created controversy. While Anguirot, Orontony, and their followers wished to remain at Sandusky, where they would be safe from the Odawas and could trade with the British in the Ohio Valley, others supported the leaders Sastaretsy and Tayachitin, who wanted to move their village to the vicinity of Montreal. The conflict intensified when, during King George's War (1744–48), Orontony and many of the Sandusky Wendats renounced the Wendats' longtime alliance with the French and sided with the rival British. After organizing an abortive attack on Detroit in 1747, Orontony and his followers left Sandusky and fled to the Muskingum River, at the site of current-day Coshocton, Ohio. Orontony's actions threatened to rend the Wendats into two rival peoples: a pro-French faction living at Detroit and a pro-British faction at Sandusky.[40] They began to distinguish between those who lived at Detroit—the *ekandechiateeronnon*—and those who moved to Sandusky— the *etionnontoutronnon*.[41] Relations between the two groups had grown so bad by 1750 that the Detroit Wendat leader Babi feared "some treasonous coup on the part of the rebels."[42] Scholars have often interpreted Orontony's exodus from Detroit as a critical moment of division within the Wendat community between "Hurons" living at Detroit and "Wendats" at San-dusky.[43]

Despite this apparent rift within the Wendat community, however, the Wendats eventually mended their disputes. A mere six years after they had left for Coshocton, the pro-British faction returned to Detroit. At a confer-ence at Detroit in April 1753, the Wendats who had gone to Sandusky "re-turned for forever" to Detroit and promised to never again "abandon their village." They also "no longer differentiate[d] our nation which now only makes one Body."[44] By the time Charles Stuart traveled through the hunt-ing camps to Sandusky and finally Detroit in the 1750s, he encountered a unified Wendake in which Wendat people moved constantly back and forth over Lake Erie in order to hunt in the Sandusky hinterlands and then return home. The Wendats therefore reaffirmed their communal identity, not as San-dusky "Wyandots" and Detroit "Hurons" but as Wendats living in the Great Lakes Region.

By the time the British regulars and Massachusetts minutemen skirmished at Lexington in 1775, then, the Wendats had carved out a homeland that em-braced the western end of Lake Erie. To the north, the Wendats continued to occupy their village site at the Pointe à Montréal on the southeastern side of the river across from the French fort. Occupied since the late 1740s, the Pointe à Montréal village—the "Chief Wondot Town," as Stuart put it—hosted the Jesuit mission and the Wendat council building.[45] Farther south and across the river from the Pointe à Montréal, the Wendats had established another village following Pontiac's War.[46] Later named after Adam Brown, a British captive whom the Wendats had adopted and who married a Wendat woman and had risen to prominence in the nation, Brownstown was situated along the Huron River. Moravian missionary David Zeisberger noted several "towns and settlements of the Wyandots" scattered along the western shore of the river.[47]

South of the lake, the Wendat homeland stretched from the mouth of the Maumee River in present-day Indiana in the west to the Scioto River water-shed in the east. The Wendats had villages at Lower Sandusky on the Sandusky River, south of the bay where they had maintained the villages of Canuta or Sunyedeand, near Pickerel Creek south of the bay, and Etionnontout or Junon-dat at the site of present-day Castilla, Ohio.[48] By 1775 the Wendats also had a village at Upper Sandusky, south and upriver from the bay. At least a few Wen-dats lived on the Little Scioto River as well.[49] During the winter, the Wendats broke up into scores of hunting camps throughout this region.[50]

CAPITALS AND SATELLITES: EXPLAINING
WENDAT EXPANSION

In creating a new Wendat homeland embracing Lake Erie, the Wendats appeared to be refiguring long-standing Iroquoian spatial organization in a new region. When the French first encountered the people whom they called "Hurons" and "Pétuns," these peoples lived in geographically extended homelands. Within these homelands, these northern Iroquoian groups divided themselves into a wide array of settlements from large, central settlements to small, seasonally occupied hamlets, and finally to seasonally occupied camps.[51]

The new homeland that the Wendats carved out after the 1730s closely resembles the tripartite categorization that archaeologist Paul Lennox has devised for precontact northern Iroquoian settlements, which sheds light on the Wendats' decision to expand to Sandusky. The first of these settlements, which Lennox calls "capital villages" or simply "villages," showed signs of intensive, long-term occupation, a diversity of economic activities, and a great deal of long-distance trade items.[52] Based on the size of these settlements—the largest of which occupied ten acres—and the presence of high-status goods, Lennox concludes that these settlements occupied a political, economic, and perhaps spiritual centrality. Noticing that the identified northern Iroquoian capital sites contained a higher concentration of long-distance trade items such as copper, Lennox concludes that the capital sites served as economic cores that absorbed the products of the outlying hamlets. The greater array of high-status goods also suggests the presence of high-status people in these capital villages.[53] In the 1630s the Jesuit missionary Paul Le Jeune noted that "large villages" in Wendake often contained "several Captains, both civil and war."[54] The presence of high-status leaders in these capital villages indicates that these sites enjoyed a political centrality within the northern Iroquoian homelands.

In addition to these capitals, Lennox also identifies smaller settlements located near the capitals, which he calls "satellites" or "hamlets." Much smaller than the larger capitals—one archaeologically identified hamlet site measures less than an acre—these settlements served a subordinate but important role for northern Iroquoians. The residents of these satellite villages focused on more specialized economic tasks, such as hunting or farming, instead of the full range of economic activities found at the capital sites. Gabriel Sagard, a Recollect priest and early visitor to Wendake Ehen, noted that the Wendats maintained "many hamlets of seven to eight cabins, built in several places convenient for fishing, for hunting, or for the culture of the soil."[55] Located near productive hunting grounds or rich soils, these hamlets both expanded the nation's economic base and reduced the pressure on the resources near the larger capital villages. In contrast to the capitals, these "satellites" appeared to lack the political influence of the capitals and assumed a subordinate position within the larger homeland. The archaeological assemblages of the northern Iroquoian satellite sites contain fewer high-status trade goods, suggesting that many of these goods found their way to the capitals from the outlying settlements. The paucity of these materials also suggests that the hamlets possessed fewer high-status individuals relative to their population.[56] Father Le Jeune confirmed that the smaller villages often had fewer chiefs than the larger villages and that these tended to be war, rather than village, chiefs. He recorded that the Wendat leader Aenons dismissed the "small hamlet" in which Le Jeune lived because it lacked a "Captain who can put you in his protection." Aenons's tone suggests that regardless of the satellites' economic importance, they assumed a subordinate political role to the capital village.[57] Finally, northern Iroquoians maintained small, seasonally occupied sites for very specific purposes, usually hunting, which left only ephemeral archaeological evidence.[58]

Archaeological and ethnographic evidence emphasizes, furthermore, that various settlements formed an integrated political and economic unit, not a collection of isolated and disconnected settlements. Lennox has found evidence of extensive trade between the satellite villages and the capitals, indicating that these places served as critical nodes within a greater economic system. He also interprets the lack of substantial palisades surrounding the satellites and camps as a sign of political unity between the satellites and capitals; when threatened by external invasion, the residents of the satellites took refuge in the more heavily fortified capital villages.[59] According to Father Le Jeune, Aenons even suggested that the separate settlements consolidate into a single entity that could better withstand Haudenosaunee invasion.[60] His suggestion presumes that these separate villages belonged to a common economic and political community. Taken together, these capitals, satellites, and camps formed a vibrant and tiered geographic entity that made use of the northern Iroquoians' territory and resources.

In expanding their homeland to Sandusky in the 1730s and 1740s, the Detroit Wendats sought to create a homeland very similar to those their northern Iroquoian ancestors had inhabited in the seventeenth century. Although more geographically extensive than the precontact homelands—the

Sandusky settlements were a three-day journey from Detroit—this new Wendake nonetheless shared much in common with the precontact model.[61] The Detroit villages served as the capital while Sandusky acted as an outlying "satellite." While the populations of Sandusky and Detroit certainly waxed and waned over time and across seasons, the Detroit settlements always remained larger than the settlements at Sandusky and elsewhere. For example, Father Potier counted thirty-three longhouses at the Detroit-area settlement (then at Bois Blanc Island, a few miles south of current-day Detroit) compared to only sixteen south of Lake Erie. Moreover, four of those were inhabited by people who also had houses at Detroit.[62] In 1755 and 1756 Stuart counted merely eleven longhouses at Sandusky, and only three of those were currently occupied by a few families. The Detroit village, however, claimed between sixty and seventy structures with 160 adult warriors, or about 640 residents.[63] Besides demographic differences, the two settlements also played different roles within the Wendat homeland. The larger Detroit settlements saw a range of economic activities, while the Sandusky settlements focused more narrowly on hunting, serving, in Stuart's words, as "the Head Quarters of the Wondot hunters."[64] Such a division of labor between large economically diversified capitals and smaller economically focused satellites reflects the precontact northern Iroquoian traditions from which the Wendats came and which they sought to reestablish in the Great Lakes region.

The political relationship between the Detroit and Sandusky settlements also fit the political relations found in precontact northern Iroquoian homelands. As had the village sites in southern Ontario, the Detroit village remained the seat of Wendat authority and power at least through the American Revolution.[65] The Wendat council house, where the Wendats conducted diplomacy with their neighbors at Detroit and elsewhere, remained at the Pointe à Montréal, suggesting the political and spiritual centrality of Detroit.[66] In the 1870s the Wendat historian Peter Dooyentate Clarke reported that the Wendats kept their collection of wampum belts (which served as a diplomatic archive) at either the Pointe à Montréal or Brownstown under the care of his grandfather, Adam Brown.[67] Moreover, the three principal village chiefs all lived at Detroit, while none lived at Sandusky.[68] This evidence points to the Detroit villages' prominence as a political—and spiritual—center of the Wendat homeland.

An unidentified Wendat leader pointedly attested to Detroit's diplomatic and political centrality over Sandusky in 1761. When two Seneca representatives proposed holding a council at Sandusky in June, the Wendat leader

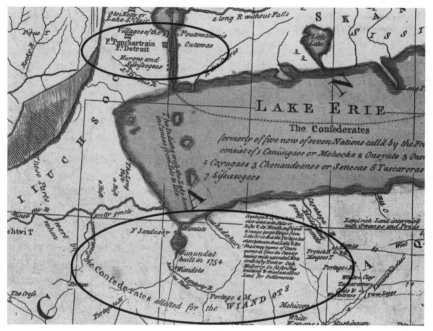

Map 2.2. Capital and Satellites of the New Western Wendake. Detail from
Lewis Evans, "Bowles's new pocket map of the following independent states
of North America: viz. Virginia, Maryland, Delaware, Pensylvania [sic],
New Jersey, New York, Connecticut & Rhode Island: comprehending also
the habitations & hunting countries of the confederate Indians" (London,
1784). Lawrence H. Slaughter Collection of English Maps, Charts, Globes,
Books and Atlases, New York Public Library, Map Div. 97-6006 (LHS 228),
ID no. 434112.

refused and insisted that they meet at Detroit instead. According to the speaker,
Sandusky was "a country of thorns. . . . It is true there have been, sometimes,
some fires, but it was by some hunters who search for their livelihood there. We
tell you we do not go there."[69] The headman's language, couched in diplomatic idioms, is suggestive. Northern Iroquoians differentiated the domestic
world of the "village" from that of the dark and dangerous "woods." By dismissing the Sandusky village as a place choked by thorns and brambles, the
speaker seems to be classifying Sandusky as marginal space unsuited for
diplomacy.[70] Detroit, not Sandusky, was the appropriate place for the kind
of diplomacy the Senecas hoped to conduct. The speakers' use of "fire" is

likewise meaningful: a "fire" referred to a place of settlement or a village. In suggesting that there had been "some fires" there, but that these had only been lit by "some hunters," the speaker likewise emphasized the subordinate role that Sandusky played in Wendat political life.

A 1769 exchange further underlines the political connection between Detroit and Sandusky and the political centrality of Detroit in that relationship. On the heels of the 1768 Treaty of Fort Stanwix, in which the Haudenosaunees alienated significant parts of the Ohio Valley (large swaths of which belonged to other peoples), a "Party of Ohio Senicas [Mingoes], Shawanese & Delawares" came to Detroit to hold a "private Council in the Huron Village." These peoples asked the Detroit Wendat headmen for some "Lands near Quiyahaga [Cuyahoga] to Plant & Hunt," which the Wendats granted them.[71] The Delawares and their Moravian missionaries, John Heckewelder and Zeisberger, later confirmed that the Wendats had given the Delawares the land they inhabited.[72] Five years later, a Shawnee band fleeing the violence known as Dunmore's War asked the senior Detroit leaders Sastaretsy and Babi to grant them "a spot of ground" near Sandusky.[73] If the Sandusky Wendats were indeed autonomous and the Sandusky settlements were separate from those at Detroit, then the Sandusky Wendat chiefs presumably held the power to grant Wendat lands south of Lake Erie. That the Delawares and Shawnees sought out the Wendat chiefs at Detroit rather than Sandusky suggests that the Delawares recognized that the Detroit village chiefs alone had the authority to grant them these lands and that the Detroit Wendat headmen concurred.

The minutes of a 1778 council between the British and several Indigenous nations likewise indicates Detroit's political preeminence over Sandusky and suggests that the principal Wendat chiefs remained at Detroit. Dutifully cataloging the chiefs present at the conference, the scribe listed the "Hurons"—presumably those from Detroit—separately from the "Hurons of Sandoskey." He counted nine Detroit Wendat chiefs, six war chiefs, and three village chiefs. While the Sandusky delegation contained four war chiefs, it included no village chiefs. Rather, all three village chiefs—Otiokouandoron/Babi, a Turtle; Dawatong/Sastaretsy, the hereditary Deer phraty leader;[74] and Shugaresse, who likely represented the smaller Wolf grouping—lived at Detroit.[75] The document therefore suggests that no village chief lived at the Sandusky settlements and war chiefs alone represented these villages.[76] The Delawares' frequent references to the "King of the Wiandots [Sastaretsy] and wise men who live at Detroit," the "great Wyondotts Chief," and the "Main Chieff Bawbee [Babi] at Detroit" likewise suggests that the principal Wendat leaders remained at Detroit, rather than Sandusky.[77] If no village chiefs resided at Sandusky, then those settlements, like the small satellite hamlets that Father Le Jeune had encountered in Wendake more than a century earlier, must have fallen under the greater authority of the village chiefs at Detroit.

The model that emerges from this evidence, then, is not one of a divided people inhabiting separate spheres but of a united Wendake encompassing a wide region, much like the precontact northern Iroquoian homelands had. The Wendats' particular geographic arrangement, in turn, served their economic and diplomatic interests well. From an economic standpoint, the Wendats' expansion simultaneously reduced their demands on the resources around Detroit and extended their resource base. By the time the Sandusky Wendats left Detroit for Sandusky in the 1730s, the Wendats had been living at Detroit for around three decades—much longer than the ten to twenty years their northern Iroquoian ancestors had occupied any single village site.[78] Such a long occupation had likely taxed the resources immediately around Detroit, particularly the wood and expansive land needed for slash-and-burn agriculture. Since the Wendats' arrival at Detroit, moreover, the post had grown from a small outpost to a rapidly growing agriculture colony. Indeed, Detroit witnessed a rapid expansion of the lands granted to French habitants in the 1730s, at precisely when the Wendats began settling around Sandusky.[79] Around 1740 the Wendats fretted about "the Sterility of their Fields."[80] The Wendats later complained that French and British settlers had encroached on their lands and had begun clearing woodlots that belonged to them.[81]

Sandusky, with its ample game and rich soils, therefore provided the resources that had become scarce at Detroit. British captive John Pattin observed in 1755 that Sandusky was "a remarkable place" both for hunting waterfowl and fishing. In addition to abundant wildlife, Sandusky also provided fertile soil for the Wendats living there. The British captive James Smith found corn planted there during the summer of 1756, and British authorities later complained that the Sandusky Wendats supplied the anti-British forces during Pontiac's War.[82] By giving access to better hunting in the Ohio Valley and opening new lands to crops, the Sandusky settlement expanded the Wendats' resource base profoundly.

At the same time, this expansion also served Wendat diplomatic interests well. Their geographical arrangement—with nodes at Detroit, Sandusky, and the scattering of smaller camps in the Ohio Valley—allowed the Wendats to insinuate themselves in the complicated geopolitics of that region. Since the 1750s the Ohio Valley region had emerged as a diplomatic center of eastern

North America as Native and European peoples from the East, South, and North converged.[83] With settlements both at Detroit and Sandusky, the Wendats were well positioned to navigate the rapidly changing political realities in the region. The Wendats living in the Ohio Valley collected and communicated information rapidly to their brothers at Detroit. Their geographic position also maintained alliances with the various peoples—the Ohio Iroquois, or Mingoes, Delawares, Shawnees, and Miamis—living in the region. Indeed, in recognition of their influence, the British and Haudenosaunees recognized the Wendats as the "Head of the Western Nations."[84] Governor Hamilton likewise noted that the Wendat Nation "is greatly respected by all the neighbouring nations," and his rebel counterpart agreed that the "Wyondats are respected by the western Indian Nations as much as the six nations are by the Northern."[85] Assuming a prominent role within the region, the Wendats pursued an ambitious diplomatic strategy and positioned themselves to influence affairs in the region. Wendat influence was at no time more apparent than during the American Revolution. When the war came to the Ohio Valley, the Wendats were well suited to navigate a violent and unpredictable world at war.

THE NEW WENDAKE AT WAR: THE WENDAT
IN THE AMERICAN REVOLUTION

The Wendats living on the borders of Lake Erie confronted the American Revolution, then, not as a collection of autonomous and rival peoples but as a political whole. Together they crafted a common Wendat strategy in which both the Sandusky and Detroit settlements played crucial roles. The Wendats' reaction to a crisis in 1779 aptly demonstrates this strategy and the political collaboration between the various settlements in the new Wendake. From the outset of the conflict, the Wendats had supported their old British allies against the "Virginians" who had been illegally encroaching on Native lands in the Ohio Valley and with whom the Wendats and their allies had been skirmishing throughout the previous decade. Yet the rebel defeat of the British at Fort Sackville (Vincennes) and the capture of Detroit governor Henry Hamilton, coupled with an imminent invasion of Sandusky by US troops, forced the Wendats to reconsider their support for their British "fathers." Using their unique geographic position and their extensive contacts within the Ohio Valley, the Sandusky and Detroit Wendats repositioned themselves in a dangerous and unstable situation, maintaining their alliance with the

British while also cultivating a relationship with the Americans—albeit tentatively and perhaps disingenuously. After the trouble had passed, they reaffirmed their alliance with the British and resumed their raids on the Pennsylvania and Virginia frontiers. The Wendats could only mount such a response because they maintained a presence in the Ohio Valley and because those Ohio Valley settlements remained integrated in a common Wendake. The Wendats' actions in 1779—and in fact throughout the war—therefore bespeak the continuing connections between the Detroit and Sandusky Wendats.

Early in the war, the Wendats formulated a strategy premised on the communication and collaboration between the Wendat branches at Detroit and Sandusky. The Sandusky war chief Orontony articulated this approach in a meeting with representatives from Virginia in July 1775. Anticipating a conflict with Great Britain, the Virginia delegates asked the Wendats and other peoples to remain neutral in the Anglo-American controversy. Orontony answered that he and his fellow Sandusky chiefs could not promise anything. Instead, he would send the Virginian's message "Over the Lakes [Erie] to our Chiefs [at Detroit] and [would] be ruled by them in our determinations." He added that it was "always a Custom with us Whatever News we hear immediately send to our head Men as we shall on this Occasion."[86] Another Sandusky leader, Donquat, repeated much the same thing to a delegation from the US Congress at Fort Pitt in October of that year. He explained that the senior Wendat leaders at Detroit could not attend the present conference but had "sent word to my People on this side of the Lake [i.e., Sandusky] to . . . [come] to the Council and Listen which is the reason you now see us here." Donquat, however, promised to relay Congress's message to "our Chiefs" at Detroit.[87] He likewise sent "messengers to Detroit, and to the chiefs of the Wyandots, near that place," to tell that they had made peace with the mostly Delaware congregation of Moravians living at Coshocton in 1777.[88] When he received another invitation to make peace with the United States in 1778, Donquat promised to "Acquaint my Chiefs of it who are over the Lakes and what ever they Bid me[,] that I shall do."[89] He dutifully transmitted this message "over the lake to the great Wyondotts Chief there."[90] In 1779 Donquat vowed he would transmit a message from the Delawares "to the Chiefs at Detroit, and what they thought fit to do, would be his rule."[91]

As these statements demonstrate, the Sandusky Wendats played a politically subordinate but essential role in the joint Wendat response to the war. Orontony and Donquat clearly testified to the subordination of the Sandusky "satellites" to the Detroit "capital." The two chiefs repeatedly reiterated that they could not make any decisions themselves but would instead be "ruled by" "our Chiefs" at Detroit and do "what ever they Bid." For this reason his European contemporaries referred to Donquat as the Wendat "Half King"; although he was an important leader, Donquat lacked the authority of the principal chiefs—or "kings" at Detroit.[92]

Despite their subordination to the Detroit leaders, however, the Sandusky leaders played a critical role in the Wendats' response to the war, serving as important conduits through which information passed and by which the Wendats projected their influence deep into the Ohio Valley. Situated in the Ohio Valley and in close proximity to the Mingoes, Shawnees, Delawares, Pennsylvanians, and Virginians, the Sandusky Wendats served as diplomatic proxies that extended Wendat reach and influence. The Sandusky Wendats kept Detroit abreast of developments in the Ohio Valley and passed "whatever News we hear immediately . . . to our head Men." Moreover, the Sandusky Wendats, and particularly Orontony at Lower Sandusky and Donquat at Upper Sandusky, served as diplomatic intermediaries for the village chief at Detroit. As Donquat reported in 1775, he had been sent by the Detroit village chiefs to "Listen" to the congressional delegates and to relay those messages.[93] The Detroit village chiefs explicitly spoke to the Sandusky settlement's intermediary status in 1785. They reminded Donquat that he was "to receive Speeches or Messages, and not to determine upon them, but to rise up and lay them before this [the Detroit Wendat] Council yourself to be settled here."[94] Donquat, the "half king," and the other Sandusky residents connected the Wendats to the Ohio Valley.

The success of this strategy, of course, depended on the regular communication between the Wendat settlements at Detroit. A sampling of the diary of Jehu Hay, the British Indian agent at Detroit, testifies to almost constant Wendat movement between Detroit and Sandusky. In 1776 alone Hay reported at least seven separate visits from the Sandusky Wendats important enough to note in his journal.[95] Donquat himself visited in March when he met with the principal Wendat chief Tetaowntarissé, known to the French and British as La Calotte, as well as Henry Hamilton, governor of Detroit. Orontony also visited Detroit at least twice that year, coming in early January and in late July and early August. "Four Hurons . . . arrived from Sandusky" in June, "Two Hurons from Sandusky" were there the following month, "a Huron arriv'd from Sandusky" in August, and "Twenty Seven Hurons from Sandusky" came in December. At Detroit these Sandusky Wendats conferred with their Detroit siblings and brought information and messages from the

Ohio Valley. In August, for instance, they brought a belt to the Detroit Wendats from the Shawnees, who promised to come to Detroit soon. Reciprocally, when the Detroit Wendats wanted to send a belt to the Iroquois in January 1777, they gave it to two Wendats "who belong'd to Sandusky" who would then take it to the Iroquois.[96] In a very real way, then, the Sandusky Wendats served as the conduits through which the Detroit Wendats interacted with the Ohio Valley.

Not surprisingly, the Sandusky Wendats, and especially Donquat at Upper Sandusky, played a critical role in the events of 1779. During these tumultuous months, Donquat, a respected Wendat leader in his own right, served as an intermediary between the Detroit Wendat chiefs and the pro-rebel Delawares, as well as a go-between with the rebels themselves. His close collaboration with the Detroit chiefs allowed the Wendats a diplomatic flexibility that prevented disaster and allowed the Wendats to navigate the vagaries of war.

Although the Wendats, and especially the Sandusky Wendats, had enthusiastically supported the British since the beginning of the war, two developments in March 1779 forced them to at least temporarily reconsider their position. First, the Wendats knew, at least by March 24, that a rebel army commanded by George Rogers Clark had defeated the British garrison at Fort Sackville (current-day Vincennes, Indiana) in early February and had taken Lt. Gov. Henry Hamilton and the popular Indian agent Jehu Hay prisoner. In fact, the acting commander of Detroit learned of the defeat from two Wendats who had been present at Vincennes.[97] At around the same time they learned of Hamilton's defeat, the Wendats had heard that an army of rebel soldiers from Fort Pitt planned to attack Sandusky sometime that spring. The rebels had advanced as far as the Tuscarawas River in late 1778 and established Fort Laurens, a mere three days' march from Sandusky, and had left a garrison of 250 soldiers.[98] By March the Wendats knew that "a large body of Virginians" was then preparing to launch a campaign against Sandusky.[99] Alarmed at the imminent invasion of their homeland, the Sandusky leaders implored both Lt. Henry Bird, the British officer at Sandusky, and Maj. Belanger Lernoult, the acting commandant at Detroit, for the aid that Hamilton had long promised them. Without British soldiers and artillery, the Wendats worried they would not be able to repel the rebel forces. Although he appealed for help from his superiors, Lernoult answered that he could do little to help the Wendats without reinforcements.[100]

The new situation required a new Wendat strategy, which Donquat signaled at a conference at Sandusky on April 1. Donquat called on his neighbors and close allies, the Delawares, among the few rebel sympathizers in the region. Irritated that the British had failed to support him, Donquat told the Delawares that his British "father" was "good for nothing & I will not listen any more to his speeches." He then asked the Delawares to relay a message to their rebel allies. Addressing his *"Brothers the Virg*[inians]*s"*—a generic term for all the rebellious colonists—he thanked them for a letter that Daniel Brodhead, the new rebel commander at Fort Pitt, had sent the Wendat chiefs offering to make peace. The Sandusky leader promised to "go to Detroit" where he would "do Good works among the Nation" by advocating for a reconciliation with the United States.[101] A few weeks later, Donquat responded to a second letter sent by Brodhead and reiterated both his support for an alliance with the rebels and his role as an intermediary for the Detroit Wendats. Written on April 8 and addressed to the principal Detroit village leader, the "Wyondot Chief Baubee," Brodhead's letter asked the Wendats to come to a council at Fort Pitt to be held in a month's time.[102] In his response Donquat told Brodhead that he had forwarded the letter "to my chief over the lake" (e.g., Babi) and that he would "assist them [the Detroit Wendat leaders] in Considering" Brodhead's invitation and a possible alliance with the Americans. Donquat's reference to "my chief" of course underlined his loyalty and subordination to the Detroit Wendats, as well as his role as a crucial conduit for the Wendats.[103]

Donquat's overture to the rebels underlines his role as an intermediary and demonstrates the particular genius of the Wendats' geopolitical strategy. Specifically, the Wendats' extensive geographic contacts in the Ohio Valley, especially the Delawares, allowed the Wendats to reposition themselves politically. Since the Delawares had settled on lands ceded to them by the Wendats in the 1760s, the two nations had forged a powerful alliance. In recognition of the Wendats' previous ownership of their territory and influence in the region, the Delawares referred to the Wendats as their "uncles" and frequently deferred to their judgment.[104] As the Delawares noted in 1775, his "Uncles the Wiandots have bound the Shawanese Tawaas [Odawas], and Delawares together and have made us as one People."[105] Given the Wendat and Delaware alliance, therefore, the Wendats naturally turned to the Delawares when they sought to reach out to the United States. A portion of the Delawares led by White Eyes had enthusiastically supported the rebels and had endeavored to convince the Wendats to abandon their alliance with the British.[106] As recently as early February 1779, the pro-rebel Delaware leader John Killbuck had sent an invitation to the Wendats to make peace with the rebels. Although Donquat chided the Delawares for supporting the United States at the time, he had changed his mind by April and called on his Delaware neighbors to mediate between the Wendats and the United States.[107] That he could do so testifies to the Wendats' extensive contacts in the region and his role as a diplomatic mediator.

True to his word, Donquat traveled to Detroit in April or May to consult with "My Chieffs," the Detroit village headmen. After a captive "Virginian" read Brodhead's letter to them, the Wendats gathered to deliberate about how to respond to the message. After four days, the Wendats decided to "make peace with the Americans" and to send out couriers to stop the war parties currently on their way to the backcountry settlements. They also wrote Brodhead, via their prisoner, that they had been forced into the war by the British and that they now put down their "War Club."[108] In the letter the senior Wendat chiefs Babi and Sastaretsy told Brodhead that they "all were very glad when we heard from you" and promised to go to the proposed conference at Fort Pitt.[109] As proof of their intentions they sent three wampum belts with John Montour, a pro-rebel operative who had long encouraged the Wendats to abandon the British in order to "conclude Peace" with the rebels.[110] Montour arrived at Fort Pitt later in May and told the rebels there "the Wyondot are on their way to Pittsburgh to make peace with the United States."[111]

The Wendat overture to the rebels, of course, probably signaled less a full-hearted renunciation of the British alliance than a political expediency. Donquat had sent his initial message to the rebels on April 1 out of sheer necessity; the congressional forces planned to leave Fort Pitt imminently and in fact only abandoned that campaign when they learned of Donquat's speech.[112] One British trader with rebel sympathies even thought that the entire peace overture was an elaborate ruse, one issued, coincidentally, on April Fools' Day. He wrote Brodhead that the Wendats "only mean to deceive You a while" and would then resume their attacks on the Virginia and Pennsylvania frontiers.[113]

More likely, Donquat and the other Wendats hoped to temporize with both the rebels and British until they could see how the situation developed.[114] The defeat of Hamilton and the near-invasion of Wendake clearly worried the Wendats. As a senior British official noted, the "unfortunate miscarriage of Lieut Gov'r Hamilton [had] strongly served to alienate [the Natives'] affections."[115] As late as August, the Hurons of Sandusky told Lernoult of their "uneasiness of Govr Hamilton's disaster & of the enemy Coming against them."[116] Moreover, Major Lernoult's failure to aid the Wendats in the time of their greatest need enraged them. In July a "Huron deputy from Sandusky," probably speaking for Donquat, reminded Lernoult that Lieutenant Governor Hamilton had frequently promised to "gather the whites and blacks [e.g., the Natives]" against any rebel invasion. When that invasion came, however, the British had taken "no step to Save us."[117] Terrified at the rebel advance toward Sandusky, irate at the inability of the British to help them, and dispirited by Hamilton's defeat, the Wendats hedged their bets while they watched developments during that year. As Alexander McCormack observed in June, the Wendats hoped "to be in on both sides" without choosing either.[118]

Without fully renouncing their alliance with the British, the Wendats quietly explored an alliance with the United States throughout the summer and fall of 1779. They frequently promised to come meet with the Americans at Fort Pitt and thereby kept the rebels from attacking Sandusky. They also largely refrained from participating in the raids on the British frontier and even encouraged their neighbors in the region to do the same. The Wendats opposed a proposed British-led campaign against Fort Lawrence, having "no mind" to join in the assault.[119] Lt. Henry Bird, the British officer put in charge of the campaign, griped that the Sandusky Wendats were "Rascals or Cowards they tell me their heads are down" and that they had "made Peace on a Belt with the Rebels."[120] Lernoult also blamed the Wendats for the "Evasions you made from Time to Time," which had undermined the campaign.[121] The Wendats also discouraged their neighbors and allies, such as the Shawnees, from going to war against the British.[122] Montour, who had helped facilitate the Wendats' peace with the Americans, told another rebel supporter that the "English call the Wyondotts Rebbels because they have turned friends with the States."[123]

At the same time they flirted with an American alliance, however, the Wendats never completely abandoned the British alliance. Despite their frequent assurances that they had quit the British father, the Wendats repeatedly deferred their promised visit to Fort Pitt. Although Babi had promised in mid-May to come "as soon as God permits," they still had not arrived by the end of the month.[124] In early June the Delawares reported that the "Hurons are on the road to this place [Pittsburgh]," and Brodhead informed his superior, George Washington, that "Peace with Wyandot [was] probable."[125] Yet when the Wendats had still not arrived by June 20, Brodhead confessed to the Delawares that he was "almost Weary of Waiting for the Wyandots."[126] In late June Babi sent a message via Donquat to Brodhead and the Delawares saying that he was at long last "ready to see You at Fort Pitt." Donquat added that he had "at all times pointed to those great Men over the Lake" and had finally prevailed on those leaders to make peace with the United States. Now he would, as the Wendat leaders' intermediary in the region, "rise up and go with them" to Fort Pitt.[127] Neither Donquat nor Babi, however, appeared at Fort Pitt in that month or the following. The Moravian minister John Heckewelder reported that there had been "No news of the Wyandot" by July 8, and the Delawares complained that it had been "three Months past since we told you to meet us here in Pittsburg" and begged them to "come without delay."[128] Although Babi did come as far as the Delaware town at Coshocton in August, there is no evidence that he actually met with British there.[129]

When, at long last, the Detroit village chiefs finally sent Donquat to speak at Fort Pitt, they seemed disinclined to make any real peace with the Americans. Speaking first, Brodhead welcomed Donquat and his entourage to Fort Pitt and "rejoice[d] that you are at last come to this great Council fire." He regretted the previous hostilities but promised that, if the Wendats delivered up their rebel prisoners and fought against the Mingoes and the English, they could finally make peace.[130] In his response, however, Donquat blithely ignored Brodhead's requests. Instead, he seemed much more interested in convincing Brodhead not to travel through Wendake when the rebel army advanced on Detroit. "Don't go the nighest way" to Detroit—via the Scioto and Sandusky—Donquat insisted. Rather, the army might choose a route that followed the Alleghany River north to Lake Erie, or perhaps swing to the west and follow the Wabash to the Maumee River and thence to Detroit.[131] Donquat's response infuriated Brodhead. He could offer no peace to the Wendats unless they pledged to fight against the British and surrender the prisoners they had taken on the Virginia and Pennsylvania frontiers. Moreover, the commander declared, "When I go to war, I will take my Choice of Roads."[132] As Brodhead guessed, the Wendats seemed more interested in protecting their homeland than in making any kind of lasting peace with the rebels.

This final diplomatic maneuver once again demonstrated the careful cooperation of the Detroit and Sandusky Wendats. At the conference Donquat reiterated his relationship with the Detroit village chiefs and his role as diplomatic intermediary. He told Brodhead that he spoke not only for himself but for "all the Huron [Wendat] Chiefs" who had sent him there. Donquat's language reiterated his important role as a go-between: "the Huron Chiefs desire me to mention," "The Chiefs desired me to tell you."[133] Donquat thereby emphasized his particular role in the Wendats' response to the war. He acted as a half king, influential in his own right but nonetheless a representative of a larger Wendat community.

The September council essentially marked the end of the Wendats' flirtation with the United States. The council itself could not have gone much worse, ending as it did with Brodhead's angry response. Although Brodhead later imagined that he could buy the Wendats' allegiance with "a few goods and trinkets," the Wendats seemed to abandon their attempts to make peace with the United States.[134] The threatened British invasion of the Shawnees— the Wendats' neighbors and "nephews"—had disturbed the Wendats.[135] More importantly, the rebel raid into Haudenosaunee territory likely both terrified and angered the Wendats, who by the eighteenth century had become close allies to the Iroquois. The Detroit Wendat chief Sastaretsy in fact met with Iroquois leaders at Niagara and vowed "never to make peace with the King's enemies."[136] The Wendats had resumed their hostilities against the back settlements by November of that year.[137] In the following years the Wendats resumed their central position, along with the Mingoes, as the Crown's most faithful supporters. In 1781 they even forced the Delawares to move to Sandusky so that the Delawares could no longer provide information to the rebels at Fort Pitt.

After September 1779 the Wendats opposed the Americans as fiercely as they ever had and continued that resistance at least until 1794. Yet their brief flirtation with a rebel alliance demonstrated the kind of flexibility that their geographic position allowed them. Most importantly, the cooperation between the Wendat core at Detroit and the periphery at Sandusky allowed the Wendats to maneuver more freely in the Ohio Valley and to act across a wider geographical stage. The Sandusky communities had served as adjuncts to the larger Wendat population at Detroit, conducting diplomacy throughout the region. Moreover, their expanded homeland and presence in the Ohio Valley paid other dividends to the Wendats. As the events in 1779 demonstrate, the Wendats had a wide communication network that stretched all the way from Detroit to Sandusky and from there to the Shawnees and Mingoes on the Scioto and the Delawares on the Muskingum. As the Wendats moved throughout this vast territory, they gathered information to be passed on to their kin at Detroit. As a result, the Wendats were well informed about events nearby that might affect them.[138] They knew, for example, about the fall of Fort Sackville before Major Lernoult did and learned about the rebels' intention to attack Sandusky in spring 1779. Their presence in the Ohio Valley also allowed the Wendats to maintain contact with the peoples of the Ohio Valley: the Mingoes, Shawnees, Delawares, Miamis, and others. Their relationship with the pro-rebel Delawares allowed the Wendats to make overtures to the United States. In short, their expanded Wendat homeland guaranteed the Wendats an important place within the Ohio Valley.

Nor were the Wendats alone in redrawing the maps of early America to their advantage. As scholars have begun to recognize, Native peoples' mobility was rarely a haphazard response to European colonialism and demographic collapse.[139] Rather, these authors contend, mobility was a powerful tool that indigenous people used to build new alliances and networks with Indigenous and European peoples and to expand their influence into contested or unclaimed areas. Most prominently, the Wendats' cultural cousins, the Six Nations Iroquois or Haudenosaunees, formed settlements far afield from their home territories. Jon Parmenter argues that the movement of (primarily) Mohawks to the Saint Lawrence Valley and (mostly) Senecas into the Ohio Valley expanded, rather than dissipated, the Six Nations' regional influence.[140] Kurt Jordan even identifies these new Haudenosaunee settlements as "colonies" established to extend influence, even if they did not practice "colonialism."[141] Likewise, as Michael Witgen demonstrates, the Wendats' Anishinaabe neighbors relied on kinship and cultural ties that stretched throughout the western Great Lakes to maintain their autonomy and assert their influence throughout "Anishinaabewaki, the lands of the Anishinaabeg."[142] The Kiskakon Odawas relied on these very connections when they were displaced by the Haudenosaunees, and the Anishinaabeg successfully used this strategy to control the "gateways" of the Great Lakes.[143] And, of course, "migration became a kind of signature" for the peripatetic Shawnees, allowing them to survive and thrive in a volatile colonial world. Moving from place to place and situating themselves on the edges of empire, the Shawnees retained and reconfigured their common identity as they moved throughout eastern North America.[144] What contemporary Europeans dismissed as hapless "wanderings" were in fact carefully orchestrated geopolitical strategies.

CONCLUSION

The story of the Wendats' continued political and social cohesion, at least through the American Revolution, has implications that reach beyond the new Wendake and help write a new narrative for Native history in early North America—a profoundly different story than that presented by previous scholars. In those tellings, the pressures of colonialism, particularly war between Great Britain and France, split the Wendats into rival factions, the "Hurons" and the "Wyandots." The implication is that at the beginning those ties binding the Wendat Nation together had been fragile. With only a little bit of pressure, the western Wendats, composed of several separate ethnic groups, split apart. Following James Clifton, historian Richard White likewise saw the Wendats' relocation to Sandusky as a defection from the larger Wendat Nation at Detroit. This defection, in turn, supported White's contention that "hammer blows" of colonialism had "shattered" the Native peoples of the Great Lakes.[145] Colonialism, according to this interpretation, had destroyed the separate identity of the Wendats, as it had for the other peoples of the region. This story is thus the familiar one of declension and dissolution.

Interpreting the Wendat settlement south of Lake Erie not as a division within the Wendat Nation but as a purposeful expansion of a Wendat homeland inverts this narrative. The Wendats' strength, not their weakness, impelled them to establish settlements south of Lake Erie, allowing them to expand their resource base into greener pastures, marshes, and forests. And, as Wendat conduct during the Revolution demonstrates, the establishment of these settlements in turn only enhanced their influence in the region. Politically integrated, the Wendats relied on their geographic position to maintain connections in the Ohio Valley. In this interpretation the Wendats did not succumb to the pressures of colonialism—although they certainly felt them. Rather, they responded to these pressures not by dissolving or dividing but by innovatively responding to the new challenges and opportunities they encountered. The Wendats showed themselves capable of responding to the rapidly changing circumstances they confronted in the eighteenth century. They also demonstrated the strength of the cultural and social bonds that held them together and made them a people.

In short, the Wendat expansion into the Ohio Valley after the 1730s, and their conduct during the Revolution, bespeaks to the Wendats' enduring strength and internal integrity. It depended, ultimately, on an undergirding cultural cohesiveness. Ultimately, of course, neither this cultural integrity nor the expanded Wendat homeland could fend off the insatiable Euro-American desire for land in the Ohio Valley. The relentless pressure for land led to further conflict with the United States, and the conflict continued into the early nineteenth century when the defeat of Tecumseh signaled the decline of Native autonomy in the region. Yet the social cohesion and innovative responses, which had formed a new Wendake in the eighteenth century, nonetheless survived the Wendats' removal to Indian Territory in the nineteenth century and the onslaught of "Americanization" in the twentieth.

NOTES

Part of this chapter is based on my PhD dissertation, "Jealous Neighbors: Rivalry and Alliance among the Native Communities of Detroit, 1701–1766," College of William and Mary, 2011. I would like to thank the Early American Reading Group at the University of Minnesota, Chris Parsons, the anonymous readers, and especially the Wendat and Wyandot commenters for invaluable feedback on this chapter. The William L. Clements Library also provided generous support for research.

    1. Charles Stuart, "The Captivity of Charles Stuart, 1755–57," ed. Beverley W. Bond, Jr., *Mississippi Valley Historical Review* 13 (1926–27): 58–81, 69–72; "Examination of Moses Moore and Isham Bernat," 1759, in Samuel Hazard, John Linn, William Egle et al., *Pennsylvania Archives* (Philadelphia: Joseph Severns, 1852), vol. 3: 632–33.

    2. For a small sample of the evidence of travel between these villages, see George Croghan, "George Croghan's Journal April 3, 1759 to April [30], 1763," ed. Nicolas B. Wainwright, *Pennsylvania Magazine of History and Biography* 71, no. 4 (October 1947): 373; Stuart, "Captivity," 78; George Croghan to Sir William Johnson, January 26, 1760, in William Johnson, *The Papers of Sir William Johnson*, ed. Alexander Flick (Albany: University of the State of New York, 1951), vol. 10: 137; George Croghan, "Journal," in Reuben G. Thwaites, ed., *Early Western Travels: Travel to the Interior of North America, 1748–1856* (Cleveland: Arthur H. Clark, 1904–7), vol. 1: 108.

    3. The Delaware leader John Killbuck referred to a Detroit Wendat man whose niece, a Sandusky Wendat woman, had been taken captive by a rebel party. Such evidence suggests that the two branches of the Wendat Nation were both figuratively and literally kin. Killbuck and the Delaware Council to Brodhead, Salem, July 19, 1780, in Louise Phelps Kellogg, ed., *Frontier Retreat on the Upper Ohio, 1779–1781* (Madison: State Historical Society of Wisconsin, 1917), 229 (hereafter cited as *FR*).

    4. "An Account of the Remarkable Occurrences in the Life and Travels of Colonel James Smith . . . during His Captivity with the Indians, in the Years, 1755, '56, '57, '58, and '59," in Samuel Drake, *Indian Captivities, or Life in the Wigwam; Being the True Narrative of Captives Who Have Been Carried Away by the Indians from the Frontier Settlements of the United States, from the Earliest Period to the Present Time* (Auburn, N.Y.: Derby and Miller, 1852), 204.

    5. Jon Parmenter, *The Edge of the Woods: Iroquoia, 1534–1701* (East Lansing: Michigan State University Press, 2010), xi; Jon Parmenter, "At the Wood's Edge: Iroquois Foreign Relations, 1727–1768" (PhD diss., University of Michigan, 1999).

    6. The Sandusky Wendats frequently referred to "our Chiefs" who lived "Over the Lakes." See also "Treaty at Pittsburgh, 1775," in Reuben G. Thwaites and Louise P. Kellogg, eds., *The Revolution on the Upper Ohio* (Madison: Wisconsin

Historical Society, 1908), 53; Baubee to George Morgan, August 16, 1778, in Louise P. Kellogg, ed., *Frontier Advance on the Upper Ohio, 1778–1779* (Madison: State Historical Society of Wisconsin, 1916), 128, 129 (hereafter cited as *FA*); Message from the Delaware and Wyandot Chiefs, December 21, 1778, in *FA* 187; Council at Detroit, February 7, 1779, in *FA* 220; John Killbuck to Lachlan McIntosh, March 13, 1779, in *FA* 248; Half King to Daniel Brodhead, [1779], in *FA* 309.

7. Richard White, *The Middle Ground: Indians, Empires, and Republics in the Great Lakes Region, 1650–1815* (New York: Cambridge University Press, 1991), 1; Gilles Havard, *Empire et métissages: Indiens et Français dans le pays d'en haut, 1660–1715* (Quebec City: Les éditions du Septentrion, 2003); Robbie Ethridge and Sheri Shuck-Hall, eds., *Mapping the Mississippian Shatter Zone* (Lincoln: University of Nebraska Press, 2009).

8. See Reuben Gold Thwaites, ed., *The Jesuit Relations and Allied Documents: Travels and Explorations of the Jesuit Missionaries in New France, 1610–1791* (Cleveland: Burrows, 1896–1901), vol. 34; Bruce Trigger, *The Children of Aataentsic: A History of the Huron People to 1660* (Montreal: McGill–Queen's University Press, 1987), vol. 2, chap. 11.

9. In challenging the narrative of dissolution and destruction posed most prominently by Richard White, this chapter contributes to the work of other scholars who have pointed out the resilience and adaptability of the so-called refugees and have questioned French influence within the Great Lakes. See, for example, William Newbigging, "The History of the French-Ottawa Alliance" (PhD diss., University of Toronto, 1995); Heidi Bohaker, "*Nindoodemag:* The Significance of the Algonquian Kinship Networks in the Eastern Great Lakes Region, 1600–1701," *William and Mary Quarterly* 63, no. 1 (January 2006): 23–52; Brett Rushforth, "Slavery, the Fox Wars, and the Limits of Alliance," in ibid., 53–80; Michael Witgen, *An Infinity of Nations: How the Native New World Shaped Early North America* (Philadelphia: University of Pennsylvania Press, 2012).

10. Conrad Heidenreich, *Huronia: A History and Geography of the Huron Indians, 1600–1650* (Toronto: McClelland and Stewart, 1971); Susan Branstner, "Decision-Making Processes in a Culture Contact Context: The Case of the Tionontate Huron of the Upper Great Lakes" (PhD diss., Michigan State University, 1991); Jules M. Boucher, "The Legacy of Iouskeha and Tawiscaron: The Western Wendat People to 1701" (MA thesis, University of Kansas, 2001); Lucien Campeau, Appendice I: Les Hurons de Détroit, in *La mission des jésuites chez les Hurons, 1634–1650* (Montreal: Editions Bellarmin, 1987), 361–67; Trigger, *Children of Aataentsic*, 2:824–25; Charles Garrad and Conrad E. Heidenreich, "Khionontateronon (Petun)," in Bruce Trigger, ed., *Handbook of North American Indians*, vol. 15, *The Northeast* (Washington, D.C.: Smithsonian Institution, 1979); James A. Clifton, *Hurons of the West: Migrations and Adaptations of the Ontario Iroquoians, 1650–1704* (Ottawa: Canadian Ethnology Service, 1977).

11. For a fuller discussion of this topic, see Andrew Sturtevant, "'Inseparable Companions' and Irreconcilable Enemies: The Hurons and Odawas of French Détroit, 1701–1738," *Ethnohistory* 60, no. 2 (Spring 2013): 219–43.

12. Registre de Sainte Anne, Detroit, February 2, 1704–December 30, 1848, Detroit Public Library, Burton Historical Collection, vol. 1: 19, 67, 132, 240; Robert Toupin, "Introduction au registre de la mission huronne," in *Les écrits de Pierre Potier* (Ottawa: Les Presses de l'Université d'Ottawa, 1996), 793; Potier, "Registre Mortuaire," in ibid., 922–23, 925. See also John L. Steckley, *The Eighteenth-Century Wyandot: A Clan-Based Study* (Waterloo, Ont.: Wilfrid Laurier University Press, 2014), 101–3.

13. Fredrik Barth, *Ethnic Groups and Boundaries: The Social Organization of Culture Difference* (Long Grove, Ill.: Waveland, 1998).

14. Sturtevant, "'Inseparable Companions' and Irreconcilable Enemies."

15. Jacques-Charles de Sabrevois, "[Memoir on the Indians between Lake Erie and the Mississippi]," 1718, in John Romeyn Brodhead, trans., and E. B. O'Callaghan, ed., *Documents Relative to the Colonial History of the State of New York* (Albany: Weed, Parsons, 1854), vol. 9: 887; Pierre-François-Xavier Charlevoix, *Journal d'un Voyage*, ed. Pierre Berthiaume, 2 vols. (Montreal: Les Presses de l'Université de Montréal, [1744], 1994), 1:541.

16. "An Indian Conference, 7–10 May 1764," in *Papers of William Johnson*, 11:179.

17. "Discours des principaux chefs huron en conseil au Major Depeyster Commandant au Detroit le 29 juillet 1781," Haldimand Papers, Correspondence and Papers Relating to Detroit, vol. 21783 (hereafter cited as HP Detroit), ff. 64–65v., Library and Archives Canada, Ottawa.

18. Janith English, personal correspondence with author, August 29, 2013, November 19, 2013.

19. This notion—and the language of clan as "technology"—comes from a conference panel, chaired by Joshua Piker, in which I participated at the 2010 meeting of the American Ethnohistorical Society. Megan McCullen and Jean-François Lozier suggested that clan exogamy served as a unifying force for the Hurons. For a discussion of the cohesive role of clanship, see Elisabeth Tooker, "Northern Iroquoian Sociopolitical Organization," *American Anthropologist* 72, no. 1 (February 1970): 93; Boucher, "Legacy of Iouskeha and Tawiscaron," 27–28.

20. Toupin, *Les écrits de Pierre Potier*, 176.

21. "sa [les Wendat] hauteur la fait haïr des autres, Et l'on ne doit pas se flatter de la r[é]concilier bien sinc[è]rement avec les Outaoüais qui soufiront [sic] toujours impatiemment sa fierté." Résumé de lettres du Canada avec commentaires des autorités métropolitaines, 1740, C11A, vol. 74, ff. 235–235v., Centre des archives d'outre-mer (hereafter cited as CAOM), Aix-en-Provence, France.

22. Aigremont to the Minister, November 14, 1708, in Michigan Pioneer and Historical Society, *Collections and Researches* (hereafter cited as *CR*), vol. 33, "Cadillac Papers" (Lansing: Wynkoop Hallenbeck Crawford, 1903), 447.

23. "de ne nous point mêler avec d'autres Nations." Paroles des Hurons du Détroit a M^r Le Mis de Beauharnois, Gouverneur général de la Nouvelle France, parlant a M. De Noyelle Commadant aud. Poste, [1740], C11A, vol. 74, f. 75v., CAOM.

24. Conseil des hurons en pr[é]sence des outaoüas, et pouteuatamis [et Sauteux] et réponse," May 13, 1753, C11A, vol. 99, ff. 75v–77v., CAOM.

25. James Clifton, "The Re-emergent Wyandot: A Study in Ethnogenesis on the Detroit River Borderland, 1747," in K. G. Pryke and L. L. Kulisek, eds., *Papers from the Western District Conference* (Windsor, Ont.: Essex County Historical Society and Western District Council, 1983).

26. Henry Hamilton to Guy Carleton, April 25, 1778, HP Detroit, f. 30.

27. David Zeisberger, *Diary of David Zeisberger, a Moravian Missionary among the Indians of Ohio,* trans. Eugene F. Bliss (Cincinnati: Robert Clarke, 1885), vol. 1: 25.

28. The Miamis claimed that the Wendats had made peace by 1729, although a 1735 report suggested that they were only then on the brink of doing so. Beauharnois au minister, July 21, 1729, C11A, vol. 51, f. 127, CAOM; Réponse à la mémoire du roi par Beauharnois et Hocquart, October 13, 1735, C11A, vol. 63, ff. 91–91v., CAOM.

29. The French official refers to the "ontati onoué onoua," which bears at least a passing resemblance to "Iontady-haga," the Iroquois name for the Hurons or "Tionontaté" ("les ontati onoué, c'est des hommes ainsi nommés par les iroquois parcequils s'entendent"). Given the Wendats' later full-time settlement here in the following years, this explanation seems likely. "Dénombrement des nations sauvages qui ont rapport au gouvernement du Canada, des guerriers de chacune avec leurs armoiries," 1736, C11A, vol. 66, f. 254v., CAOM; Erminie Wheeler-Voegelin, *Indians of Northwest Ohio: An Ethnohistorical Report on the Wyandot, Potawatomi, Ottawa, and Chippewa of Northeast Ohio* (New York: Garland, 1974), 30–31.

30. Réponse à la mémoire du roi par Beauharnois et Hocquart, October 13, 1735, C11A, vol. 63, f. 92v., CAOM.

31. Stuart noted that the Maumee River marked the boundary between the Odawa and Wendat hunting territories. Stuart, "Captivity," 73. On his 1754 map, the British cartographer Thomas Jefferys indicated that the lands south and west of Lake Erie were recently "allotted for the Wiandots," even though they had clearly been hunting there since at least the 1730s. See Thomas Jefferys, "A General Map of the Middle British Colonies in America," 1758, Edward E. Ayer Collection, 133 39 1758, Newberry Library, Chicago.

32. Stuart, "Captivity," 72.

33. Joseph-Gaspard Chaussegros de Léry, "Journal de la Campagne," 1754–55, in Pierre-Georges Roy, ed., *Rapport d'Archiviste de la Province de Québec pour 1927–1928* (Québec: L. Amable Proulx, 1928), vol. 7: 409.

34. Smith, "An Account of the Remarkable Occurrences," in Drake, *Indian Captivities.*

35. "quelques chasseurs, qui y cherchoient leur vie." "Report of Indian Council," June 18, 1761, in Louis Waddell, John Tottenham, and Donald Kent, eds., *The Papers of Henry Bouquet,* vol. 5, *September 1, 1760–October 31, 1761* (Harrisburg: Pennsylvania Historical and Museum Commission, 1984), 593.

36. Pierre Potier, "Journal de Voyage," in Toupin, *Les écrits de Pierre Potier,* 164; Pierre-Joseph Céloron de Blainville to Pierre Potier, September 8, 1750, in ibid., 635–36; Potier to Céloron, September 8, 1750, in ibid., 637; Potier to Céloron, September 17, 1750, in ibid., 643.

37. Toupin, *Les écrits de Pierre Potier,* 164; Wheeler-Voegelin, *Indians of Northwest Ohio,* 91–92.

38. "Indian Affairs at Detroit in the Years 1738–1741," *CR* 34:201.

39. Pierre Potier, "Recensement des Hurons," in Toupin, *Les écrits de Pierre Potier,* 200–226.

40. Clifton, "Re-emergent Wyandot"; Andrew K. Sturtevant, "Jealous Neighbors: Rivalry and Alliance among the Native Communities of Detroit, 1701–1766" (PhD diss., College of William and Mary, 2011), chap. 4.

41. Pierre Potier, "Journal de Voyage," in Toupin, *Les écrits de Pierre Potier,* 162, 164.

42. "il Croignoit quelque Coup de traitre de La part des rebelles," Potier à Pierre-Joseph Céloron de Blainville, September 11, 1750, in Toupin, *Les écrits de Pierre Potier,* 642–43.

43. Anthropologist James Clifton interpreted the movement of Nicolas Orontony and his followers to Sandusky as a crucial moment of Wendat dissolution. Clifton noticed that many of the Sandusky faction belonged to the Turtle phratry, one of the three multiple-clan groupings in the Wendat social structure. Accordingly he speculated that the movement signaled a split between the members of the Wendat Confederacy and the other Iroquoian-speaking refugees who had joined them after 1649. Indeed, he noted, European observers referred to the Sandusky people as "Wendats," rather than Hurons, suggesting an ethnic distinction between them. In that sense, it was a "re-ethnogenesis" of that community. Clifton, "Re-emergent Wyandot," 1–15. Yet Clifton draws too neat a division between the members of the Turtle phratry clan and those of the two other Wendat phratries, ignoring the fact that many Turtles remained at Detroit. See Toupin, *Les écrits de Potier,* 176; Sturtevant, "Jealous Neighbors," 238–39. Moreover, the Wendats at Detroit had long identified themselves as "Wendats," suggesting that the Sandusky Wendats were claiming no new affiliation by doing the same. See John Steckley, "How the Huron Became Wyandot: Onomastic Evidence," *Onamastica Canadiana* 70, no. 198 (1988): 59n2; Charles Garrad and John Steckley, "A Review of *The Re-Emergent Wyandot,*" *Kewa: Newsletter of the London Chapter, Ontario Archaeological Society* 84, no. 7 (October 1984): 10–14; Boucher, "Legacy of Iouskeha and Tawiscaron," 14–18; Potier, "Journal de Voyage," in Toupin, *Les écrits de Pierre Potier,* 162; Steckley, *Eighteenth-Century Wyandot,* 40–48. Finally, he neglected to mention that most of these "reemergent" Wendats returned to the Detroit community in the following years.

44. "nous ne distinguons plus nôtre nation qui ne fait a pr[é]sent qu'un m[ê]me Corps." "Conseil des hurons en pr[é]sence des outaoüas, et pouteuatamis [et Sauteux] et réponse," May 13, 1753, C11A, vol. 99, ff. 76–77v., CAOM.

45. Stuart, "Captivity," 73; Peter Dooyentate Clarke, *Origin and Traditional History of the Wyandotts and Sketches of Other Indian Tribes of North America: True Traditional Stories of Tecumseh and His League in the Years 1811 and 1812* (Toronto: Hunter, Rose, 1870), 18, 37, 66–67; Sturtevant, "Jealous Neighbors," 225.

46. The Wendats moved to the vicinity of "otter River, Thirty Six Miles from Detroit," around the spring of 1765. "Conference between Bradstreet and the Wendots,"

September 29, 1764, in *Papers of Sir William Johnson*, 4:548. The Wendat leader called Old Calotte lived "10 leagues" from Detroit, likely at the same settlement. Hamilton to Gen. Guy Carleton, November 30, 1775, in Thwaites and Kellogg, *Revolution on the Upper Ohio*, 128.

47. *Diary of David Zeisberger*, 1:33. A British officer bought a tract of land from Wendats near the mouth of the Detroit River in 1784. See Haldimand to Hay, August 14, 1784, in *CR* 20:246.

48. Erminie Wheeler-Voegelin carefully lays out the relative positions of these two settlements. Although she claims that they had both been abandoned by 1764, the Wendats' later presence here suggests that they may have maintained a presence here after that. Wheeler-Voegelin, *Indians of Northwest Ohio*, 92, 157.

49. A 1778 document identifies the leader Snipe as the "Wyandatt War Chief from Scioto." "Council held at Detroit June 16 1778 with the Ottawas, Chippeways, Hurons, Pouteouattamis, Delawares, Shawanese, Miamis, Mingos, Mohawks, and the Tribes of Ouashtanon (Ouiatenon), Saguinan—Delawares—Senecas," HP Detroit, f. 50. See also Samuel Montgomery, "The Journal of Samuel Montgomery," *Mississippi Valley Historical Review* 2, no. 2 (September 1975): 262–73; Wheeler-Voegelin, *Indians of Northwest Ohio*, 201.

50. Wheeler-Voegelin, *Indians of Northwest Ohio*, 94–96.

51. Trigger, *Children of Aataentsic*, 1:31–32; Gary Warrick, *A Population History of the Huron-Petun*, A.D. *500–1650* (Cambridge: Cambridge University Press, 2008), 93–96.

52. Lennox, "The Bogle I and Bogle II Sites: Historic Neutral Hamlets of the Northern Tier," Archaeological Survey of Canada, Paper No. 121, National Museum of Man Mercury Series, Ottawa, 1984, 258–72. The closely related Haudenosaunees likewise maintained this range of settlements within and beyond their homelands. Kurt Jordan, "Incorporation and Colonization: Postcolumbian Iroquois Satellite Communities and Process of Indigenous Autonomy," *American Anthropologist* 115, no. 1 (March 2013): 29–43; Kurt Jordan, *The Seneca Restoration, 1715–1754: An Iroquois Local Political Economy* (Gainesville: University Press of Florida, 2008); Kurt Jordan, "Not Just 'One Site against the World': Seneca Iroquois Intercommunity Connections and Autonomy, 1550–1779," in Laura L. Scheiber and Mark D. Mitchell, eds., *Across a Great Divide: Continuity and Changes in Native North American Societies, 1400–1900* (Tucson: University of Arizona Press, 2010), 79–106.

53. Although Lennox introduces this model in a discussion of settlement patterns among the Neutrals, a northern Iroquoian people, it has applications to other Northern Iroquoians. Lennox, "Bogle I and Bogle II Sites," 258–72.

54. Paul Le Jeune, "Relation de ce qui s'est passé en la Nouvelle France, en l'année 1636," *JR* 10:230.

55. "plusieurs hameaux de sept à huict cabanes, bastis in divers endroits commodes pour la pesche, pour la chasse, ou pour la culture de la terre." Gabriel Sagard, *Histoire du Canada et voyages que les frères mineurs récollects y ont faicts pour la conversion des infidèles: depuis l'an 1615* (Paris: Libr. Tross, 1866), vol. 3: 802; Paul Lennox, ed., "MTO Contributions to the Archaeology of the Late Woodland Period in

Southwestern Ontario," Research Report No. 24, Museum of Archaeology, London, 1995; Paul Lennox, "Bogle I and Bogle II Sites."

56. Lennox, "Bogle I and Bogle II Sites," 267.

57. Le Jeune, "Relation," 234–40, quotations on 240.

58. Despite their often ephemeral nature, archaeologists have identified a few of these temporary settlements. See Lennox, "MTO Contributions," "Bogle I and Bogle II Sites."

59. Lennox, "Bogle I and Bogle II Sites," 267–69.

60. Le Jeune, "Relation," 240.

61. British colonist James Smith noted that he and his captors traveled from Sandusky to Detroit in three days. "Smith Captivity," in Drake, *Indian Captivities,* 233.

62. A 1732 sketch of the Wendat village at Detroit located 28 or 29 longhouses at the village. Henri-Louis Boishébert, "Plan du Village des hurons au Detroit, Erie," 1732, Bibliothèque nationale de France, Paris. Reprinted in Brian Dunnigan, *Frontier Metropolis: Picturing Early Detroit, 1701–1838* (Detroit: Wayne State University Press, 2001).

63. Stuart's estimate of structures at Detroit in 1755 is curious. It is more than double those of 1732 or 1747, although the population was about the same. Either Stuart miscounted or the Wendats had begun living in smaller structures rather than the traditional longhouse. Stuart, "Captivity," 72, 73.

64. Ibid., 80.

65. Ibid., 72.

66. Conference at Detroit, 1761, in *Wisconsin Historical Collections* (Madison, Wisc.; Democrat Printing Company, State Printers, 1888), vol. 18: 246–47; Clarke, *Origin and Traditional History of the Wyandotts,* 37.

67. Clarke, *Origin and Traditional History of the Wyandotts,* 37, 38, 66–67.

68. A 1778 document listed no "village chiefs" for the Sandusky Wendats, while there were three at Detroit. "Council held at Detroit June 16 1778" (n. 49).

69. "un pays des eronces... il est vray quil Si ai [sic] allumé quelque fois; quelque feu, mais c'est par quelques chasseurs, qui y cherchoient leur vie. nous te dissons nous y allons point." "Report of Indian Council," June 18, 1761, in Waddell et al., *Papers of Henry Bouquet,* 5:593.

70. Parmenter, "At the Wood's Edge," 1.

71. George Croghan to Sir William Johnson, December 22, 1769, *Papers of Sir William Johnson,* 6:316.

72. "Treaty at Pittsburgh, 1775," in Thwaites and Kellogg, *Revolution on the Upper Ohio,* 86; "Council at Detroit," February 7, 1779, in *FA* 220; Delawares to Washington and Congress, May 10, 1779, in *FA* 320; John Heckewelder, *A Narrative of the Mission of the United Brethren among the Delaware and Mohegan Indians* (Philadelphia: McCarty and Davis, 1820), 115, 154.

73. "Speech of Sastaretsy King of the Hurons, with Baby, Andrew and five of the principal Chiefs of their Nation to Richard Berringer Lernout," Detroit, August 19, 1774 (enclosed in Belanger Lernoult to William Gage, August 13, 1774), Thomas Gage

Papers, American Series, vol. 120, William L. Clements Library, University of Michigan, Ann Arbor.

74. In 1778 Hamilton identified the leader as "Dawatong or Sastaharitze [Sastaretsy]." *Henry Hamilton and George Rogers Clark in the American Revolution with the Unpublished Journal of Lieut. Gov. Henry Hamilton*, ed. John D. Barnhart (Crawfordsville, IN: R. E. Banta, 1951, 104. When entering this man's death during an epidemic in 1783, the priest to the Wendat mission referred to him as "Daouatont Roy des hurons." The title of "king of the Hurons" usually referred to the current Sastaretsy. In fact, when Dawatong's successor, "Ignace oatsénon sastarestsi," died later that year, the missionary likewise identified him as "Roy des hurons." See Registre Mortuaire, in Toupin, *Les écrits de Pierre Potier,* 931.

75. The Wendats organized themselves into three separate groupings, or phratries, each of which contained three or four separate clans. For a fuller discussion of this tripartite division of Wendat political culture, see John Steckley, "The Clans and Phratries of the Huron," *Ontario Archaeology* 37 (1982): 29–34; Clifton, "Re-emergent Wyandot," 12–13; Campeau, "Appendice I: Les Hurons de Détroit," 361–67; Boucher, "Legacy of Iouskeha and Tawiscaron," 154–59; Sturtevant, "Jealous Neighbors," 181–82.

76. "Council held at Detroit June 16 1778."

77. "Treaty at Pittsburgh, 1775," in Thwaites and Kellogg, *Revolution on the Upper Ohio,* 101; John Killbuck [Delaware] to Lachlan McIntosh, March 13, 1779, in *FA* 248; Delawares to Daniel Brodhead, June 17, 1779, in *FA* 362.

78. Warrick, *Population History of the Huron-Petun,* 60–61.

79. Lina Gouger, "Le peuplement colonisateur de Détroit, 1701–1765" (PhD diss., Université Laval, 2002), 94, 97, 99–100; Dunnigan, *Frontier Metropolis,* 21.

80. "la Stérilité de leurs Champs." Although the Marquis of Beauharnois, then governor of New France, doubted the legitimacy of this complaint, the Wendats' sincere desire to move elsewhere lends credence to the complaint. The growing presence of French and Native settlers, the increase in the Wendat population, and Wendat farming practices all contributed to a growing need for fresh soil like those offered around Sandusky. Beauharnois à Richardie (copy), August 30, 1741, C11A, vol. 75, fol. 105–105v., CAOM.

81. Journal of Colonel Croghan's Transactions with the Western Indians, 1765, in John R. Brodhead, Berthold Fernow, and E. B. O'Callaghan, eds., *Documents Relating to the Colonial History of the State of New York* (Albany: Weed, Parsons, 1856), vol. 7: 784; James Stevenson to Sir William Johnson, December 18, 1770, *Papers of William Johnson,* 7:1040; [Jehu Hay], Journal, July 10, 1776, Henry Hamilton Papers, vol. 1, Burton Historical Collection, Detroit Public Library (hereafter BHC). Although identified as the journal of Henry Hamilton, this journal appears from internal evidence to be that of Jehu Hay, the Indian agent at Detroit.

82. "Indian Affairs at Detroit in the Years 1738–1741," [1741], in *CR* 34:201; Smith, "An Account of the Remarkable Occurrences," in Drake, *Indian Captivities,* 202; Thomas Gage to Sir William Johnson, April 22, 1764, in *Papers of William Johnson,* 4:403.

83. Michael N. McConnell, *A Country Between: The Upper Ohio Valley and Its Peoples, 1724–1774* (Lincoln: University of Nebraska Press, 1992).

84. "Minutes of the Proceedings of Sir William Johnson Bart with the Indians on His Way to, and at the Détroit in 1761," *Papers of William Johnson,* 2:494; "Address to the Hurons of Sandusky," [July 10, 1779], HP Detroit, f. 240.

85. Hamilton to Gen. Guy Carleton, November 30, 1775, in Thwaites and Kellogg, *Revolution on the Upper Ohio,* 130; Brodhead to Washington, May 6, 1779, in *FA* 311.

86. "Treaty at Pittsburgh, 1775," in Thwaites and Kellogg, *Revolution on the Upper Ohio,* 52–53.

87. Ibid., 91. Donquat did in fact transmit the belt to the senior Detroit Wendats. In January 1776, La Collette, a Detroit leader, produced several wampum "Belts sent to him for the Huron Nation from the Treaty at Fort Pitt in October last." [Jehu Hay], Diary, January 16, 1776, Hamilton Collection, Folder One, BHC. The diary lacks page numbers, so citations are based on the date of entry.

88. Heckewelder, *Narrative,* 161.

89. "Message from the Delaware and Wyandot Chiefs," December 21, 1778, in Kellogg, *Frontier Advance,* 187; John Killbuck to John Gibson and George Morgan, February 9, 1779, in ibid., 223.

90. John Killbuck to Lachlan McIntosh, March 13, 1779, in ibid., 248.

91. Arundel to Capt. Lernoult (containing the messages of the Delawares to the Hurons), July 31, 1779, HP Detroit, f. 259.

92. To call the Wendat leaders "kings" vastly overstates their influence within the consensus- and merit-based Wendat political culture. For a further discussion of Donquat and the notion of "half kings," see James A. Clifton, "Dunquat," in John A. Garraty and Mark C. Carnes, eds., *American National Biography* (New York: Oxford University Press, 1999), vol. 7: 105–7. An Ohio Seneca, or Mingo, leader named Tanaghrisson also carried the title of "half king" in the 1740s and 1750s. Michael McConnell, *Country Between,* 75.

93. "Treaty at Pittsburgh, 1775," in Thwaites and Kellogg, *Revolution on the Upper Ohio,* 53, 91.

94. "Indian Council," September 20, 1785, in *CR,* 11:466.

95. [Jehu Hay], Diary, Hamilton Collection, Folder One, BHC.

96. Ibid., January 6, March 24, June 6, July 21, August 2, August 20, December 24, 1776; January 3, 1777.

97. Belanger Lernoult to unknown, April 8, 1779, in *CR* 10:328.

98. Lt. Col. Mason Bolton to Gen. Frederick Haldimand, November 18, 1778, in ibid., 19:366; John Killbuck to John Gibson, January 29, 1779, in *FA* 213; Bolton to Haldimand, February 12, 1779, in *CR* 19:274; Henry Bird to Belanger Lernoult, March 12, 1779, in *FA* 252; Bolton to unknown, March 24, 1779, in *CR* 10:310–11; Lernoult to unknown, March 26, 1779, in ibid., 10:328.

99. Bolton to unknown, March 24, 1779, in *CR* 10:310; Belanger Lernoult to unknown, April 8, 1779, in ibid., 10:328.

100. Henry Bird to Belanger Lernoult, March 12, 1779, in *FA* 251–52; Lernoult to unknown, March 26, 1779, in *CR* 10:328.

101. Wyandot Indians to Delawares, April 1, 1779, in *FA* 265–66.

102. Daniel Brodhead to the Wyandot and Ottawa Chiefs, April 8, 1779, in *FA* 278–79.

103. Half King to Daniel Brodhead, n.d., in *FA* 309–10.

104. For a few examples of the Delawares referring to the Wendat "uncles," see "Conference held by The Honourable Brigadier General Monckton with the Western Nations of Indians," August 12–15, 1760, in Hazard et al., *Pennsylvania Archives,* 3:744–50; "Treaty at Pittsburgh, 1775," in Thwaites and Kellogg, *Revolution on the Upper Ohio,* 85–87; Heckewelder, *Narrative,* 115, 135; Daniel Brodhead to the Wyandot and Ottawa Chief, April 8, 1779, in *FA* 279; Big Cat to Daniel Brodhead, May 28, 1779, in *FA* 348; Daniel Brodhead to Big Cat, June 3, 1779, in *FA* 358; Daniel Brodhead to Delaware chiefs returning from Congress, June 5, 1779, in *FA* 359.

105. "Treaty at Pittsburgh, 1775," in Thwaites and Kellogg, *Revolution on the Upper Ohio,* 86.

106. Colin G. Calloway, *The American Revolution in Indian Country: Crisis and Diversity in Native American Communities* (New York: Cambridge University Press, 1995), chap. 6.

107. John Killbuck to John Gibson and George Morgan, February 9, 1779, in *FA* 223.

108. Guillaume Montforton to Belanger Larnoult [Lernoult], May 7, 1779, HP Detroit, ff. 228–29.

109. Wyandot Chiefs to Daniel Brodhead, May 12, 1779, in *FA* 324. The letter identifies "Bawbee and Dawaschet." While the identity of the second leader, "Dawaschet," is unclear, it bears at least a superficial resemblance to "Dawattong," a secondary name for the current Sastaretsy, leader of the Wendat Deer clan and purported king of the nation.

110. Montforton to Lernoult, May 7, 1779, in HP Detroit, f. 229; Genl. Montforton to Lernoult, May 14, 1779, in *CR* 19:412; George Morgan to John Jay, May 28, 1779, in *FA* 343; John Montour to John Dodge, May 28, 1779, in *FA* 346.

111. Summary of a letter from John Heckewelder to Brodhead, May 28, 1779, in *FA* 347; Big Cat [Delaware] to Brodhead, May 28, 1779, in *FA* 348.

112. Lachlan McIntosh reported that he intended to "proceed to Sandusky and destroy the Wyandott Towns," if Donquat had not asked for peace. Lachlan McIntosh to George Washington, April 3, 1779, in *FA* 269–70; "List of Indian Conferences," in *CR* 20:133.

113. Alexander McCormack to Daniel Brodhead, June 20, 1779, in *FA* 382.

114. The Wendats had kept the door open to a rebel alliance even before 1778. They had consorted with known rebel sympathizers John Dodge and John Montour and had pressured Governor Hamilton to release these men when the governor imprisoned them early in the war. More seriously, they had made half-hearted overtures to the rebels via the Delawares in the summer of 1778, which Donquat mentioned in September 1779. See Baubee [Babi] to George Morgan, August 16, 1778, in *FA* 129; Heckewelder, *Narrative,* 186–90; Zeisberger to the Commissioners at Fort Pitt, August 19, 1778, in *FA* 119; "Copy of a Council at Fort Pitt the 17th and 18th of Sept. 1779 brought to Detroit by Duentate a chief of the Huron Nation," HP

Detroit, f. 279. The Delaware leader Big Cat wrote that he was confident that "our Uncles are Earnest this time," suggesting that they were not earnest at the other times. Big Cat [Hingwapooshees] to Daniel Brodhead, May 28, 1779, in *FA* 348.

115. Haldimand to George Germain, September 13, 1779, in *CR* 10:359.

116. "List of Indian Conferences," in *CR* 20:133.

117. Donquat also accused the British of treating them as "hunting dogs animated by the voice of their master." "Discours d'un députe huron de Sandoské au Captn d'Ernoult Comm^{dt} et aux nations Sauvages assemblées," July 19, 1779, HP Detroit, ff. 248–49. At the April 1 conference, Donquat also noted that "at Night they tell me he [his British Father] is here & in the morning he is gone & no one knows where but I cant find him," bespeaking his sense of betrayal. Wyandot Indians to Delawares, April 1, 1779, in *FA* 266.

118. McCormack to Brodhead, June 20, 1779, in *FA* 382.

119. Maj. Frederick Vernon to Daniel Brodhead, April 29, 1779, in *FA* 298; Big Cat [Delaware] to Brodhead, May 4, 1779, in *FA* 308.

120. Lt. Henry Bird to Col. Mason Bolton, [1779], in *CR* 19:413. Some Wendats did apparently participate in the siege of Fort Laurens in May, however. George Morgan to John Jay, May 28, 1779, in *FA* 343.

121. Lernoult to the Hurons of Sandusky, HP Detroit, f. 241.

122. Delawares to the Shawnees, April 8, 1779, in *FA* 281; Delawares to Brodhead, June 17, 1779, in *FA* 363; Brodhead to Washington, May 6, 1779, in *FA* 311.

123. John Montour to John Dodge, May 28, 1779, in *FA* 346. Both Montour and Dodge had spent time incarcerated at Detroit because of their support for the American cause.

124. Wyandot Chiefs to Daniel Brodhead, May 12, 1779, in *FA* 324.

125. Brodhead to Delaware Chiefs, June 5, 1779, in *FA* 358; Summary of Brodhead to Washington, June 5, 1779, in *FA* 360. For other statements regarding the Wendats' expected arrival at Fort Pitt, see Summary of Brodhead to Archibald Lochry, June 3, 1779, in *FA* 357; Delawares to Brodhead, June 17, 1779, in *FA* 362.

126. Daniel Brodhead to the Delawares, June 20, 1779, in *FA* 366; Delaware Chiefs to Big Cat [Delaware], in *FA* 367.

127. The opening discourse is from the "head of the Wyandotts," likely meaning Babi, who seemed to be the most influential Wendat chief at the time. Yet the document does not identify him as the speaker, suggesting instead that although the message came from Babi, it was probably delivered by Donquat, who was present at the conference. Big Cat to Brodhead, June 24, 1779, in *FA* 379–81, quotations on 380.

128. Summary of Heckewelder to Brodhead, June 30, 1779, in *FA* 386; Arundel to Capt. Lernoult (containing message of the Delawares to the Hurons), July 31, 1779, HP Detroit, 260.

129. The Delaware chiefs informed Brodhead and George Morgan, an Indian agent for the Continental Congress, that Babi had arrived at Coshocton. Yet there is no evidence of a meeting between Babi and a rebel representative. Delaware Chiefs at Coshocton to Brodhead and Killbuck, August 11, 1779, in *FR* 46–47. Another Delaware leader reported that he had prevented a Wendat party from attacking the

rebels at around the same time. Capt. Johnny [Delaware] to Brodhead and Kill-buck, August 9, 1779, in *FR* 45.

130. Brodhead's Speech to the Wyandot Chiefs, September 17, 1779, in *FR* 66–67.

131. "Copy of a Council held at Fort Pitt the 17th and 18th of Sept. 1779 brought to Detroit by Duentate a chief of the Huron Nation," HP Detroit, ff. 278–79.

132. Maghingive Kesbuck [Brodhead] to Doonyantat [Donquat] principle chief of the Wyandots, September 18 1779, HP Detroit, ff. 279v–80.

133. "Copy of a Council . . ." (n. 129), HP Detroit, f. 279.

134. Summary of Brodhead to Joseph Reed, September 23, 1779, in *FR* 76.

135. The Wendats, in fact, urged Brodhead not to send a war party against their Shawnee brothers at the September meeting. Ibid.; "A Speech delivered by the Chiefs of this [Shawnee] Village to Lieutenant Caldwell," December 26, 1779, HP Detroit, ff. 302–302v.

136. Arendt De Peyster to Alexander McKee, November 2, 1779, in *CR* 10:371. They had transmitted the belt by January 13. "A Meeting at Pickance," January 10, 1780, HP Detroit, ff. 303–303v.

137. Summary of Brodhead to Timothy Pickering, November 3, 1779, in *FR* 109.

138. Jon Parmenter similarly argues that the Iroquois's outlying settlements in the Saint Lawrence and Ohio Valleys facilitated communication. Parmenter, "At the Wood's Edge," xxxiv–xxxv, 12.

139. See, for instance, Kathryn M. Labelle, *Dispersed but Not Destroyed: A History of the Seventeenth-Century Wendat People* (Vancouver: University of British Columbia Press, 2013).

140. Parmenter, *Edge of the Woods: Iroquoia,* xi.

141. Jordan, "Incorporation and Colonization"; Jordan, *Seneca Restoration;* Jordan, "Not Just 'One Site against the World.'"

142. Witgen, *Infinity of Nations,* 1.

143. Bohaker, "*Nindoodemag*"; Newbigging, "History of the French-Ottawa Alliance."

144. Stephen Warren, *The Worlds the Shawnee Made: Migration and Violence in Early America* (Chapel Hill: University of North Carolina Press, 2014), 3.

145. Clifton, "Re-emergent Wyandot"; Richard White, *Middle Ground.*

CHAPTER 3

Maintaining Connections

LORETTE DURING THE EIGHTEENTH CENTURY

Thomas Peace

During the eighteenth century, the Wendats at Lorette felt similar pressures as those who lived west of Lake Erie. Located just nine miles from the administrative center of France's North American empire, these people increasingly confronted military conflicts and the expansion of agricultural settlements as the colonies of Canada and New England grew in size and drew more focused metropolitan interest and involvement. This chapter examines the lives of two Wendat men, André Otehiondi and Louis Vincent Sawatanen, to explore how the Wendats at Lorette responded to these external influences. Through their lives, we can see how the Wendats adopted a diverse set of territorial, diplomatic, and cultural strategies as a way to maintain, and perhaps even strengthen, their presence and influence within the Lower Great Lakes and Saint Lawrence Valley.

Before developing this argument, however, it is important to take a step back to where the first chapter of this book left off. Too often, study of the Wendat migration into what is known today as the Saint Lawrence Valley is situated within a context that assumes a permanent European colonial presence by the mid-seventeenth century. But as John Reid reminded us nearly three decades ago in his work on the marginal colonies of Acadia, Maine, and New Scotland, the existence, strength, and resilience of colonies during this period should not be presupposed. "Successful colonization," Reid observes in his conclusion, "required both physical strength, in terms of numbers, organization, and economic prosperity, and a reconceptualization of American land to give it a European identity."[1] Though with hindsight we can see that many of these processes were under way by the 1640s, there remained considerable contingencies that could have derailed France's colonial efforts. The later success of a colony should not be projected onto its beginning years. In the 1640s, 1650s, and 1660s, what was becoming the Saint Lawrence Valley continued as an important geographic area for the region's diverse Indigenous peoples.

When they left Wendake Ehen in the 1640s and 1650s, André Otehiondi's and Louis Vincent Sawatanen's ancestors arrived at a place whose new French names, the Saint Lawrence and Saint Charles Rivers, were likely unknown. Instead, they might have called these important places by their Wendat names, the Lada8anna and Oria'enrak Rivers.[2] At the time of their arrival, the area had few French colonists, and the French seigneurial system was just becoming established under the auspices of the New France Company.[3] With little land cleared, the recent French migrants had only a small and tentative foothold in North America. Around the French settlement at Quebec, the Wendats made up slightly less than one-third of the population.[4] It would be another decade before the French regime began to directly administer the handful of settlers who had crossed the Atlantic to begin the fledgling colony. Indeed, it is quite possible that this place would have looked little different to the Wendat migrants than it had to their Saint Lawrence Iroquoian ancestors a century earlier.[5]

Much changed over the next fifty years, however. By Otehiondi's and Sawatanen's grandparents' generation, in the late seventeenth century, the French population had tripled. French *habitant* life increasingly dominated the banks of the river now known as the Saint Lawrence.[6] French farms extended farther inland and the seigneurial system became firmly entrenched as the primary method through which land was managed. Wendat society had also changed. Increasingly, they began to call this place home, an eastern Wendake.[7] In this new Wendake, they hunted in the countryside, planted fields, and created meaningful places around their burgeoning town. But alongside this deepening entrenchment within the Laurentian landscape, the community also faced significant disruption, which kept their population unstable. Haudenosaunee (Iroquois) raids, Christianity, Jesuit duplicity and conniving over the status of Wendat land (specifically, legal title to Sillery), and the Wendats' attachment to relatives living elsewhere encouraged some to leave the community and others to arrive.[8] Amidst this transitory process, the community moved several times, finally establishing itself at Lorette in 1697.

The move to Lorette was unusual. In Wendake Ehen, the Wendats moved their towns every eight to twelve years due to soil exhaustion and for access to firewood and protection from enemy attack.[9] Although this practice of community movement was somewhat disrupted by their longer-distance migration during the 1640s and 1650s, it continued after the Wendats moved to the north banks of the Lada8anna River, only ending once their town was established at Lorette. After 1697 the town became a permanent component of the Laurentian world, and the Wendats have remained at this place ever since. Today, the town is known as Wendake, its affairs managed by the Conseil de la Nation huronne-wendat.

By Otehiondi's and Sawatanen's parents' generation, in the early eighteenth century, these changes began to take their toll. Situated at the northern extent of an increasingly colonized seigneurial landscape, the Wendats had little good agricultural land available to which they could move. To their north, the land was poorly suited for growing crops. To their east, west, and south, the land was bound into seigneurial censives increasingly farmed by French habitants. In 1739 there were 549 French habitants and 120 Wendats living in the five seigneuries northwest of Quebec.[10] Unlike in Montreal, where the ratio between Indigenous and French populations was much more balanced and a common ground existed between Indigenous and colonial societies, here the Wendats were significantly outnumbered. In Montreal there were about 2.7 settlers for every Indigenous person.[11] Around Lorette, by the mid-eighteenth century, the ratio was nearly double at 4.6 to 1. When the neighboring seigneuries and town of Quebec are considered, the population difference is even more marked. Around Quebec there were sixty-one settlers for every Wendat person.[12] Their French neighbors were demographically overwhelming.

The Wendats responded to this transition by developing a flexible culture that integrated past practices with new ways of relating to space and neighbors. This culture developed through three broad strategic approaches used to maintain a Wendat place on the Laurentian landscape. First, they acquired legal title to nearby censives in order to ensure access to agricultural land and forest resources. Second, they maintained and strengthened ties with neighboring Indigenous peoples, such as the Wendats at Detroit and the Abenakis and Mohawks in the Saint Lawrence Valley, who along with the Wendats participated in a confederacy known as the Seven Fires. Third,

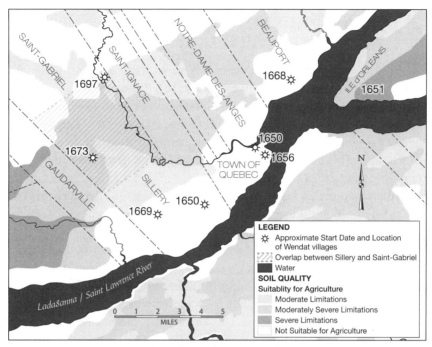

Map 3.1. Seigneuries and Soil Quality around Lorette. Based on maps by Michel Lavoie, "'C'est ma seigneurie que je réclame': le lutte des Hurons de Lorette pour la seigneurie de Sillery, 1760–1888" (PhD thesis, Université Laval, 2006), appendix; and Canada Land Inventory, National Soil DataBase, Agriculture and Agri-Food Canada. 1998, http://sis.agr.gc.ca /cansis/nsdb/cli/index.html (accessed January 7, 2016). The Canada Land Inventory is based on maps created between 1960 and the early 1980s. In this map, present-day urban areas, which were farmed in the seventeenth and eighteenth centuries, are represented as unsuitable for agriculture. Map by Tom Jonas. Copyright © 2016 University of Oklahoma Press.

they embraced a host of diverse economic and cultural strategies such as the manufacturing of equipment, including canoes, sleighs, and snowshoes, as well as deploying schooling and alphabetic literacy to better understand the legal workings of the French, and later British, colonial regimes. Taken together, these three strategic approaches helped maintain a distinct Wendat identity and gave the nation greater political power than their demographic weight would suggest.

TWO WENDAT LIVES: ANDRÉ OTEHIONDI
AND LOUIS VINCENT SAWATANEN

The Wendats' strategic decision making is most clearly seen in Otehiondi's and Sawatanen's lives. Both men were born at Lorette but spent much of their lives elsewhere. Importantly, though, while they were away, they maintained ties with and continued to be seen as part of the community at Lorette. Otehiondi was considerably older than Sawatanen, and although he retained a connection to his home community after he left, he never returned to live there permanently. Sawatanen, on the other hand, lived away from Lorette for about two decades, between 1772 and 1791. Taken together, their experiences span much of the eighteenth century and represent two possible paths that a Wendat man had available to him during this period.

André Otehiondi was likely born in the 1730s. Although we know little about his parents or family life, a 1773 letter from his uncle, Paul Tsa8enhohi, one of the Wendats' longest-serving grand chiefs, points us toward some semblance of family life.[13] The word "uncle," however, which also has diplomatic overtones (seen clearly in the previous chapter), should be interpreted with caution. The term may refer to the social and political relationship between the two men—a formal moniker reflecting the position of the grand chief—rather than being symbolic of a family connection. Nonetheless, in the absence of clear evidence to the contrary, the moniker suggests that Otehiondi was possibly born into a politically prestigious clan. It is significant that Tsa8enhohi was Otehiondi's uncle rather than father. In Wendat society clan membership and leadership were determined through the female line. Fathers often came from a different clan than their children, while uncles shared the same clan as their sister's children. It makes sense in this context that Otehiondi's uncle rather than father would contact him about his personal or family affairs. If representative of this type of matrilineal structure, this letter points to considerable continuity in Wendat social and political structure over the late seventeenth and eighteenth centuries. It also points to continuities with longhouse structures despite an architectural shift to French-style homes in the early eighteenth century (as will be discussed shortly).

Otehiondi first appears in the historical record east of Lake Erie during the 1760s. After the fall of New France, he worked for the British as a messenger to the Shawnees, Haudenosaunees, and Delawares and also between Fort Pitt, Detroit, and Sandusky (the latter two both being places with sizeable Wendat communities).[14] When hostilities broke out during Pontiac's

War, Otehiondi made haste to the British. He wanted to ensure that he was not considered part of the uprising.[15] Shortly after peace returned to the region, Otehiondi married. John Steckley's analysis of marriage records from Detroit indicates that in 1767 he married Marie-Anne Dastarron in a Catholic ceremony. Dastarron was a Wendat from the area and a member of the Porcupine clan.[16] Although he held land near Lorette, Otehiondi lived with his wife at Detroit until his death in 1775. Given that the Wendats practiced matrilocal marriage, it is possible that this relationship is what originally drew Otehiondi to, and kept him at, Detroit. The fact that on his death his wife sent a delegate to administer his affairs rather than travel to Lorette herself suggests that she did not have a strong connection to the community there.[17] The letter from his uncle two years before he died makes it clear that few people expected his return; Grand Chief Tsa8enhohi asked whether Otehiondi's land should be sold.[18]

Sawatanen was about a decade younger than Otehiondi. He too seems to have come from a relatively prestigious family. Although his mother, Marguerite Bergevin, was a Canadien, his father, Vincent Aronchiouann, was part of a family that held an important place in the community's life. A chief named Vincent, for example, extinguished the council fire at Kanesatake in 1740, reclaiming Wendat wampum belts that had been kept there.[19] Five years later, a chief by the same name led a Wendat war party in a French attempt to retake Annapolis Royal in British-occupied Mi'kma'ki/Acadia (present-day Nova Scotia).[20] In Sawatanen's old age, another Vincent, Tsawenhohi (Nicolas Vincent), became the village's grand chief.[21] Although some scholars believe that Tsawenhohi was Sawatanen's son, genealogist Serge Goudreau's work indicates that this was not the case.[22] Both men were related through their common uncle, Jean Vincent, and if a father-son connection existed between Sawatanen and Tsawenhohi (as some historic documents indicate), it was likely a symbolic relationship between the two men.

Jean Vincent's relationship with Sawatanen was important. He was not only Sawatanen's uncle but also his surrogate guardian after Sawatanen's father died in the mid-1760s.[23] It was this relationship, explored in greater detail later in this chapter, that brought Sawatanen down to New Hampshire in 1772 to attend Moor's Indian Charity School. Shortly after arriving, the American War of Independence broke out. Both Jean Vincent and Sawatanen fought alongside the colonial rebels. In 1778 Sawatanen served as an interpreter to the Abenakis and Mi'kmaq for the Continental Congress before returning to school. He graduated from Dartmouth College, the more prestigious and colonist-centered offspring of the Charity School, in 1781. With his studies complete, Sawatanen met the Anglican missionary John Stuart and began teaching school and translating the Bible at Stuart's Mohawk mission near Montreal and later on the shores of the Bay of Quinte. In 1791, as the last Jesuit missionary prepared to leave Lorette, Sawatanen returned home. For the next thirty years, he ran a local school attended by nearly all of the community's youth.

Initially, it might appear that the lives of André Otehiondi and Sawatanen were quite different. Otehiondi moved away from Lorette to live among the Wendats at Detroit. When conflict arose between the region's Indigenous communities and the British, Otehiondi sided with the British, working for them as a messenger. In contrast, Sawatanen moved away from Lorette to go to school, possibly reinforcing old family connections developed by Jean Vincent (and definitely building them) with the Abenakis and Mohawks living on land that would eventually become New Hampshire, Vermont, and New York. When war broke out between colonists and the British empire, Sawatanen chose to side with the colonists, working for them in a capacity similar to Otehiondi. His attendance at Dartmouth also gave him a more prominent place in the documentary record. Though there are only a handful of documents created by him, we know much more about his life.[24] Because of this, Sawatanen's life and experiences are discussed more regularly throughout this essay.

The difference in the decisions these men made should not surprise us. In *Indians in the American Revolution*, Colin Calloway emphasizes the diversity of experiences and decisions Indigenous peoples had to make as Europeans and Euro-Americans dramatically reshaped the colonial world at the end of the eighteenth century. Few Indigenous communities were single-minded in their responses to European conflict. In order to ensure continued access to their homeland and its resources, these communities had to carefully balance and negotiate their social and political relationships. Situating long-standing cultural and political practices within this rapidly changing colonial world fostered the development of a flexible culture where community members often took radically different approaches to evolving social, political, and environmental contexts. Though varied and often not unified, this tactic allowed the Wendats as a whole to retain a distinct identity while remaining on what had become a new Wendake.

TERRITORIAL STRATEGIES: NOTARIES
AND SURVEYORS

Otehiondi and Sawatanen's ancestors had used the land around Quebec for decades before French settlement expanded much beyond the town site at Quebec. As French farms got closer to their community, the Wendats sought to entrench their position. In order to maintain a presence on the land, individual Wendats sought legal title to seigneurial lots known as censives. Although purchased individually, the acquisition of this land was clearly a community strategy. Usually three or more Wendats acquired neighboring parcels of land at the same time; seldom was it acquired in isolation. Here again, both Otehiondi and Sawatanen serve as useful examples for how this process worked: Otehiondi had legal title to a house in town, while Sawatanen had a larger parcel of land in the northern part of Saint-Gabriel seigneury. In all cases noted here, the Wendats hired notaries and surveyors to clearly determine the boundaries of their property.

Otehiondi's house was on a small two-arpent lot located in the northwestern but central part of Lorette; his land was bound by Pierre Romain's property, the church, and the common, which was used for livestock. Although we know little about the house's architecture, most homes in the community resembled those of their French neighbors. Owning a home and small property in the town was common, and by the 1720s some people in the town had begun to live in French-style houses.[25] The transition from the longhouses of their ancestors to French-style construction was slow and corresponded with the end of town movement rather than the initial Wendat migration to the Lada8anna Valley. The style of the eighteenth-century home in the community varied. Pehr Kalm, who visited in 1749, claimed that although some homes were made of stone, most were wooden.[26] During his extended absence in Detroit, Otehiondi's house seems to have been cared for by his uncle, the Grand Chief Paul Tsa8enhohi, or perhaps the community as a whole.[27]

In addition to adopting French architecture, the Wendats also hired surveyors to clearly demarcate boundaries between property, both within and outside the town limits. Though certainly marking significant cultural change, this shift in property and architecture reflects the end of Wendat town movement and greater stability within Wendat society during the eighteenth century. In a world where the town itself could no longer be moved, more permanent and rigid structures were needed to maintain access to resources and soils suitable for agriculture. The end of town movement, caused by the marked decline in unoccupied fertile soil around Quebec, is far more important to understanding eighteenth-century Wendat life than the somewhat related issue of Canadienization, which tends to be the focus of visitors and scholars who describe the community. Without the option of moving their town again, the Wendats needed to develop new strategies to feed their families and heat their homes.

Much like the Wendats who built French-style homes, many community members also acquired land around Lorette. Sawatanen, for example, acquired 90 arpents (3 by 30 arpents) of land north of the town in 1794.[28] He was not alone. Between 1730 and 1800 about sixty people acquired similar parcels of land.[29] The majority of these people acquired their land together in groups of three or more within the seigneury of Saint-Gabriel, demonstrating the communal and strategic nature of this land acquisition. Some Wendats, however, acquired land in the neighboring non–Jesuit-controlled seigneuries of Gaudarville and Saint-Ignace. Although it is difficult to know when these people took up land outside of the seigneury, the earliest discovered documents are eight concessions in Gaudarville, the seigneury to the village's west, made in 1733.[30] The earliest known document from the seigneury of Saint-Ignace, a land sale between two Wendats, Barthélémie Picard and Ignace, dates from 1746.[31] While most Wendat landholders seem to have moved from Gaudarville by 1784,[32] Wendats continued to hold land in Saint-Ignace well into the nineteenth century. A newspaper clipping collected by another Sawatanen, the Wendat priest Prosper Vincent, lists François-Xavier Picard and Philippe Vincent, Wendat chiefs and traders, as living there rather than in the village itself.[33] These examples suggest that although the village remained the center of community life, Wendat families increasingly lived beyond its boundaries while remaining active in Wendat social and political life.

Legal title to land beyond the town limits was an important aspect of eighteenth-century Wendat life. Altogether in the post-conquest period, the community held as much as three thousand square arpents of land, or ninety arpents per family.[34] This was exactly the same amount Sawatanen was conceded in 1794. If distributed evenly among all the Wendats living in the community, the average Wendat family had access to more land than their French neighbors. In 1781 the average French family in Saint-Gabriel cultivated twenty-two arpents.[35] Although the Wendats likely did not bring it all under cultivation, agricultural practices probably continued and, without firm evidence, should not be easily dismissed.

This was a significant amount of land. Traditionally historians have suggested that Wendat agricultural practices declined over this period, but increased attention to Wendat landholding suggests that the situation was more complicated.[36] George Heriot, a Scottish artist who visited in the early nineteenth century, was one of the few people to describe the scope of Wendat agriculture. He observed that the community sowed about 240 arpents of corn.[37] These fields were likely located on 1,600 square arpents of land granted communally to the town in 1742 (most often called the forty arpents).[38] As a communal grant and collective space, Heriot's assessment likely excluded the 1,700 arpents doled out to individuals in the concessions described above. Because they were spread out, it was unlikely a visitor such as Heriot would have observed land use on these smaller parcels. It is quite possible, then, that he underrepresented the extent of agriculture.

Nonetheless, even if an underestimate, taken alone, Heriot's observations suggest that the Wendats cultivated about 7.5 square arpents per household.[39] A government report somewhat confirms these numbers, indicating that each family at Lorette cultivated about three to four arpents of land.[40] This was slightly less than Otehiondi's and Sawatanen's early seventeenth-century ancestors required before their migration away from Wendake Ehen. Conrad Heidenreich determined that the Wendats needed 2.3 acres of land per person (2.7 arpents) in the early seventeenth century, while Heriot's observations suggest that each person used between 1.4 and 2 acres (1.6 and 2.4 arpents) at Lorette.[41] Given that they also had access to additional parcels of land in Saint-Gabriel and other neighboring seigneuries, it seems reasonable to conclude that as late as the early nineteenth century, the Wendats maintained a similar amount of land under cultivation as they had two centuries earlier.

As settlers encroached on the town, the Wendats living there had less and less access to land and resources. Surveying the land into individual parcels and the private acquisition of property through notarial contracts became a useful strategy for accommodating the town's small size, while further entrenching the Wendat presence in the region. Private parcels of land within the town, such as Otehiondi's, provided clearly demarcated space on which the Wendats could live without interference from neighbors. The acquisition of seigneurial censives, such as Sawatanen's, allowed the Wendats to farm or

harvest available resources as they had before the nearby landscape was settled by colonists. That they expanded beyond the Jesuit-controlled seigneury
(Saint-Gabriel) in which their town was located demonstrates how Wendat
spatial practices pushed against the settler-imposed landscape and jurisdictions developing around Quebec at the time.

DIPLOMATIC MOBILITY: WENDATS, THE SEVEN FIRES, AND ANGLO-AMERICA

Just as residing in the town did not exclusively define community membership, neither were proximity of residence or frequency of visits limiting
factors. André Otehiondi was not the only Wendat during this period to hold
property in absentia. Jean Vincent, Sawatanen's uncle, also held land at Lorette, despite making frequent forays south of the Lada8anna River. According to Serge Goudreau, in addition to spending significant amounts of time
in the Green and White Mountains (present-day Vermont and New Hampshire), he also held land in both Gaudarville and Saint-Gabriel seigneuries.[42]
In both of their cases, Otehiondi and Vincent maintained their property
around Lorette despite spending relatively long periods of time away from the
town. Through a community network, like the one that existed between Otehiondi and Tsa8enhohi, they maintained legal title while they were away and
living elsewhere.

As we saw in earlier chapters, by the eighteenth century mobility was a
well-used Wendat strategy for survival. It is unlikely that Otehiondi, Vincent,
and Sawatanen were unique. Wendat individuals often moved in and out of
the town, and it was not unusual for the population to vary significantly.
Comparing a list of families that supported the British during the American
Revolution with a nominal census taken five years later indicates significant
differences in the size of specific families. The 1779 list—which includes only
seven families with children—suggests that the average family size was 5.3
people, whereas in the 1784 census it was 4.7. Although the larger sample size
in the census partially accounts for this difference, it does not fully explain
it. Only three people on the 1779 list have the same number of children in the
census. Four people are listed as having one or fewer children than in 1779,
and one does not appear on the census at all.[43] There is no indication of the
population having declined due to disease or warfare, suggesting that something else was taking place within the community, possibly migration,
though also perhaps poor enumeration.

Notarial records reflect an even wider gap between the census and the number of people who were identified as part of the village. Of the sixteen people involved in land transactions during the 1790s, only seven appear in the 1784 census of the village; only six appear in a list of all the men living in the village in 1819 (three of whom were not listed in the 1784 census).[44] If we expand this group to include the men in all of the post–British conquest notarial records, there are seventeen people whose names do not appear on the census and five who are listed in the census but not in any notarial records.[45] Even accounting for name changes, this suggests that more people—possibly nearly two-thirds more—identified as part of this community than appear in archival documentation.

It is a mistake, then, for historians to rigidly adhere to European accounts of the village population. European officials with only a distant relationship to the Wendat community usually recorded censuses, notarial records, and other official written documentation. Similarly, as documents anchored in a specific moment in time, these records account poorly for children becoming adults, death, or people arriving and departing the community. This latter point is most critical for understanding the Wendats. At any given time, a significant portion of the population might be away hunting or fishing, farming, trading, or visiting relatives. Or, as we will see shortly, living in a distant allied community.

The central point here is that presence in the town was not a critical component determining community membership. Tsawenhohi (Nicolas Vincent) made this specific point in testimony before a committee of the Lower Canadian Assembly in 1819. In describing the village's population, he claimed that there were "about 35 Families, 20 persons or thereabouts are absent—those who are absent and even settled out of the Village would have the same right to the Land belonging to the Tribe as those that remain, on their returning among us."[46] Tsawenhohi was describing community members such as André Otehiondi, Jean Vincent, and Sawatanen. Although they lived for extended periods away from the village, all three men maintained their kinship connections and rights as community members.

Not only did these men maintain their relationship with the Wendats who remained at Lorette, but they also expanded the community's influence in the Northeast and lower Great Lakes. With community members living among allied Indigenous communities, the Wendats were able to maintain connections with other Indigenous groups and strengthen their diplomatic position with both the French and, more importantly in the late eighteenth century, the British. With such a small population, this was an important strategy for maintaining a distinct identity and military and political relevance in the face of rapidly expanding European settlement.

Otehiondi and Sawatanen are not isolated examples. Other Wendats, for example, lived at Detroit. In 1747 Pierre Potier, the Jesuit missionary there, took a census of the western Wendats. Though his enumeration is considered deeply flawed—mainly because it was taken during the Wendat hunting season amidst a time of political upheaval—the census indicates that two families from Lorette were living at Detroit. Toutsaint lived there with his three daughters and five grandchildren, and Sohendinnon, who was known as the Lorrétain, lived separately from his wife a little ways from the main village.[47] According to John Steckley, this man, who was noted as being able to speak French, was known as "Quarante Sols," a prominent title in the Bear clan. He was also a war chief and shaman at Detroit.[48] These people helped facilitate the relationship between the Wendats in Quebec and Detroit. That such figures were present in the western community is not altogether surprising. Potier noted that at least twenty-six non-Wendat people, including Meskwaki, Haudenosaunees, and Anishinaabeg, also lived in the village, reminding us of the cosmopolitan nature of eighteenth-century Detroit.[49]

In addition to the three families that lived at Detroit during the eighteenth century, Wendats from Lorette sometimes traveled back and forth to the French fort. Some of these people may have lived there for a time during these visits. During the War of the Austrian Succession in the 1740s, Sieur Delestre—a French military official—arrived back in Canada from Detroit accompanied by a number of Wendats from Lorette. They left the winter before to help bring unity to the divided western community.[50] The following year, two Wendats accompanied Father Richardie, the Jesuit missionary at Detroit, on his return journey from Quebec. Once they arrived, the two men asked to remain in Detroit.[51] Potier's writings may record the names of these men. Though he does not make this link explicitly, he recorded seven "hurons de Lorette" in a separate enumeration from the Wendat village. In addition to Otehiondi, the Wendats from Lorette were Vincent 8tactetanion, Antoine Ts8ta8aj, Romain Tachiendae'te, Mathias Hendisentandi, Louis Barthelemi Hatsoenhaarenn'ia, and Ignace Anien8indet. Although Otehiondi eventually settled in the community, a note later in Potier's records indicates that the first four men listed, which included Otehiondi, were part of a larger Laurentian delegation that traveled down to the community in 1747.[52] It is tempting to infer that the others traveled down with Richardie, though this is not stated in the records. In any case, these examples demonstrate that Laurentian Wendats who went west remained in the area for multiple months—sometimes choosing to remain there—and that they were involved in western diplomacy.[53] At least some Wendats from Lorette were likely familiar to those people living in the western communities throughout the eighteenth century.

Although these examples only provide a brief glimpse into the relationship between the Wendats at Lorette and Detroit, they help contextualize André Otehiondi's experiences later in the century. Lorette's attachment to Detroit was political. During the War of the Austrian Succession, Lorettan Wendats accompanied imperial officials up the Lada8anna River and across the Great Lakes. During Pontiac's War and the American War of Independence, men from Lorette such as Otehiondi served as couriers between British outposts.[54] During both the French and British regimes, the Wendats served as liaisons between the European crowns and Indigenous peoples living west of Lakes Ontario and Erie.

All of this curried favor with imperial officials and prevented this small town from being ignored. Indeed, when, at the end of the Revolution, one British official proposed abandoning the practice of giving gifts to the Wendats at Lorette, John Johnson, the superintendent of the Indian Department in Quebec, quickly responded, "I . . . wish my promise to them fulfilled not only on account of the light they would conceive it in, but on account of their connection with the Hurons of Detroit, and the effect any evil representation of theirs might have on the minds of those people and others connected with them."[55] By maintaining their connections with the Wendats at Detroit, the Wendats from Lorette ensured that the politically powerful imperial officials residing at Quebec would meet them with respect and consideration.

While Otehiondi's life helps us better understand the relationship between eastern and western Wendat communities, as well as Lorette's position relative to imperial power, Sawatanen's experiences in the borderland between the Lada8anna Valley, New England, and New York represent a slightly different strategy of mobility, though it too is similarly tied to the Wendats' migration from Wendake Ehen. As Kathryn Labelle demonstrates in chapter 1, the Wendat dispersal from Wendake Ehen was multifaceted and varied. Not only did the Wendats move to Quebec and Michilimackinac (and then Detroit), but many also joined with the Haudenosaunees and later settled in places such as Kahnawake and Kanesatake, Catholic missions around Montreal similar to Lorette. Sawatanen's move down to Moor's Indian Charity School was embedded in this history of migration and the diverse relationships between Wendats in the other Laurentian towns.[56] His time away from Lorette strengthened regional ties between northeastern Indigenous communities.

By the mid-eighteenth century the Wendats were part of a broad political entity known as the Seven Fires Confederacy. This confederacy was made up of eight towns allied with Catholic missions along the Lada8anna River. Known to the French as *les villages domiciliés,* these towns were culturally diverse and primarily composed of peoples who moved into the Lada8anna Valley following France's initial settlement at Quebec. The Algonquins and Nipissings lived near the Mohawks at Kanesatake (Lac-des-Deux-Montagnes); the Mohawks at Kahnawake (Sault Saint Louis), Akwesasne (Saint Regis), and Oswegatchie (La Présentation); Algonquins at Pointe-du-Lac; Abenakis at Wôlinak (Bécancour) and Odanak (Saint François); and the Wendats at Wendake (Jeune-Lorette).[57] The Wendats had many ties with these communities, and in the late eighteenth century this confederacy served as a principal diplomatic body for negotiating with the British.[58]

Serge Goudreau's recent genealogical work, derived from the 1784 Lorette census, sheds some light on the interconnections between these communities. Of the twenty-eight people listed in the census, six had direct connections through their spouses to other Seven Fires communities, particularly the confederacy's principal village at Kahnawake. Some of these people also had children who similarly maintained these connections. For example, Charles Simonete and Martine Te8aratas, as well as two children of Zacharie Otesse and Charlotte Aren8ara, eventually settled at Kahnawake. A generation later, the son of Zacharie Thomas married an Algonquin woman from near Trois Rivères and was buried near Kahnawake. Two women, Marie Soenronk and Geneviève Teannonnens, married Abenaki and Maliseet men. Their families remained at Lorette, suggesting that, much like the marriage between Otehiondi and Dastarron in Detroit, the traditional matrilocal residency pattern continued in the community. While another Wendat couple, Joseph Vincent and Anne Jacques, lived for a period at Lorette, they spent at least six years living outside of the community, mostly at Kanesatake.[59] Although Wendats with kinship connections to outside communities did not quite make up the majority of the population, the 1784 census makes clear that kinship networks with allied communities were important to the community as a whole.

These extended relationships reflect the important role the town played for Indigenous peoples in the Northeast. By the nineteenth century these broader

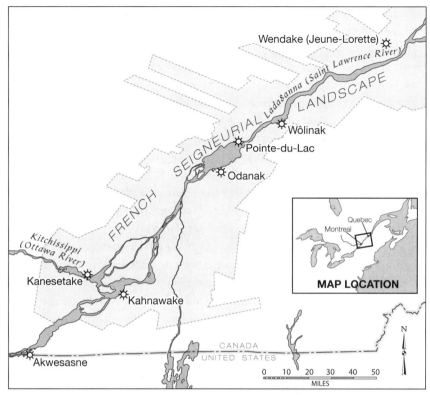

Map 3.2. Members of the Seven Fires Confederacy. Map by Tom Jonas. Copyright © 2016 University of Oklahoma Press.

connections shaped community life. The community's schoolmaster at the time, likely Ferrier Vincent, told one visitor "that among the Indian villages in Canada, few and widely scattered as they are, a tolerably active intercourse is maintained. An Indian of Upper Canada, or New Brunswick, or Nova Scotia, should his affairs bring him to Quebec, seldom fails to pay a visit to the men of his race at St Lorette, and thence arise frequently marriages or other connections, which account for the circumstance that the offspring of so many other tribes are to be found here."[60] It seems likely that this type of kinship connection drew Sawatanen down to Moor's Indian Charity School. Located at the confluence of the White and Connecticut Rivers, the school was located firmly on Abenaki territory.

Although his introduction to Moor's Indian Charity School is usually associated with the school's first recruiting drive to the Lada8anna Valley in

1772, Sawatanen had family ties to the region through Jean Vincent. The little we know about Sawatanen's uncle suggests he was familiar with much of the territory that today forms the northern parts of Maine, New Hampshire, Vermont, and New York. Put another way, he knew Mohawk and Abenaki territory well. Indeed, despite hailing from Lorette, he was well integrated into Abenaki society. When the War of Independence broke out, just three years after Sawatanen arrived at the school, his uncle took up a captaincy leading the Abenakis of Odanak in support of the Continental Congress.[61] Sawatanen was similarly involved with the Abenakis, fighting in Timothy Bedel's regiment and serving as a translator to the Penobscots in 1778.[62] When the Revolution subsided, Jean Vincent remained in the region. He died in Mendon, Vermont, about fifty kilometers from Moor's Indian Charity School, in 1810.

Through the Seven Fires, Sawatanen was also connected to the Mohawks. Indeed, he was recruited by Wheelock's missionaries at the Mohawk community of Kahnawake and began his studies alongside eight other boys from the community. On arrival at the school, the less-than-fluent missionaries considered him an expert in both the Wendat and Mohawk languages.[63] Although it is unclear just how accurate this description was, or how important connections with the Mohawks were in drawing Sawatanen to the school—he was only in the village by coincidence when the missionaries were there recruiting—his connections to these people strengthened during his time in New Hampshire.[64] By the time he graduated from the college in 1781, he had developed enough skill in their language to both work as a teacher among the Mohawks and help the Anglican missionary John Stuart translate the Gospel of Matthew into their language.[65]

Sawatanen's relationship with Stuart was a result of his time at Dartmouth College. It was also likely facilitated by the Mohawk leader Thayendanegea (Joseph Brant). Though about a decade apart in age, Thayendanegea and Sawatanen had many similarities. Both men, for example, attended Moor's Indian Charity School. Despite disagreements between Wheelock and the Mohawks, Thayendanegea maintained his connections with the school, sending his son and nephew there in the early nineteenth century. Both men also worked with Stuart on his translations of the Bible. Stuart served the Mohawk community at Fort Hunter, where Thayendanegea's sister and Sir William Johnson's wife Koñwatsiʔtsiaiéñni (Molly Brant) lived. As supporters of Britain, following the Revolution, Stuart, Koñwatsiʔtsiaiéñni, and the rest of the Mohawks from this community moved to Montreal, where they met Sawatanen (perhaps not for the first time). All three then moved to Lake

Ontario's north shore, where the Mohawks settled on the Bay of Quinte, while Stuart and Koñwatsi'tsiaiéñni lived at Cataraqui (present-day Kingston, Ontario).

Another possibility may explain how Sawatanen became involved with the Brant family. As this book suggests, many dispersed Wendats maintained connections with each other after their separation. It is possible that Thayendanegea, Koñwatsi'tsiaiéñni, and Sawatanen were connected through kin or social networks maintained after the Wendat Confederacy dispersed in 1650. John Norton, who followed Sawatanen as the schoolteacher among the Mohawks on the Bay of Quinte, claimed that Thayendanegea was born to "Wyandot prisoners adopted by the Mohawks both on the father and mother's side."[66] Perhaps a connection was maintained between this Haudenosaunee leader, a child of Wendat parents, and some Wendats from Lorette. This explanation would help contextualize Jean Vincent's mobility throughout Abenaki and Mohawk territory as well as illuminate why he was frequently mistaken as being from a Mohawk community.[67] Perhaps members of the Vincent family moved between Wendat and Mohawk societies with some ease, causing the confusion over Jean Vincent's identity and helping explain Sawatanen's connection to the Mohawks who settled on the Bay of Quinte. Either way, it is reasonable to suggest that Thayendanegea and Sawatanen knew each other and that it was through Thayendanegea that Sawatanen met John Stuart.

Sawatanen's relationship to the Mohawks, especially the Loyalist Brant-Johnson families, demonstrates well how mobility served as a useful Wendat survival strategy. The fact that Sawatanen fought for the Americans during the Revolution and then taught school among the Loyalist Mohawks immediately following the war's conclusion indicates that we cannot understand Wendat identity and Indigenous alliances using a Euro-American frame of reference. Rather than being defined by Euro-American events, people, and places, Sawatanen's migration down to New Hampshire, and later to the Bay of Quinte, was determined by the Indigenous networks in which he was situated. The questions Sawatanen faced were not whether he should remain loyal to the British Crown or American settlers, but rather what would be of most benefit to him and his people. His response to these questions was not just determined by the needs of his specific village, but also reflect an understanding of the broader situation in which Indigenous people found themselves in the late eighteenth century. Here mobility served as a strategy for maintaining and strengthening connections with neighboring Indigenous peoples.

Sawatanen's experiences during the twenty years he was away from Lorette were significant for the Wendats. On his return in 1791, the community began forty years of petitions to the Crown demanding legal title to the seigneury of Sillery and education for their children. Sillery was a seigneury originally conceded to the Indigenous peoples residing in the Jesuit missions around Quebec in the mid-seventeenth century. By the century's end, however, it had been transferred directly to the Jesuits without consultation with the original landholders. Community memory, and some historic documents, suggest that Sawatanen was responsible for bringing about these petitions.[68]

Three experiences while he was away shaped his decision to submit formal written petitions to the Crown. First, his experience as an interpreter for the Continental Congress gave him a keen understanding of European diplomacy. Working among the Abenakis and Mi'kmaq, Sawatanen learned (or perhaps had reinforced) the importance of writing as a tool that could determine the outcome of diplomatic relationships. Oral agreements held little weight with the British. Both the Abenakis and Mi'kmaq had learned the hard way that what mattered in these negotiations was the words Europeans put down on the page, not what came out of officials' mouths. Oral agreements were only as good as the officials who made them. By the late eighteenth century, British duplicity had demonstrated the importance of writing in diplomatic protocol.

Second, Sawatanen's relationship with the Mohawks introduced him to the territorial nature of British diplomacy. Before the Mohawks and other Loyalist migrants could settle on Lake Ontario's northern shore, the 1763 Royal Proclamation required the British to negotiate with the Mississaugas for their land. These treaties traded access to land for gifts and medals. Up until this point, neither the British nor the Seven Fires had connected land, loyalty, and compensation. Having seen much of their land and resources transformed into an agricultural landscape, the British-Mississauga treaties caused some of the Seven Fires to ask why "my father [does] not love me like my brother."[69] After the 1780s it became increasingly clear that Indigenous people needed to (and could) ensure British legal title and compensation for land quickly being overrun by Europeans.

Third, Sawatanen's connection to the Stuart family paid dividends decades later when John Stuart's two sons occupied prominent government positions in Lower Canada. Andrew Stuart, a prominent leader in the Parti Canadien, supported the Wendats as they mounted their petitions to the Crown, while his older brother James, Lower Canada's attorney general and a member of the executive council, opposed their claims. For the decade between 1820 and 1830, Andrew was heavily invested in the Wendat cause. At times he served on assembly committees evaluating their claims, and at other times he wrote letters on their behalf.[70] Although we cannot be sure that either man established a meaningful relationship with Sawatanen or the Wendats at Lorette, their family's heavy involvement in Indigenous affairs along the Lada8anna River and shores of Lake Ontario make it clear they would have been familiar with many of the important issues facing Indigenous people at this time. Furthermore, it is likely that Andrew Stuart maintained a closer connection with the community than his brother. Photographic evidence of Andrew Stuart's son (also named Andrew) in the traditional dress of a Wendat chief suggests that Sawatanen's time with Stuart and the Mohawks began a relationship between the community and the Stuarts that lasted at least three generations.[71]

Sawatanen's broad network throughout the Northeast best demonstrates the importance of mobility for a small community such as Lorette. By having community members such as Sawatanen, Otehiondi, and Jean Vincent embedded in neighboring communities, the Wendats at Lorette were able to learn from the experiences of their neighbors and allies. By learning from the mistakes and successes of others, the Wendats were able to make choices that otherwise might not have been available to them. Much like how their relationship with Detroit maintained their political importance and continued British gift giving, learning from neighbors provided the community with political capital allowing them to maintain a distinct place in the Quebec landscape. Although it would have been impossible for them to have anticipated the specific outcome this strategy would have on their community, these networks of people embedded in different societies made the survival of their community more certain in the face of their diminishing demographic significance around Quebec.

CULTURAL STRATEGIES: ECONOMICS, ADOPTION, AND EDUCATION

In addition to diplomatic mobility and territorial strategies, the Wendats at Lorette also selectively engaged with French and New England cultures and economies in order to maintain their distinct presence on the land. They did this in three ways: First, they extended their fur-trading relationships into other areas of the colonial economy, primarily by attaching their community's identity to the manufacturing of small handicrafts and tools. Second, they were open to integrating outsiders into community life. Initially they incorporated people from other Indigenous communities, but eventually they also included captives from New England and spouses from French Canadian society. Finally, they sought to use European institutions, particularly those providing a colonial education, to their advantage. As Linda Sioui's work well illustrates, many of these strategies continue into the present.[72]

By the eighteenth century the Wendats had begun to participate in the market economy around Quebec. Referring to a different context, historian John Lutz uses the term "moditional economy" to discuss this new type of economic practice. He defines a "moditional economy" as one that "combined the traditional modes of reproduction and production (for subsistence, prestige goods, and exchange—trade was always a part of the pre-European economy) with new modes of production for exchange in a capitalist market. . . . Historically, people have engaged in multiple modes of production at different times of the day and year: they hunted, fished, gathered, farmed, raised their children, and exchanged their labour in different combinations, and as opportunities presented themselves."[73] This definition suitably describes the evolution of the Wendat economy as the community at Lorette grew closer to French society over the seventeenth and eighteenth centuries. In addition to their agricultural production, gathering, fishing, and hunting, the Wendats also began to sell manufactured goods.

Manufacturing products could be quite lucrative. During the War of the Austrian Succession, for example, the community sold at least 338 sleds, 250 snowshoes, 125 paddles, and 75 canoes to the French military. This was essential equipment for quick travel over the North American landscape, and the French paid handsomely. In 1745 and 1746, for example, the community earned 1,610 livres tournois (lt) by supplying 42 canoes. The following year they made just over 5,150 lt. If distributed evenly, this would have amounted to approximately 270 lt per family, nearly one-third the annual income of a small farmer at the time.[74]

Beyond the amount earned by the community, at least seven Wendats sold goods individually. Most of these men made less than one hundred lt. Two men, Vincent and Jacques, however, earned significantly more. Jacques made 361 lt supplying canoe gum and building sleds, while Vincent, a key canoe builder, was paid 390 lt (over two years) for nine canoes. When added to the amount earned by the community as a whole, the total value of these goods was just over 7,800 lt. Without counting other income, the Wendats made about three times more than the local seigneur in 1746 and 1747.[75] Although the wartime conditions suggest this revenue was somewhat irregular, its size relative to seigneurial income suggests its importance.

During the eighteenth century, evidence of this type of manufacturing is sparse and almost always related to the supply of European armies.[76] But, as Brian Gettler demonstrates later in this book, as the nineteenth century progressed descriptions of the village increasingly reveal the manufacturing of goods for market sale. Joseph Bouchette's early nineteenth-century description of the town, for example, points to an extensive list of Wendat goods. The village made moccasins, sashes, baskets, sleighs, caps, mittens, and dolls, in addition to the products that they had been making nearly a century earlier (snowshoes, paddles, and canoes).[77] Although Bouchette paints a rather dismal view of town life, the end of his description suggests that this trade had once been more lucrative, suggesting its beginnings in the eighteenth century. "For these articles they occasionally find a sale," Bouchette wrote, "but at half the price they formerly obtained." In addition to manufactured goods, the Wendats also sold their surplus agricultural produce.[78] All of this was done in conjunction with a burgeoning fur trade.[79]

With Lorette set permanently in place and declining access to the resources on which they had traditionally relied, the moditional economy provided the Wendats with an opportunity to ensure the well-being of their families. The list of goods they produced demonstrates that they capitalized on a European need for equipment and clothing suitable for the Laurentian environment. Much like their acquisition of land, this practice was an extension and application of their material culture to a new and evolving cultural setting around Lorette. Here there was continuity, just as much as there was change.

The development of a moditional economy was partially fueled by the adoption and integration of Europeans into Wendat society. Like other Iroquoian people, the Wendats compensated for their small numbers by adopting outsiders.[80] Two types of adoption occurred in Lorette. Adoption of Indigenous and English captives during military campaigns was most common. The other type of adoption came from the local French population, when French parents occasionally abandoned children born out of wedlock to the community. It is difficult to determine how frequently this second form of adoption occurred. Official French correspondence suggests that it was less common and diminished in the early eighteenth century, but the parish records from the early 1760s indicate that it continued as an important element of village life through much of the eighteenth century.

The adoption of captives was a relatively common way to sustain the population. Used as a tool to bolster Iroquoian populations at times of dramatic population loss, the incorporation of New England captives and others into Wendat society played an important role in defining this community's identity.[81] It is unclear just how many people in the village were captives or descendants of captives, but anecdotal evidence suggests the number was significant. In the twenty years between 1730 and 1750, there were at least five captives living permanently at Lorette. In 1734, for example, the Wendats adopted a Meskwaki woman.[82] A decade later William Pote, a New Englander taken captive at Annapolis Royal, learned that the Wendats hoped he would join their community. Pote's captor told him "he hoped I Should make as Good a heron. As one John Honewell an English man that had Lived with ym Near thirty years, and was married amongst them and had Severel Children."[83] Honewell was likely the same person who guided Pehr Kalm around the Quebec countryside. Kalm claimed his guide had been taken captive as a child thirty years earlier in order to replace a member of their community killed in battle.[84] Similarly, in early 1746 Pote described a conversation with Jacob, who lived at Lorette but had fought with John Gorham's company before being captured by the Wendats.[85] In 1750 two additional English captives were listed at Lorette. Both had integrated into Wendat society.[86]

In addition to these wartime captives, the Wendats also integrated members of the local French population through marriage and the adoption of children. Although racial prejudices made it illegal for a French habitant to give an unwanted child to an Indigenous person after 1717, evidence from the parish records suggests that this practice did not stop.[87] Of the thirty baptismal entries that involved the Wendats between 1760 and 1765, eight (slightly more than one in four) involved adopted children.[88] Although the nature of these adoptions remains unclear, these acts demonstrate that adoption continued to play a significant role in shaping the community's population. This evidence contextualizes the periodic references to the presence of French people living in the community. Although some of these people were spouses of community members, others were French children brought up by Wendat parents.[89] Some of these children became well integrated into community life. Serge Goudreau's genealogical work, for example, demonstrates that the mother of Etienne Ondiaraété, a prominent chief at the end of the eighteenth century, was likely a French girl who grew up in the community.[90]

Aside from adoption, the Wendats also built bridges with their French neighbors through marriage. Although we know little about this aspect of village life, intermarriage was an important strategy for ensuring a strong network with the diverse peoples of the Saint Lawrence Valley. We have already seen a number of examples of marriage that drew Indigenous communities together. Goudreau's work also indicates extensive intermarriage with French neighbors. He suggests that of the twenty-eight people enumerated in the 1784 census, as many as twelve marriages had one partner (almost always the wife) who was French. Goudreau's research resonates strongly with Franquet's description of the village in the early 1750s. The military officer observed: "Today their blood is mixed. Accordingly, there are English men and women slaves captured and adopted during wartime who take on their characteristics and marry into their society. There are also French women who marry natives; furthermore, there have been cases of bastards being taken to the community, growing up with native manners and having none of our nation's customs. It is easy to distinguish all of these foreigners by the colour of their skin which is white and that of the natives is tanned."[91] Sawatanen's own family fits this description. Both his mother and wife were from French families.[92] Importantly, though, Sawatanen never self-identified or was labeled by others as anything other than Wendat. Indeed, all of the people listed in the 1784 census were described as Wendat and continued to identify as such over the course of their lives. Regardless of the ethnicity of their parents or spouses, of the two cultures living around Quebec, all of these people chose to identify as Wendat rather than Canadien.

Franquet's words summarize the variety of strategies that this community used to integrate outsiders. Whether by marriage, infant adoption, or captivity, these practices brought new blood and new ideas into the community. Their presence helped to better situate the community within both French and Indigenous worlds. Drawing people from the outside—particularly adults with a different set of perspectives—helped the Wendats acquire skills and build relationships to better negotiate and integrate into the colonial environment. In many ways, this was the inverse of the strategy of mobility embodied by Otehiondi, Vincent, and Sawatanen. In addition to sending their people away, the Wendats also integrated outsiders.

This type of flexibility and adaptability were the characteristics in Wendat society that led Sawatanen to seek out schooling. The Wendats at Lorette had engaged with Christianity for more than a century by Sawatanen's lifetime. Initially proselytized by the Jesuits in the early seventeenth century, the

Wendats continued to live near—and later within—a Jesuit mission after they moved to Quebec. The Jesuits had a rich tradition of teaching and learning. By the mid- to late eighteenth century, the Wendat language had been transcribed into Roman script, and some community members could read and write.[93] Following the conquest, however, the status of the Jesuits was in question. Amid a near global ban, the British tolerated the Jesuit presence in the colony while ensuring that they did not increase in numbers. In the mid-1760s there were only sixteen priests in the colony, and by 1800 there were none.[94]

It was the combined context shaped by the new British imperial presence and the declining Jesuit influence that pointed Sawatanen toward Moor's Indian Charity School. Although it is often thought that missionaries from Moor's Indian Charity School recruited all of their students in the early 1770s, the missionaries' own accounts demonstrate that their encounter with the Wendats was more by luck than intention. Sylvanus Ripley, the missionary sent by Wheelock to the Lada8anna Valley, had been convinced by Quebec's lieutenant governor, Hector Theophilus de Cramahe, that the strong Catholic influence at Lorette made the Wendat community not worth a visit. On returning to Kahnawake after failing to visit Lorette while he was at Quebec, Ripley met Sawatanen and his brother Bastien. The boys had left Lorette five weeks earlier in order to visit Sir William Johnson. Their goal in visiting Johnson was to attend "a School where they might get knowledge."[95] Having learned of Ripley's mission, they postponed their visit to Johnson and awaited Ripley's return to Kahnawake. Their recruitment to Moor's Indian Charity School demonstrates that as British influence increased and Jesuit influence declined, the Wendats actively sought out new opportunities for a colonial education. Bastien only attended the charity school for a handful of years, while Sawatanen remained for nearly a decade.

Within the community, colonial education also remained important. By the 1790s, as their Jesuit missionary neared death, the Wendats as a whole were at risk of permanently losing access to colonial structures of teaching and learning. They used two strategies to replace the Jesuits and continue their children's education. First, they petitioned the Crown to fund the education of their children at the Petit Séminaire, a prestigious church-run boarding school in the heart of Quebec. Second, Sawatanen returned to the community from the Bay of Quinte in order to start a day school. Both strategies marked continuities with the community's past while establishing a foundation for its future.

In 1791, when the Wendats first petitioned the Crown in writing, they asked for title to their lands and access for their children to the Petit Séminaire.[96] Although they never did receive title to the seigneuries of Sillery or Saint-Gabriel, the doors of the school were opened relatively quickly. Ferrier Vincent, Sawatanen's replacement as schoolmaster in the 1820s, attended the school the longest. He was there for at least seven years.[97] But he was not alone. Between 1797 and 1806 four children attended the school; three attended for more than three years.[98]

Although we know little about these students' experiences at the school, what evidence exists suggests it was a disappointment. The Petit Séminaire's revenue and expenses for the students do not match. The school seems to have made a tidy profit on their Wendat charges. While the government paid 1,285 livres and 14 sous to cover the students' annual costs, the school spent only half that amount.[99] In addition to the discrepancy in their funding, the school's structure was also quite rigid. As a boarding school, students were seldom allowed to return home.[100] With Lorette less than a day's travel away, it is likely that this rule caused problems for Wendat families who wanted to spend time with their children. These two factors likely provided the motivation that encouraged the Wendat council to pull their youth from the school in 1806,[101] although, as will be discussed in subsequent chapters, individual Wendats periodically attended the school throughout the nineteenth century.

The failure at the Petit Séminaire contrasts with the success of Sawatanen's day school. Beginning in 1791 or 1792, Sawatanen appears to be one of the first Indigenous schoolmasters in what would become Canada. His school, which he held on church property, was fairly well attended.[102] The few documents that describe it indicate that the school served between twenty-five and thirty students, both boys and girls, amounting to most of the community's children under the age of 14.[103] By the 1820s a handful of Algonquin, Mohawk, Abenaki, Maliseet, and Mi'kmaw students also attended the school, demonstrating how the village was connected to other northeastern Indigenous nations.[104] At that time, the students were taught to read in French, but they had no instruction in the Bible—a point that one Protestant visitor and fellow Dartmouth College graduate, Thaddeus Osgood, found alarming and sought to remedy.[105] Importantly, Sawatenen's successor, Ferrier Vincent, taught in both Wendat and French languages. The school's curriculum therefore seems to have maintained an important connection to Wendat culture.[106]

Examining education reveals many of the trends seen in other chapters. The Wendats were not exclusively focused on following or building relationships with any one group. Instead, the community capitalized on the diverse resources around it. When, after the conquest, an opportunity arose for Sawatanen to attend Moor's Indian Charity School, the Wendats developed and strengthened their relationship with New Englanders, the Abenakis, and the Mohawks. When Jesuit influence declined, they capitalized on Sawatanen's education and local resources to provide additional opportunities for their children at the francophone Petit Séminaire. In both cases, the Wendats sought out these opportunities in order to equip their community with the tools they needed to maintain their place within an increasingly colonized landscape. As their own school developed, other communities with whom they were linked through trade and kinship, such as Kahnawake, Odanak, and the Maliseets, also sent their children for an education.

CONCLUSION

In the mid-nineteenth century Sawatanen's cousin and Jean Vincent's grandson, Zacharie Vincent, was declared the last "pure-blooded" Wendat.[107] Indeed, from the time of their dispersal to the present day, the general discourse about this community continues to be focused on their gradual "Canadienization" and assimilation into the neighboring francophone society. This way of looking at the community privileges the French presence along the Lada8anna Valley and completely ignores the continued Wendat influence over the past four centuries. With the rapid increase of French settlement, the Wendats required new strategies to maintain their place on the landscape. But rather than seeing these people solely as immigrants reacting anew to life in a landscape defined by French colonialism, the evidence presented here suggests it is more appropriate to see eighteenth-century changes as continuous with their seventeenth-century past.

The Wendats developed a moditional economy and culture that integrated the needs of the present into their past practices. They did not merely adopt European peoples, architecture, and economy as individuals; rather, as a community and nation, they used these new tools to strengthen relationships with both their European and Indigenous neighbors. Rather than eroding the distinct nature of their society and their place on the Laurentian landscape, the relationships that people such as André Otehiondi, Jean Vincent, and Sawatanen cultivated, the decisions they made, and the strategies they developed were used to strengthen the Wendat position within this space. Sawatanen's return to the community did not merely mark the beginning of a day school; it also began a four-decade period of petitioning for Wendat legal title to parts of the seigneurial landscape. Indeed, relative to the dearth of source material on this community in the eighteenth century, the period between 1790 and 1830 appears as a veritable renaissance of Wendat identity and political agitation. This was certainly a significant period of cultural transformation, but the general discourse toward "Canadienization" and assimilation misses important avenues of continuity. The eighteenth and early nineteenth centuries were a period when the Wendats maintained, developed, and strengthened their place within the Laurentian landscape.

NOTES

This chapter is based on my PhD dissertation, "Two Conquests: Aboriginal Experiences of the Fall of New France and Acadia," York University, 2011. I would like to thank Jonathan Lainey, Jean-François Lozier, and Andrew Sturtevant for sharing their insights, research, and useful primary source material, as well as Serge Goudreau for generously sharing his genealogical research. Research for this paper was conducted with the support of the American Philosophical Society's Phillips Fund for Native American Research and the Social Sciences and Humanities Research Council. I am particularly grateful to the staff at the Rauner Library and Special Collections at Dartmouth College and the faculty in Dartmouth's Native American Studies program for the dynamic intellectual environment they fostered as the ideas for this book and chapter came together.

Just as this chapter was finished, Alain Beaulieu, Stephanie Bereau, and Jean Tanguay published *Les Wendats du Quebec: Territoire, Economie et Identité, 1650–1930* (Quebec City: Les Editions GID, 2013). Chapters 2, 3, and 4 of their book cover similar terrain, though sometimes reaching different conclusions. Any reader drawing on this chapter would be wise to also consult their work.

1. John G. Reid, *Acadia, Maine and New Scotland: Marginal Colonies in the Seventeenth Century* (Toronto: University of Toronto Press, 1981), 186.

2. As outlined in the introduction, in order to clearly make this point about the Wendats' arrival in the region, I have chosen to use Wendat names for the local landscape around Lorette rather than the more common French terminology. Unless otherwise noted, this toponomy comes from Jean Poirier, *La Toponymie des Hurons-Wendats* (Quebec City: Commission de Toponymie du Québec, 2001).

3. The seigneuries around Lorette were all granted around 1650. Saint-Gabriel and Saint-Ignace were both granted in 1647, Sillery in 1651, and Gaudarville in 1652. See Joseph Bouchette, *A Topographical Dictionary of the Province of Lower Canada*, in Joseph Bouchette, *The British Dominions in North America; or a Topographical*

and Statistical Description of the Provinces of Lower and Upper Canada, vol. 2 (London: Longman, Rees, Orme, Brown, and Green, 1831).

4. According to the 1665–66 census, there were 984 people living in and around Quebec (excluding Île d'Orléans), while in 1650 about 300 Wendats migrated into the region. These numbers do not include the presence of other Indigenous peoples at places such as Sillery, suggesting that this ratio was likely higher than one-third. Statistics Canada, *Families, Population, Sexes, Conjugal Condition, 1665–66 All settlements*, Census of New France, E-STAT (accessed March 21, 2012). The government of Canada discontinued the E-STAT service in 2013, but Queen's University's library agreed to continue it. These resources are available at http://library.queensu.ca/data /census-1665-1871 (accessed December 1, 2015).

5. James Pendergast, "The Confusing Identities Attributed to Stadacona and Hochelaga," *Journal of Canadian Studies* 32, no. 4 (1998): 149–67; Gary Warrick, *A Population History of the Huron-Petun, A.D. 500–1650* (Cambridge: Cambridge University Press, 2008), 194–204. For examples of Wendat visits to the Saint Lawrence Valley before their dispersal in 1650, see Bruce Trigger, *The Children of Aataentsic: A History of the Huron People to 1660* (Montreal: McGill–Queen's University Press, 1976), 246–47, 326–27, 398–99, 430, 476–85, 522–26, 604–5, 615–16, 799.

6. Statistics Canada, *Statement of Population, 1706*, Census of New France, E-STAT (accessed November 30, 2011).

7. "Wendake" is primarily used as a noun to refer to the Wendat homeland on the shores of Georgian Bay or to their present-day reserve, which is still located at Jeune-Lorette. Here I use the word loosely drawing on its broader meaning: "where the Wendat live." See Poirier, *La Toponymie des Hurons-Wendats*, 43.

8. For more on Jesuit conniving and duplicity as it relates to Sillery, see Michel Lavoie, *"C'est ma seigneurie que je réclame": Le lutte des Hurons de Lorette pour la seigneurie de Sillery, 1658–1890* (Montreal: Boréal, 2009).

9. Conrad Heidenreich, *Huronia: A History and Geography of the Huron Indians, 1600–1650* (Toronto: McClelland and Stewart, 1971), 213–16.

10. Statistics Canada, *NF—Statement of the Population of Canada, 1739—New France* (table), Census of New France, E-STAT (accessed September 22, 2010). A censive is a parcel of land leased from the seigneur by a French settler.

11. By 1754, at the end of the French regime, the population of Kahnawake was 1,500 and that of Montreal only 4,000. See Jan Grabowski, *The Common Ground: Settled Natives and French in Montreal, 1667–1760* (PhD diss., University of Montreal, 1993), 67; Statistics Canada, *NF—Statement of the Population, 1754—New France* (table), Census of New France, E-STAT (accessed September 22, 2010).

12. This number was calculated by adding the population for 1739 from Champigny, Gaudarville, Jeune-Lorette, Notre-Dame-des-Anges, Charlesbourg, Saint Bernard, Saint-Gabriel, Saint-Ignace, Sainte-Foy, Sillery, Beauport, and the town of Quebec. The total comes to 7,355. Statistics Canada, *NF—Statement of the Population of Canada, 1739—New France*, Census of New France, E-STAT (accessed September 22, 2010).

13. Paul Tsa8enhohi to André Otehiondi, June 11, 1773, Division des archives de l'Université de Montréal, Baby Collection, U 5266; "La Mosaïque de Grands Chefs Hurons," n.d., Archives du Conseil de la Nation huronne-wendat (ACNHW), Collection François Vincent, FV/105/6/c.

14. William Murray to Andrew, a Huron [of Lorette?], December 11, 1764, *William Johnson Papers*, ed. Alexander Flick (Albany: University of the State of New York, 1925), vol. 4: 628; [Hay], "Diary of the Siege of Detroit," in Franklin B. Hough, *Diary of the Siege of Detroit* (Albany: J. Munsell, 1860), 51–54, 82, 89, 112–13.

15. Anonymous [Robert Navarre], *Journal of Pontiac's Conspiracy*, ed. M. Agnes Burton (Detroit: Published by Clarence Monroe Burton under the Auspices of the Michigan Society of the Colonial Wars, [1912]), 230, 236.

16. John Steckley, *The Eighteenth-Century Wyandot: A Clan-Based Study* (Waterloo, Ont.: Wilfrid Laurier University Press, 2014), 123.

17. André Genest, July 1, 1775, Bibliothèque et Archives nationales du Québec à Québec (BAnQ-Q), Fonds Cour supérieure, District judiciaire de Québec, Greffes de notaires, CN 301, S115.

18. Paul Tsa8enhohi to André Otehiondi, June 11, 1773 (n. 13).

19. Lettre de Beauharnois au ministre, September 21, 1741, Centre des Archives Outre-mer (CAOM), C11A, vol. 75, ff. 138–142v; M. de Beauharnois to Count de Maurepas, in E. B. O'Callaghan, ed., *Documents Relative to the Colonial History of the State of New York* (hereafter *DRCHSNY*) (Albany: Weed, Parsons, 1855), vol. 9: 1069–70. See René Bélanger, "Vincent," *Dictionary of Canadian Biography* (*DCB*), http://www.biographi.ca/en/bio/vincent_3E.html (accessed December 1, 2015).

20. William Pote, *The Journal of Captain William Pote Jr.* (New York: Dodd and Mead, 1896).

21. It is important to note that both Sawatanen and Tsawenhohi were hereditary names. This can be seen most clearly in the similarity in names between André Otehiondi's uncle, Paul Tsa8enhohi, and Nicolas Vincent Tsawenhohi, both grand chiefs of the Wendat Nation at Lorette. The number "8" often signifies a *ou* or *w* sound, meaning that although they are spelled differently, they would have been pronounced similarly. Likewise, in the nineteenth century the first Wendat Catholic priest, Prosper Vincent, was also known as Sawatanen. Louise Vigneault and Isabelle Masse, "Les autoreprésentations de l'artiste huron-wendat Zacharie Vincent (1815–1886): icons d'une gloire politique et spirituelle," *Journal of Canadian Art History* 32, no. 2 (2011): 65; see also Fonds Prosper Vincent, Musée de la Civilisation (MC), P20/190/15.

22. "Death Notices," *Salem Gazette*, May 17, 1825, 3; Georges Sioui, "Nicolas Vincent," *DCB*, http://www.biographi.ca/en/bio/vincent_nicolas_7E.html (accessed December 1, 2015); Serge Goudreau, personal correspondence, July 19, 2009.

23. Serge Goudreau, "Les Hurons de Lorette au 18e siècle," *Mémoires de la Société généalogique canadienne-française* 63, no. 2 (Summer 2012): 131.

24. For a more detailed biography of Sawatanen's life, see Jonathan Lainey and Thomas Peace, "Louis Vincent Sawatanen: premier bachelier autochtone canadien,"

in Gaston Deschênes et Denis Vaugeois, eds., *Vivre la Conquête: Des parcours individuels* (Quebec City: Les éditions du Septentrion, 2013), 204–14. A translated and extended version of this essay appears as "Louis Vincent Sawatanen: A Life Forged by Warfare and Migration," in Kristin Burnett and Geoff Read, eds., *Aboriginal History: A Reader,* 2nd ed. (Toronto: Oxford University Press, 2016), 106–16.

25. Alain Beaulieu, *De la maison longue à la maison canadienne: Le cas des Hurons de Lorette* (Neufchâtel: Ministère de la Justice du Québec, Direction du droit autochtone, 1995), 27.

26. Peter Kalm, *Travels into North America,* vol. 2, 2nd ed., trans. John Reinhold Forester (London: T. Lowdens, 1772), 307–8. This is supported by two additional eyewitness accounts. Louis Franquet, a French military engineer who visited in 1752, claimed that Wendat homes were built using the same *pièce-sur-pièce* construction technique as the French settlers, while Louis-Antoine de Bougainville, another army officer who visited four years later, claimed they were built of stone. Louis Franquet, *Voyages et mémoires sur le Canada* (Quebec City: A. Côté et Cie, 1889), 107; Edward P. Hamilton, ed., *Adventures in the Wilderness: The American Journals of Louis-Antoine de Bougainville, 1756–1760* (Norman: University of Oklahoma Press, 1964), 75.

27. André Genest, July 1, 7, 8, 1775, BAnQ-Q, CN 301, s115.

28. Jean-Baptiste Panet, May 5, 1794, BAnQ-Q, CN 301, s206. See also "Acte de concession d'une terre . . . ," BAnQ-Q, Fonds Ministère des Terres et Forêts, Gestion des terres publiques, Biens des Jésuites, Seigneurie de Saint-Gabriel, district de Québec, E21, S64, SS5, SSS6, D524. An arpent is a term of measurement. One arpent equals about 5/6 acres.

29. For a list see Thomas Peace, "Two Conquests: Aboriginal Experiences of the Fall of New France and Acadia" (PhD diss., York University, 2011), appendix 2.

30. Noel Duprac, October 21, 1733, December 28, 1733, July 4, 1734, October 16, 1736, October 6, 1737, September 14, 1745, BAnQ-Q, CN 301, s94. Benoît Grenier notes that Marie-Catherine Peuvret kept these documents in a separate workbook from the contracts that she made with French settlers; they were also listed as part of the inventory of her goods taken on her death. See Benoît Grenier, *Marie-Catherine Peuvret: Veuve et seigneuresse en Nouvelle-France, 1667–1739* (Quebec City: Les éditions du Septentrion, 2005), 128, 218.

31. Contrats et recette pour le fief St Ignace, 1731–1855, Les Archives des Augustines; André Genest, October 10, 1746, BAnQ-Q, CN 301, s115.

32. The final document associated with these concessions is Jean-Baptiste Panet, March 20, 1784, BAnQ-Q, CN 301, s206.

33. Fonds Prosper Vincent, MC, P20/190/23.

34. This number should be used cautiously. Most notarial records tell us only when the land was acquired, but we know little about how long it was held. The three thousand arpents of land assumes that no land was sold between 1760 and 1800, and it includes the forty arpents held communally by the Wendats at Lorette. The per-family calculation is derived by dividing the total land acquired by the thirty-two families noted by Joseph Bouchette in 1821. See Bouchette, *Topographical Dictionary,*

n.p. [484, Wendats are listed under "Indians"]; Table B-1: Huron-Wendat Land Transactions: 1730–1800, in Peace, "Two Conquests," 414.

35. Registre avec index contenant l'État général des biens des Jésuites dans la province de Québec, comprenant l'aveu et dénombrement de 1781, BAnQ-Q, E21, S64, SS5, SSS1, D284.

36. Léon Gérin, "Le Huron de Lorette," in Denis Vaugeois, ed., *Les Hurons de Lorette* (Quebec City: Les éditions du Septentrion, 1996), 22–23.

37. George Heriot, *Travels through the Canadas, Containing a Description of the Picturesque Scenery on Some of the Rivers and Lakes; with an Account of the Productions, Commerce and Inhabitants of Those Provinces* (Philadelphia: M. Carey, 1813), 93. Heriot estimates about two hundred acres, which I have converted into arpents in order to standardize the measurements used in this chapter.

38. *Appendice du Quatrième volume des journaux de l'Assemblée Législative de la Province du Canada du 28 Novembre 1844, au 29 mars 1845, ces deux jours compris et dans la Huitième année du Règne de Notre Souveraine Dame La Reine Victoria: Première session du second Parlement Provincial du Canada* (Montreal: L. Perrault, 1845), EEE-23; *Appendix to the Sixth Volume of the Journals of the Legislative Assembly of the Province of Canada, from the 2nd Day of June to the 28th Day of July 1847* (Montreal: R. Campbell, 1847), T-82, T-83.

39. This calculation is derived by dividing the land under cultivation by the thirty-two families observed by Joseph Bouchette in 1821. Bouchette, *Topographical Dictionary*.

40. "Rapport sur les Affaires des Sauvages en Canada, sections 1ère et 2ème. Mis devant l'Assemblée Législative, le 20 Mars 1845. #6: Hurons de la Jeune-Lorette," in *Appendice du Quatrième volume des journaux de l'Assemblée Législative de la Province du Canada du 28 Novembre 1844, au 29 mars 1845, ces deux jours compris et dans la Huitième année du Règne de Notre Souveraine Dame La Reine Victoria: Première session du second Parlement Provincial du Canada* (Montreal: L. Perrault, 1845), appendix EEE.

41. Heidenreich, *Huronia*, 198. This is a crude comparison; a deeper understanding of the soil fertility in the two places is required. Nonetheless, there is some similarity between Wendake Ehen and Jeune-Lorette, which makes this superficial comparison useful. Both sites were located on predominantly sandy loam soil structures, which made agriculture somewhat marginal. For more information on soil in these two places, see ibid., 195–200; Gérin, "Huron de Lorette," 22–23; Cole Harris, *The Seigneurial System in Early Canada: A Geographical Study* (Montreal: McGill–Queen's University Press, 1966), 16–17.

42. Goudreau, "Hurons de Lorette au 18e siècle," 138.

43. Girault to Haldimand, October 21, 1779, Library and Archives Canada (LAC), MG 21, Haldimand Papers, vol. 21777, ff. 165–67.

44. There were 28 people listed in the census and 37 listed in the petition. See Registre contenant un recensement nominatif pour les paroisses situées dans les seigneuries des Jésuites en 1784, BAnQ-Q, E21, S64, SS5, SSS1, D288; "Petition of the

Huron for the seigneurie of Sillery. Written at Lorette on the 26th January 1819," in *Eighth Report of the Committee of the House of Assembly* (Quebec City: Neilson and Cowen, 1824), i.

45. I have determined unique individuals by removing all cases in which only the first or last name has been provided, unless no other person within thirty years shares a similar first name. I have not included individuals named in Wendat surveys (BAnQ-Q, CA 301).

46. *Eighth Report of the Committee of the House of Assembly* (n. 44), 13.

47. Robert Toupin, *Les écrits de Pierre Potier* (Ottawa: Les Presses de l'Université d'Ottawa, 1996), vol. 1: 170–265, esp. 193, 198.

48. Steckley, *Eighteenth-Century Wyandot*, 72–73.

49. Toupin, *Les écrits de Pierre Potier*, 171.

50. "Abstract, in form of a Journal of the most interesting occurrences in the Colony," in reference to military movements, and of the various intelligence received, since the departure of the ships in November, 1746," in *DRCHSNY* 10:116.

51. "Journal (de La Galissonière et Hocquart) concernant ce qui s'est passé d'intéressant dans la colonie de novembre 1747 à octobre 1748," CAOM, C11A, vol. 87, f. 185; "Journal of whatever occurred of interest at Quebec in regard to the operations of the war, and the various intelligence received there since the sailing of the ships in November, 1747," in *DRCHSNY* 10:145.

52. Toupin, *Les écrits de Pierre Potier*, 236, 265.

53. It is important to note, however, that Jean-François Lozier highlights the absence of Wendats from Lorette in warfare in the Great Lakes and farther west during the French regime, suggesting that this relationship needs to be probed more deeply. See Jean-François Lozier, "Les origines huronnes-wendates de Kanesatake," *Recherches Amérindiennes au Québec* 44, nos. 2–3 (2014): 111.

54. Joseph Vincent to Matthew, Lord Aylmer, November 1, 1832, LAC, RG 10, vol. 85, 33791, in Denys Delâge and Jean-Pierre Sawaya, *Les Traités des Sept Feux avec les Britanniques: droits et pièges d'un héritage colonial au Québec* (Quebec City: Les éditions du Septentrion, 2001), 93; "At a Meeting with a Deputation from the Hurons of Lorette," November 30, 1775, LAC, MG 19 F35: Superintendent of Indian Affairs, lot 611, 4.

55. John Johnson to R. Matthews, April 3, 1783, LAC, Haldimand Papers, vol. 21775 ff. 88.

56. For more on how the Wendats shaped the development of these towns, particularly Kanesatake, see Lozier, "Les origines huronnes-wendates de Kanesatake."

57. The names in parenthesis are alternative names used either by the French or by the descendants of the Seven Fires for their present-day communities.

58. See Jean-Pierre Sawaya, *La fédération des Sept Feux de la vallée du Saint-Laurent: XVIIe au XIXe siècle* (Quebec City: Les éditions du Septentrion, 1998); Jean-Pierre Sawaya, *Alliances et dépendance: Comment la couronne britannique a obtenu la collaboration des Indiens de la vallée du Saint-Laurent entre 1760–1774* (Quebec City: Les éditions du Septentrion, 2002).

59. Goudreau, "Les Hurons de Lorette au 18e siècle," 125–47.

60. J. G. Kohl, *Travels in Canada, and through the States of New York and Pennsylvania*, trans. Mrs. Percy Sinnett (London: George Manwaring, 1861), vol. 1: 177–78.

61. Colin G. Calloway, *The American Revolution in Indian Country: Crisis and Diversity in Native American Communities* (New York: Cambridge University Press, 1995), 76, 79. Calloway considers Vincent as being from Kahnawake, but documentation from Lorette suggests that he was in fact a Wendat man. This ambiguity seems to be a case where Vincent carried multiple identities (likely explained by the interconnections between Seven Fires communities outlined briefly above). See Goudreau, "Hurons de Lorette au 18e siècle," 125–47; Peace, "Two Conquests," 352–53.

62. "Vincent, Louis, Bedel's New Hampshire Regiment," Compiled Military Service File, US National Archives and Records Administration, Washington, D.C.

63. Eleazar Wheelock to John Thornton, October 20, 1775, Rauner Library and Special Collections (hereafter RLSC), Dartmouth College, 775570.

64. Wheelock to Trustees, October 22, 1772, RLSC, 772572.

65. C. M. Johnston, "John Deserontyon, (Odeserundiye)," in *DCB*, http://www.biographi.ca/en/bio/deserontyon_john_5E.html (accessed December 1, 2015).

66. *The Journal of Major John Norton, 1816*, ed. Carl F. Klinck (Toronto: Champlain Society, 1970), 105.

67. On Jean Vincent, see H. P. Smith and W. S. Rann, *History of Rutland County Vermont* (Syracuse, N.Y.: D. Mason, 1886), 636–37. Smith and Rann suggest he was from western New York; a historical marker on Route 4 near Mendon, Vermont, indicates that Vincent was from Kahnawake (Caughnawaga). See also note 61.

68. "Timeline of the Huron community," n.d., ACNHW, Collection François Vincent, FV/104/6/b6; see also Georges Boiteau, "Les chasseurs hurons de Lorette" (MA thesis, Université Laval, 1954), 56–57, 61; Denis Vaugeois, *The Last French and Indian War* (Montreal: McGill–Queen's University Press, 2002), 74. Boiteau went so far as to suggest that Sawatanen became someone on whom all of the hope of the community was placed (61). This is clearly an exaggeration; many of his contemporaries were equally involved in these claims and, based on some of their signatures, may have been similarly educated. Nonetheless, his role in the community was important, as was the emphasis that he placed on education.

69. "Récit du Conseil adressé à Monsieur le Colonel Campbell Surint Genl des Affaires Sauvages," December 16, 1791, LAC, MG 19 F35, Superintendent of Indian Affairs, series 2, lot 694, author's translation. Delâge and Sawaya have observed that the difference between the treatment of Indigenous land in Upper and Lower Canada was significant. Although Lord Dorchester (Guy Carleton) told some of these communities that they would be compensated, there is no evidence that any compensation ever occurred. See Delâge and Sawaya, *Traités des Sept Feux*, 227–33; "Réponse du Lord Dorchester aux Sauvages du Lac des deux Montagnes," August 28–29, 1794, LAC, MG19, F35, Superintendent of Indian Affairs, series 2, lots 698, 699.

70. *Eighth Report of the Committee of the House of Assembly*; A. Stuart, "Remarks upon the several REPORTS made from time to time by the Law Officers of the Crown of His Majesty's Province of Lower Canada upon the Claim of the Christian Indians settled at Lorette to the Seigniory of Sillery, under a Grant from His most

Christian Majesty, bearing date the 13th day of March 1651, and comprising a portion of what now is called the Seigniory of St. Gabriel," November 25, 1829, in *Aboriginal Tribes (North America, New South Wales, Van Diemen's Land and British
Guiana)* (London: HMSO, 1834), 106–13.

71. Collection de la famille Aubert de Gaspé, LAC, MG18-H44.

72. Linda Sioui, *Réaffirmation de l'identité wendate/wyandotte à l'heure de la
mondialisation* (Wendake: Hannerorak, 2012).

73. John Sutton Lutz, *Makúk: A New History of Aboriginal-White Relations*
(Vancouver: University of British Columbia Press, 2008), 23–24.

74. "État des munitions qui ont été fournies par les particuliers ci-après nommés
pour munir les magasins de Québec à l'occasion de la guerre depuis le 20 octobre
1745 jusqu'à pareil jour 1746," October 26, 1746, CAOM, C11A, vol. 117, ff. 49–65; "État
des munitions qui ont été fournies par les particuliers ci-après nommés pour munir
les magasins de Québec à l'occasion de la guerre depuis le 20 octobre 1746 jusqu'au
10 octobre 1747," October 15, 1747, CAOM, C11A, vol. 117, ff. 95–116. The amount per
family is based on Franquet's estimate that there were twenty-five families in the village. Franquet, *Voyages et mémoires,* 107. Gregory Kennedy, whose work focuses on
farming societies in Acadia and the Loudunais, has compiled annual budgets for
these regions that provide a good point of comparison. In the 1760s revenue for an
average day worker in the Loudunais (in livres) was 349.8 and for a plowman 1,872.47.
In Acadia the income in 1707 of a small farmer was 776.33 and 1,647.07 for a large
farmer. See Gregory Kennedy, "French Peasants in Two Worlds: A Comparative Study
of Rural Experience in Seventeenth- and Eighteenth-Century Acadia and the Loudunais (PhD thesis, York University, 2008), appendix A. This paragraph modifies
and updates conclusions drawn in Thomas Peace, "The Slow Process of Conquest:
Huron-Wendat Responses to the Conquest of Quebec, 1697–1791," in Phillip Buckner
and John G. Reid, eds. *Revisiting 1759: The Conquest of Canada in Historical Perspective* (Toronto: University of Toronto Press, 2012), 119.

75. Dépouillement fait les 8, 9 et 10 mars 1756 des sommes dues tant pour les
arrérages de cens et rentes que des droits de lots et ventes, 1755 compris, BAnQ-Q,
E21, S64, SS5, SSS6, D1419; Registre avec index contenant l'État général des biens des
Jésuites dans la province de Québec, comprenant l'aveu et dénombrement de 1781,
BAnQ-Q, E21, S64, SS5, SSS1, D284.

76. Evidence of Wendats supplying the British can be found in Girault to Haldimand, September 20, 1778, Haldimand Papers, ms. 21777, f. 36. In this letter Etienne Girault, the missionary at Lorette, informs Frederick Haldimand that it was a
good time to order snowshoes from the village.

77. Bouchette, *Topographical Dictionary.*

78. J. Long, *Voyages and Travels of an Indian Interpreter and Trader* (London:
self-published, 1791), 154.

79. General Murray's Report of the State of the Government of Quebec in Canada, June 5, 1762, in Adam Shortt and Arthur G. Doughty, eds., *Documents Relating
to the Constitutional History of Canada, 1759–1791* (Ottawa: J. Taché, 1918), vol. 1: 73.

See also Jean Tanguay, "La liberté d'errer et de vaquer: Les Hurons de Lorette et l'occupation du territoire, XVIIe–XIXe siècles" (MA thesis, Université Laval, 1998), 53.

80. Daniel K. Richter, *The Ordeal of the Longhouse: The Peoples of the Iroquois League in the Era of European Colonization* (Chapel Hill: University of North Carolina Press, 1992), 32–35.

81. For more on the Haudenosaunee mourning war as a method of population replacement, see ibid., 3, 32–35, 60–66.

82. Lettre de Beauharnois et Hocquart au ministre, October 7, 1734, CAOM, C11A, vol. 61, ff. 89v–90.

83. Pote, *Journal,* 20. Jean Langlois is one of the Wendats who appear in the documentary record relatively frequently. His name and his engagement with the French suggest that he might have been the person to which this Wendat man referred.

84. Kalm, *Travels into North America,* 300.

85. Pote, *Journal,* 86.

86. "Minutes of the Exchange of Prisoners, 1750: General Return of the English prisoners detained in the government of New France," in *DRCHSNY,* vol. 10, 214–15.

87. "Requête de Martin de Lino, procureur du roi de la Prévôté de Québec, au Conseil de Marine, [1717]," CAOM, C11A, vol. 38, ff. 226–227v; "Résumé de lettres du Conseil et de Bégon et délibération du Conseil de Marine," April 20, 1720, CAOM, C11A, vol. 41, ff. 259–261bis. Serge Goudreau has written most extensively about this case and the issues that develop from it. See Serge Goudreau, "Le village huron de Lorette: une crèche pour les enfants canadiens du XVIIIe siècle," *Mémoires de la Société généalogique canadienne-française* 51, no. 1 (Spring 2000): 7–12.

88. Hubert Charbonneau and Jacques Légaré, *Répertoire des actes de baptême, mariage, sépulture et des recensements du Québec ancien* (Montreal: Les Presses de l'Université de Montréal, 1986), vol. 33: B-464.

89. There are no parish records for the period before 1760, which makes it impossible to adequately address the issue of intermarriage.

90. Serge Goudreau, "Étienne Ondiaraété (1742–1830): Un chef huron du village de Lorette," *Mémoires de la Société généalogique canadienne-française* 54, no. 3 (Winter 2003): 270.

91. Franquet, *Voyages et mémoires,* 107, author's translation. Goudreau uses this quotation and another similar one from James Murray's 1762 report on Quebec to illustrate this same point. See Goudreau, "Le village huron de Lorette," 12.

92. Goudreau, "Hurons de Lorette au 18e siècle," 131.

93. Peace, "Two Conquests," 363–65. For a good example of this script see "Receuil de chants Hurons" [avant 1838], MC, Fonds d'archives du Séminaire de Québec, SME 13/MS-66.

94. Roy C. Dalton, *The Jesuits' Estates Question, 1760–1888: A Study of the Background for the Agitation of 1889* (Toronto: University of Toronto Press, 1968), 6.

95. Wheelock to Trustees, October 22, 1772, RLSC, 772572.

96. Huron chiefs to Guy Lord Dorchester, July 22, 1791, MC, SME 1/2/12a.

97. Mathieu Chaurette, *Les premières écoles autochtones au Québec: Progression, opposition et luttes de pouvoir, 1792–1853* (master's thesis, Université du Québec à Montréal, 2011), 36.

98. Livre des dépenses du Séminaire de Québec commencé le 1er janvier 1782, MC, SME c. 37.

99. Journal des recettes de 1771–1801, MC, SME, c. 36.

100. MC, SME 13.1 f. 47; see also Noël Baillargeon, *Le Séminaire de Québec de 1760 à 1800* (Quebec City: Les Presses de l'université Laval, 1981), 144.

101. MC, SME 1/2/12c. De Salaberry provides notice that the Huron council was removing their children from the seminary, in a note dated July 5, 1806.

102. Requête de Louis Vincent, maître d'école à la Jeune-Lorette, adressée aux commissaires des biens des Jésuites, December 9, 1800, BAnQ-Q, E21, S64, SS5, SSS2, D1623; Brouillon de procès-verbaux de réunions de la commission responsable de l'administration des biens des Jésuite, June 8, 1802, BAnQ-Q, E21, S64, SS5, SSS2 D62.

103. There were thirty children under fourteen in the 1784 census. See Registre contenant un recensement nominatif pour les paroisses situées dans les seigneuries des Jésuites en 1784, BAnQ-Q, E21, S64, SS5, SSS1, D288.

104. Kohl, *Travels in Canada*, 177.

105. Thaddeus Osgood, *The Canadian Visitor Communicating Important Facts and Interesting Anecdotes Respecting the Indians and Destitute Settlers in Canada and the United States of America* (London: Hamilton and Adams, [1829?]), 23–24.

106. Chaurette, *Premières écoles autochtones au Québec*, 36; see also Robert Christie to Duncan C. Napier, December 7, 1844, LAC, RG 10, vol. 599, ff. 47710–47711.

107. David Karel, Marie-Dominic Labelle, and Sylvie Thivierge, "Zacharie Vincent," *DCB*, http://www.biographi.ca/en/bio/vincent_zacharie_11E.html (accessed December 1, 2015).

CHAPTER 4

Wendats, Presbyterians, and the Origins of Protestant Christianity on the Sandusky River

Michael Leonard Cox

Despite Christianity's colonial origins and all of the multifaceted arguments about its use as a tool of assimilation, the Indigenous peoples of the Eastern Woodlands have lived with Protestant Christianity for more than two centuries. Indeed, many, including many Wendats, have come to embrace Protestantism as *their* religion, shaping its tenets to meet their needs. To understand this spiritual legacy, we must consider the long-term influence of Christianity on traditional practices, traditional practices on Indigenous Christianity, and the coexistence and commingling of beliefs and traditions. Such changes and alterations are the natural products of historical religious change. Clyde Holler made this observation thirty years ago: "all living religions change in response to new circumstances and challenges. This has been especially true of Native American religions, which have changed rapidly and drastically in response to forced cultural change and contact with Christianity . . . a religion that ceases to change is a religion that is already dead or in danger of extinction."[1] In the Eastern Woodlands, contact between spiritual traditions, in this case driven by the arrival of Protestant missionaries at Sandusky, paved the way for changes in Wendat religious practices. In the two centuries since the arrival of Protestant missionaries in the region, Protestantism has become traditional for many Wendats and other Indigenous peoples.[2]

Framing Protestantism as "traditional" does not imply that non-Christian traditional spirituality and cultural practices were unimportant or ceased to function; neither does it ignore the very real damage that the introduction of Protestantism wrought on Indigenous cultures and territory.[3] There is little doubt that Christianity—both Catholic and Protestant—introduced Euro-American cultural practices and the subsequent loss of homelands during this period. What emerges from this story, though, is that for most Wendats, the interplay between Christianity and Indigenous spirituality was not an either/or choice. Many Wendats and others felt (and continue to feel) connections to both traditions in very real, very fluid ways. Holler's argument about the Lakota spiritual leader Black Elk's conversion to Christianity is particularly relevant. Holler explains that Black Elk's "commitment to Christianity does not necessarily imply any lessening of his commitment to traditional Lakota religion. This is clearly the understanding of conversion assumed by the missionaries, but it was not necessarily that of the Indians themselves."[4] Allan Greer, one of the leading scholars of early Indigenous religious conversion, adds that understanding conversion "in bipolar terms—successful or unsuccessful, real or false, a sign of assimilation or evidence of covert resistance—with 'syncretism' occasionally invoked to cover any intermediate result" is inherently limiting and inaccurate. The complexities and ambiguities of religious contact, in Greer's view, are where the real indigenous engagement with Christianity occurred.[5] While it is difficult to pinpoint the stance many Wendats took on Protestantism, particularly in light of historiographical reliance on (mostly) missionary-produced records, one need not make a leap of faith to argue that the Wendats engaged with Protestantism with nuance, rather than simply assimilating the new religion. By re-examining the first decade of Protestant Christianity among the Wendats along the Sandusky River, this chapter addresses the multiple levels on which Wendat people chose to engage with Protestantism. This approach forces us to see early converts not simply as "outcasts," "corrupted," or "inauthentic"[6] but rather as individuals and small groups forming the cornerstones of what became a new Indigenous religious tradition within the community.[7]

CHOICES AT THE TURN OF THE
NINETEENTH CENTURY

Following the Treaty of Greenville in 1795, the Indigenous peoples of Ohio faced the realities of a constricted land base and the encroachment of white settlers into what would soon become the state of Ohio, depleting the available hunting resources.[8] One possibility for forging a tenable way of life in light of these new realities was to selectively adapt to Euro-American culture.[9] Many of the Sandusky Wendats, like a number of other Native groups east of the Mississippi, had begun to consider adaptation critical to their own future survival. Euro-American expansion was rapidly transforming the Ohio frontier (a middle ground) into a white-dominated contact zone.[10] The greatest potential source for gaining critical skills, primarily education in the English language and colonial agricultural techniques, proved to be the growing missionary movement among American Protestants.[11] While the Ohio Wendats had some fleeting contacts with other Protestants in the late 1790s, most notably the Society of Friends (Quakers), the first sustained Protestant missionary dialogue that ultimately bore the fruit of a missionary station came through a series of encounters with Presbyterians at the turn of the nineteenth century.[12]

The first contact between the Wendats and what would become the Presbyterian mission likely took place in 1800.[13] Reverend Joseph Badger of the Connecticut Missionary Society preached to the Wendats at Lower Sandusky in October. Badger immediately broached the subject of establishing a permanent linkage between his faith group and the Wendats. On this initial visit he claimed to have "had a talk with the Chiefs on the Subject of having a minister live with them, and teach their children to read, & c. was fully persuaded that this was the only way in which they could be led to any valuable improvement. At the close of our talk they expressed a wish to hear from us again."[14] Badger's initial visit was the beginning of a long dialogue between the Sandusky Wendats and Christian missionaries about a more permanent missionary arrangement. Between 1801 and 1805 Presbyterian missionaries repeatedly visited the Wendat people along the Sandusky, with a few venturing into Michigan to visit Wendat people at Brownstown and Monguagon. In addition to preaching to the Wendats, they also preached regularly to other Indigenous peoples, local white settlers, and a small African American community located near Upper Sandusky.

What clearly emerges from the extant records of these initial years of contact is a pattern of "feeling out" by both the Wendats and missionaries, both of whom considered the other only one of several potential partners for co-operation. For their part, many missionaries argued that the Wendats were better primed for a mission than other Indigenous groups. For example, in September 1801 Reverend Thomas Hughs noted that the Sandusky Wendats "are more civilized, and have more information than any we met with. The Roman Priests have been among them, and have baptized some of them." Hughs met with assembled chiefs at Upper Sandusky, where an unnamed headman asserted, "they [the Wendats] had been talking among themselves about our preaching, and were all pleased, and wishing that a minister would come and live with them."[15] After gaining an audience with the assembled chiefs, and speaking through a chain of interpretation (George Bluejacket translated English to Shawnee, and a Wendat man who understood Shawnee translated to Wendat),[16] the chiefs promised to go to Lower Sandusky and give a formal response regarding the presence of a minister and/or school-master among them. Most of the council never made it to Lower Sandusky, however, complaining of sickness as the culprit for their absence.[17] Without their presence or participation, consensus could not be reached, prompting the same "old chief" to state: "we think it not best to give our answer yet: if we did, the chiefs from the upper town, who are the Head-Chiefs, might come upon us and say, *Why did you give your answer so soon?* We think best to wait a little longer. . . . You, *brothers,* come and want to preach to us: this is good; we thank you for it. You want to send a schoolmaster to teach our children, and a minister to teach us how to serve God: this is all good, *brothers;* we thank you for it."[18] Beyond the notable perpetuation of traditional community decision-making procedures into the nineteenth century, it is also clear that the Wendat Nation dictated the proper setting for discussion of the issue of a mission, and the missionaries were powerless to speed the process. All told, it required nearly four years of give-and-take discussions before the Wendats accepted the development of a mission among them.[19]

ESTABLISHING THE MISSION

In the summer of 1805 Joseph Badger returned to the Sandusky.[20] He "talked with the Indians on the subject of civil improvements, both in learning to read, write, and number by figures, and cultivating their lands more extensively, raising cattle, and making of cloth."[21] As all missionaries had attempted before, Badger met with a Wendat council to propose a missionary establishment. This time, however, the Wendats gave a definite answer:

They have given their full consent to have a Minister reside with them and have a school to teach their children. their reasons for not accepting the offer before are in these words 'we were So bad, we were afraid to have a Minister live with us, we were all drunkards So that he would not preach to us but a few times we were afraid Some of our young men when intoxicated would Stagger to his house hooping & Yaling So as to put him in fear, and make him uncomfortable. but now we are determined to quit drinking alltogether.'—There is no difficulty now in the Way, on the part of the Wyandots of having the Gospel Staiedly amongst them, and also a school for their children, if a grant of a piece of the reserved land can be made by Congress to the Missionary who would Setle here.[22]

Though Badger's statement simplifies the numerous reasons why the Wendats had yet to select a missionary on the Sandusky, his comment reveals that the Wendats (at least enough of them to effectively sway the community) were now committed to allowing both religious and practical instruction from the Western Missionary Society, marking the first solid determination on the part of the Wendats to receive full-time Protestant missionaries.[23] Badger received tribal approval to build his mission anywhere on the western side of the Sandusky River at Lower Sandusky, providing that he "should not go off the Reserve to improve any land, or bring any other white people but such as I needed to assist in the mission."[24] The Wendats were willing to host the mission, but only with a small mission family in a narrowly defined space.[25] The Wendats, at least their tribal leaders, attempted to control cultural adaptation by choosing and sanctioning the Presbyterians on their own terms. As became clear during the life of the mission, allowing it to be built meant neither acceptance of Christianity nor rejection of other possibilities.

While the missionary establishment made an impact among the Sandusky Wendats, a number of other religious possibilities existed alongside the mission. Some of these alternative pathways had little to do with the mission, while others presented direct challenges to Wendat engagement with Christianity. At times, these challenges came from within the mission itself, or more broadly from Euro-Americans. In other cases, these alternatives and challenges originated in the Indigenous world.

As we have seen in earlier chapters of this book, Catholicism has an important legacy among the Wendats. By the early nineteenth century the Wendats had been in contact with Catholic missionaries, particularly the Jesuits, for nearly two hundred years.[26] Many Wendats had long incorporated facets of the Catholic religion into their own society, with Ohio missionaries observing aspects of Catholic ritual and practices cropping up among the Wendats there. In the Michigan Wendat communities of Brownstown and Monguagon, closer to Detroit, many Wendats retained a connection to the Catholic Church through contact with nearby French Canadian Catholics and their priests.

Knowledge of Catholicism's important place in these societies discouraged some missionaries from even attempting to preach at Brownstown, because they "knew that they were attached to the Roman Catholic religion." Sandusky Wendats, who lived farther from Detroit and lacked a priest stationed among them in recent decades, appear to have had much weaker attachments to Catholicism for the most part. Nonetheless, the long legacy of Catholicism shaped the Wendat understanding of Christianity. At Lower Sandusky a number of Wendats assembled to hear a Presbyterian sermon in 1801. Afterward a woman asked the missionaries to baptize her child. The interpreter told the missionary that the Wendats "would be displeased if it would not be done."[27] He attempted to explain that Protestants would not baptize any of them until they converted and had a deep understanding of the Bible. During the same missionary tour, a young man also asked whether the sin of murder could ever be pardoned, likely thinking along the lines of Catholic confession. Confronting these and other Catholic-based rituals became a recurring theme in the missionary record.

The most prevalent direct challenges to the mission came not from Indigenous—or even religious—sources but from local traders. Several traders assailed Badger and the mission due to fears that Badger's sermons against liquor would cause the alcohol trade to collapse. Badger likewise held most traders in low regard as particularly poor examples of white Euro-American culture, leading to personal friction beyond the more structural challenges caused by his sermons. In 1806 Badger weathered accusations levied by a local trader that he had disparaged the Quakers and discouraged the Wendats from communicating with them.[28] Later, another trader accused Badger (a married man) of committing adultery with a local widow.[29] By 1808 the continuous allegations of impropriety levied by the traders seemed to be having an impact in the Wendat community. Badger noted in his own journal that his enemies told the Wendats that "their land would all go to pay me for what I was doing, if they permitted me to stay." The Wendats assured Badger that they did not believe the traders, claiming "they were glad to have missionary aid."[30]

Despite such assurances, one particular trader soon transmitted a speech by the chiefs at Upper Sandusky to Governor of Michigan Territory William Hull, accusing Badger of mismanaging "a large sum of [donation] money . . . for the use of the Indians; that the good people of Ohio had sent a number of cattle for them; and that Mr. Badger kept the cattle for his own use, and had never given them one dollar of the money."[31] Hull forwarded the speech to the Western Missionary Society, who formed a committee to visit the mission and investigate.[32] When questioned about the contents of the letter, Tarhe—a noted Wendat leader—admitted that the chiefs at Upper Sandusky "do not know much about it here, only what we hear from flying stories." Other than his preaching occasionally at the upper town and administering medicine to the sick there, Tarhe claimed to have little regular contact with Badger. As to the claims against Badger, "we cannot prove anything; we have heard them only from white people (meaning the traders)." The committee explained that the money and livestock were collected "for the sole purpose of furnishing the missionaries and the school with provisions."[33] Badger and the laborers at the mission were to "assist the Indians to plough, to show them how to do their work, and to assist them in working as much as . . . [they] could find time to do" after completing the work necessary for the mission to function. Following the explanation, Tarhe expressed relief that the charges were false and that "we have been told by several traders that the cattle and hogs were sent for our use, and that Mr. Badger brought seven hundred dollars with him to hire hands and purchase tools to do our work for us, and that he was keeping that money for himself. . . . We will not listen to any more of these stories."[34] While the missionaries managed to assuage Wendat apprehensions, conflict with traders remained a hindrance to the missionary establishment.

While the mission faced external difficulties from traders' tales, it also encountered internal problems that threatened to divide the mission family and the Wendat people. A key difficulty was that the mission was regularly without an interpreter, which limited the missionary's influence. None of the Presbyterian missionaries spoke Wendat or any other Indigenous language, nor was any effort made to train missionaries to speak Wendat. No missionaries spent enough time among the Wendats to pick up their language. Even Badger required a translator.[35]

As was true in most other Indigenous missionary contexts, it was absolutely necessary to have a reliable interpreter. Speaking an entire sermon through an interpreter seems to have been awkward and tedious enough, but the missionaries had few alternatives.[36] Occasionally, individuals such as

Hampton Northrop, Samuel Sanders, and Elizabeth Whitaker would interpret, but they were not available for day-to-day duties at the mission.[37]

In the end, their only viable choice was to hire a full-time interpreter. As
the Western Missionary Society's hiring of William Walker demonstrates, in-
terpreters in the contact areas occupied "the same place that the learned do
in a civilized society. Of course their services are estimated at a very high rate.
Four hundred dollars per annum will be required by the person in view
[Walker]."[38] Walker's desirability as interpreter included not only his skill but
that of his wife Catherine, "a serious woman; [who] can read and interpret
well." The Walker children were already bilingual and were thought to "be of
very great service in the school."[39] If Walker is any example, being an interpreter was not just a full-time career but also a family trade.

The hiring of an interpreter points to a related problem faced by the mission. It rarely had enough funds to support its efforts, which were expensive
and involved a significant amount of nonspiritual work. Additionally, the
startup costs required to build the infrastructure of a new mission drained
the scant funds available. Numerous Christian donors were willing to support a spiritual mission, but fewer were willing to bankroll costs incurred to
build missionary houses or to teach Indians farming, basic mechanical skills,
and household arts. The Missionary Society recognized this dilemma and
sought to address it. In an 1808 report, for example, they were very careful to
assure potential donors that all of the nonreligious aspects of the missionary
enterprise were merely "handmaids of religion," tools used to both attach the
Wendats to Christianity and enable them to succeed in "proper" society.[40]
Despite such assurances, raising the funds necessary to conduct the work of
the mission effectively proved difficult.

INDIGENOUS CHALLENGES TO THE MISSION

Besides the difficulties within the mission, some Wendats opted to explore
alternative spiritual powers that existed outside of (and sometimes conflicted
with) the Presbyterian mission. One such power was the prophetic movement
of Handsome Lake.[41] Handsome Lake, a Seneca prophet, experienced a series of visions in 1799 to 1800 that led him to call for, in part, a return to "traditional" forms of worship.[42] Wendat interest in Handsome Lake's religion
emerges often in the missionary records. For example, in 1804 Hampton
Northrop informed Reverend George Scott that some of the Wendat chiefs
had "sent for a pretended prophet in the Cornplanter's nation, a brother to

the Cornplanter . . . with a design to hear him in order to form a choice who would be their teacher."[43] By August 1805 missionary John Anderson noted "both popish & pagan influence is exerting to keep them in the way to destruction. An Imposter, who is called the Propht [sic] of the Six nations, is much talked of by the ignorant. He will endeavour to revive and uphold their old heathenism, in opposition to Christianity."[44]

Handsome Lake continued to attract Wendat attention in the latter years of the Presbyterian mission. For example, while on an 1808 inspection of the mission, the reporting committee experienced the arrival of "the celebrated Seneca Prophet . . . with upwards of thirty chiefs and warriors." From the missionaries' perspective, the arrival of Handsome Lake proved deleterious. All of the Wendats were so preoccupied with the visit "that they could not pay much attention to the concerns of the mission." Even more disturbing to the missionaries was their perception that Handsome Lake's arrival "encouraged the party who were attached to paganism. Their expectations of the beneficial wonders which the prophet would perform were bounded by nothing short of raising the dead. . . . Friendly Indians were in confusion, and the prophet's party were impertinent."[45] By examining Handsome Lake's religion, the Wendats were exploring another option that would allow them to cope with the cultural upheaval created by the encroachment of American society.

Another potential challenger for spiritual adherence arrived in the person of Tenskwatawa, the Shawnee Prophet, in May 1806.[46] Tenskwatawa had experienced a prophetic vision in early 1805. He endorsed a return to the "Indian" lifestyle by rejecting the acculturationists and their white allies.[47] He arrived in the community in response to requests from some Wendats who had solicited his services as a witch finder. The people who sought out Tenskwatawa, usually cited as "young men," were involved in a witch hunt designed to rid the tribe of the causes of disease.[48] These witch hunters also wanted to identify causes of the reduction in game animals and the subsequent decline of "traditional" Wendat culture. By mid-May the Prophet had labeled four women at Lower Sandusky as witches and ordered their execution. As is true in most American-generated documents, these women are difficult to identify, but Joseph Badger commented that they were "four of the best women in the nation," which probably means that they were among the more acculturated in the community and likely among those who regularly attended Christian services. Tarhe and the other Wendat chiefs decided to intercede to stop the executions.[49]

The presence of the Shawnee Prophet and the events surrounding his activities reveal a degree of conflict among the Sandusky Wendats. Some obviously supported the Prophet or he would not have been asked to come to Lower Sandusky. This support may have been expressed as interest in his spiritual movement or more general discontent with the Wendat leadership's 1805 decision to cede land to the United States, as well as frustration with the slow process of adaptation. Nonetheless, a larger portion of the tribe, including the tribal leadership, disapproved of the Prophet's activities. From a religious perspective, some simply did not believe in his message or his spiritual legitimacy. Others likely resented the Prophet as an uninvited upstart—especially the tribal leadership, who had not officially sanctioned Tenskwatawa's efforts. In their view, he challenged their authority and interfered with their efforts to move the tribe in an adaptive direction. After his 1806 visit, Tenskwatawa's influence remained and grew. Badger continued to note in his journal that he "found them [the Wendats] in great confusion about their prophet: part of them will not listen to him [but] others will." On another occasion, Badger stated: "the Indians still keep up their pow-wow dances in obedience to the prophet."[50] It is clear that Tenskwatawa, like Handsome Lake, continued to find an audience among the Wendats. His followers often found themselves at odds with the mission and its program.[51]

Along with (and alongside) burgeoning interests in Native prophetic movements, traditional practices continued, likely as the most common form of spiritual expression. It is difficult to identify many specific references to the perpetuation of traditional practices, as they often overlapped and intersected with missionary observance of the prophetic movements, which dominated their attention. A few examples we have, again from Badger's journal, take note of "great confusion among the Indians by reason of their dreams and prophets."[52] On one occasion, mission laborer Quintus F. Atkins witnessed the "Indians . . . dancing to their God, on another, dancing before Sabbath service."[53] This latter observation points to a mixture of nativistic practices with missionary instruction. It again demonstrates that the Wendats exerted great freedoms in the spiritual realm.

A MULTIRELIGIOUS MILIEU

The realities of the religious "stew" percolating in the Wendat world emerge clearly in the early nineteenth century. Perhaps James Hughs recorded the

best example in the spring of 1805. Hughs preached to a large assembly gathered at Tarhe's home. He preached on the singularity of God, countering
information he had obtained that some Wendats believed there were two
gods, one who created white people, and the other (called the Warrior) who
created Indians.[54] Tarhe supported his sermon in a long speech in which he
"exhorted his people to receive it, for he believed it was all true, and that it
was the word of God."[55] It is interesting to ponder, though unclear, whether
Tarhe meant the specifics of the sermon were true, or if he simply believed
the notion that there was only one God. Tarhe also spent a great deal of time
emphasizing the duties parents had to their children, which can perhaps be
read as an endorsement of the educational possibilities offered through the
missionaries.[56] The competing religious visions emerged again a few days
later, when Hughs was required to wait outside the council house while those
inside "engaged in some kind of worship." Afterward, as Hughs preached his
sermon, he noted an image of the Warrior god "set up by the side of the council house, to which they pay some kind of homage when they worship. They
say they do not consider it a God, but have it there to put them in mind of
their God. Most of them seemed to acknowledge only one, the true God."[57]
As he preached a number of Wendats, especially chiefs, exclaimed "neh toah"
[that's right] frequently. From this account, it seems that many Wendats may
not have considered it apocryphal to believe in multiple spiritual visions simultaneously, and to both honor and believe seemingly incongruous conceptions of creation.

This notion of a broad acceptance of multiple faiths is supported by Tarhe's response to the sermon. He urged the people to "obey what our father is
teaching us, and what our ancient chiefs have told us; for it is all one substance. Let us all be of one mind; one god made us all, he made us all of one
blood. It is true we Indians serve the Warrior; we hold to the Warrior." Tarhe
urged his people to remember that "we are all one nation, and we should not
abuse or despise one another."[58] This speech seems a remarkable example of
both an effort to salve the growing spiritual tensions within the community
and a statement on the compatibility of divergent spiritual opinions and
practices, all under the umbrella of one God who created all people, while
also acknowledging that the Wendats worshipped the Warrior. While seemingly contradictory from some perspectives, Tarhe's appeal makes sense if
considered from the context of a people able to incorporate multiple spiritual
perspectives without deeming them incompatible. The impact of the mission,

therefore, may not have been to define Wendat people as Protestants. Rather, it added the Protestant perspective, and the Christian choice, to the Wendat spiritual milieu of the time.

Before weighing the potential spiritual benefits some Wendat people derived from the mission, it is important to consider the extraspiritual dimensions of the Wendat-Presbyterian relationship. From his first visits to the Sandusky country, Badger found that the Wendats wanted far more than spiritual guidance from him. It quickly became clear that the Wendat missionary would have to wear a variety of hats, serving as a scribe, letter reader, doctor, and technical instructor, among other tasks. When considering the broad nonspiritual uses that Wendat people made of the missionary presence, we must look beyond what happened in sermons or religious meetings.

The Wendats made particular use of the mission as a source of labor. Atkins recorded that he labored for a number of individuals during his term as a mission laborer from 1806 to 1807. In 1806 he drew logs for Boldson, later helping him make shingles for his roof. He plowed for Snow, Polly, the Wasp, Big Arms, and a white captive "in habits and dress no way different from the Indians."[59] He later made a door for "Snaygys big daughter a wiandot woman."[60] Badger noted in late 1806 that the mission family had "helped them . . . build several houses."[61] During the 1807 planting season, Atkins plowed for a number of days for Boldson and three other Wendats. He plowed for a day for "Cherokee mans wife," and in the Indian cornfield as well.[62] By February 1807 Badger reported that the mission had plowed a cornfield of 24 to 25 acres for the Indians, as well as about five acres for the mission itself. They had completed a house for the mission family and were at work on a schoolhouse as well.[63]

The laboring relationship between the mission and the community clearly worked both ways. Badger notes, for example, that some "Wyandots came and laid up my house ready to lay on the joists. I gave them dinner."[64] Atkins mentioned that on June 13, 1806, a number of Wendats helped plant the mission fields after planting their own. He also noted that on June 4, 1807, he "labored with a number of the Wiandots at putting up the schoolhouse we got it up the jin [joist] this evening." A few days later "John Bird a negro man from the upper town of Wiandots" assisted in shingling the roof.[65] An ethic of cooperative labor seems to have developed between the mission family and the Wendats living in close proximity to the mission.

In addition to physical labor to help plant and manufacture, the Wendats made use of Badger's medical knowledge and access to medicine. A number of specific instances in the record describe Wendats seeking Badger's medical skills. Sickness was so prevalent in the spring and summer of 1807 that Badger was employed almost daily on healing business. Badger treated Tarhe with wine and sweet water in late May 1807. He administered care to "a girl about fifteen years of age [who] lies very sick with a nervous fever." A man named Barnet, whom we will meet shortly, was also violently ill during the season, as was "a young man very sick" whom Badger watched and nursed for a number of days. By August 1807 Badger wrote that his son "and several Indian children" were sick. The frequency of his caregiver duties led Badger to complain, "I am often hindered most of a day to give them medicine or inform them about some trifling business."[66]

While his medical duties might have been taxing, they were arguably vital to the success of the mission. John Anderson, a fellow missionary who briefly preached at the mission alongside Badger in August 1805, saw Badger's medical skills as a key to his acceptance by the Wendats. He noted: "Mr. Badger has gained the confidence of the Indians by giving them medicines which has, in every instance, cured their disorders."[67] While his success rate undoubtedly was not 100 percent, his healing capabilities became an important avenue of interaction between Wendat people and the mission.

Along with labor and healing, the Wendats also drew on Badger's proficiency in English. Much like Sawatanen, the Wendat schoolteacher from Lorette discussed in the previous chapter, the Sandusky Wendats frequently asked Badger to write to government officials on their behalf. The Wendats used Badger, a well-versed and educated man, as a conduit to convey their thoughts and present their concerns to the American government. For example, Tarhe called on Badger to read papers regarding a land claim by a white adoptee and write a letter on Tarhe's behalf to the governor of Michigan. The same day, the Wendats again used Badger's services as scribe, this time to request of the president, as per the Treaty of Greenville, a blacksmith who could "do all kind of work from the gun to the hoe," as well as a trader "who would not cheat them."[68] The Wendats also later called on Badger to write "in answer to Some proposals made to them by the Quakers to give them and the Delawares a thousand dollars worth of Goods of their own manufacture including building them a Mill which proposals in their answer accepted."[69]

Wendat leaders felt free to call on his services whenever they required them, particularly to read and respond to communications from the US government. Badger was conflicted about these requests. He saw them as both an annoyance and an opportunity to couple his religious message with his duties as scribe and interpreter. In one case, he was called on to read a speech from the governor of Michigan for Tarhe and Walk-in-the-Water, an important Michigan Wendat chief. He used the occasion as an opportunity to discuss the potential of expanding missionary operations into Michigan. In another instance, he took letters that had arrived at Lower Sandusky from Governor Hull and traveled to find the chiefs in their winter encampment near present-day Columbus.[70] With no government officials at Lower Sandusky, other than the factor at the US trading house that opened for a few years there, Badger—like the Jesuit missionaries at Lorette—was the closest thing to an American official in residence, making him a good source of information and a good conduit for communication with American government officials.

The aspect of the mission establishment that both the Wendats and the mission family were most anxious to see come to fruition was the school for Wendat children. Unfortunately, it also was one of the last things the missionaries were able to execute. The mission family suffered from the same bout of illnesses that struck the Wendats in 1806 and 1807, delaying the construction of the schoolhouse significantly. By late 1806 Badger estimated that he would probably open the school in the spring of 1807.[71] Badger planned for the school to accept both boys and girls from all of the tribes near Lower Sandusky. The boys would "cultivate a garden plot to [?] proportion to their number + age." The girls would be taught "knitting, sewing, Spining, and making Cloth."[72]

Despite Badger's optimism, it was well into the summer of 1807 before the schoolhouse was complete. Because of Wendat economic practices, students would not come to the school in earnest until winter at least. The major problem preventing the timely completion of the schoolhouse was a high degree of laborer turnover, which left too few hands to perform the necessary work.[73] When Badger began to prepare for the school to finally open, he again discussed the matter with the tribal council. Tarhe "said if he had a child to go to school he would put it under [the mission's] care: I found several willing to send." Badger desired a national agreement to support the school, but Tarhe told him: "every family must act their pleasure about having their children learn."[74] Therefore, there would be no compulsory attendance, nor even a guarantee of a minimum number of attendees. As such, the school struggled with inconsistent attendance, some of it fostered by "pagan devotees, called prophets," who worked to discourage women from enrolling their children in the school.[75]

Despite the inauspicious beginnings of the educational program, by 1809 the school had grown to fifteen students, with a mission report comparing the children to other children in any school setting: "some are dull; some arise to mediocrity, and some higher." The report noted that the children made significant progress learning English. The children of William Walker Sr., the recently hired interpreter for the mission, made an important difference in the school's success because they "can speak both the English and Wendat language very well." The schoolmaster indicated that the students spent most of their day in academic lessons, with regular prayer mixed in. The only manual labor duties mentioned in the report were after school when "we have our handmill to attend to, to grind corn for our supper."[76]

WENDAT SPIRITUAL ENGAGEMENT WITH THE MISSION: BARNET

While support for the establishment of the mission was far from universal in the first years of the nineteenth century, the spiritual transition of some Wendat people along the Sandusky seems to have begun to take root. According to the missionary record, a man named Barnet became the most important Christian convert on the Sandusky. He is, therefore, a transitional figure in the history of the Sandusky Wendats. Barnet was one of very few males known to have attached themselves spiritually to Presbyterianism. He was also among the first Wendat males to fully embrace the Euro-American version of yeoman agriculture championed by Thomas Jefferson and diligently taught by the missionaries. Additionally, his story circulated throughout the eastern United States in a variety of Christian periodicals and became a significant component of the spread of Presbyterian missionary endeavors in the first decade of the nineteenth century. Barnet's story was sufficiently well known in Christian circles that Harvey Newcomb, a noted children's author, selected Barnet as the subject of a Christian primer in the 1830s, more than twenty years after his death.[77]

As authors such as William McLoughlin have noted, the early Indigenous converts to Christianity were often of Métis ancestry and may have had an extra affinity for facets of Euro-American culture.[78] It is important to keep in mind that this possible affinity had less to do with "race" and more to do with the connections people of mixed ancestry maintained with European relatives and culture. According to William Connelley, a noted ethnographer among the Wendats in the late nineteenth and early twentieth centuries, Barnet's father "was a white man, who had been made prisoner by the Indians almost in infancy. Always residing among them, he knew nothing of his parentage, and was a complete Indian in all his habits of thought, feeling, and action."[79] The Wendats fully integrated the elder Barnet into the community; he married a Wendat woman and their son was born circa 1770. Very little is recorded about the younger Barnet (also called Eunonqu or Flying Arrow) before 1800, other than his first marriage to a Wendat woman, with whom he had his eldest son, John.[80] The couple had divorced by 1800 (apparently at her insistence) and Barnet quickly remarried, this time to a Shawnee woman. The couple lived near Lower Sandusky, the northernmost Wendat town on the Sandusky River, and eventually had three children.[81] Barnet's relationship to the mission unfolds throughout its history. For its duration, he never strayed far from the thoughts of the missionaries and seemingly never severed his connections to Protestantism. Through words and actions, he persistently identified with the missionaries and their spiritual and cultural work.

Barnet appears in nearly every mission report. In September 1803 Barnet hosted missionary George Scott in his own home. During this meeting, he confided privately to Scott that he wished to know more about Christianity and that "he had been for a considerable time under deep convictions," but "he was under great temptations to conceal his sentiments on religion from his father's family and the other Indians, because they laughed at him." Despite his reticence to face the ridicule of his contemporaries, Barnet fervently desired a permanent mission among his people. He even declared, "if ever a council should be called for this purpose, if the chiefs refused, he was determined to speak to them publicly; though this was contrary to their law and custom."[82]

Perhaps the most telling example of Barnet's growing devotion is what happened when no missionaries were in the Sandusky communities. In a letter Barnet dictated to a local trader soon after Scott's departure, he explained that God urged him to speak out for the mission at both Lower and Upper Sandusky. He felt compelled to take the matter to the chiefs at Upper Sandusky, where "some of the chiefs rose and said that it was right." Barnet, along with another pro-mission Wendat, Little Cornstalk, then spoke publicly to the people of Upper Sandusky, where "a number of the people . . . came forward and gave wampum to support the cause." As he did not have the personal authority to endorse the mission, Barnet lamented: "my eyes are steady shed-ing [sic] tears, that I cannot say in my letter come."[83] On a return visit, where Scott delivered a sermon in Barnet's home, he and Scott had a lengthy con-versation. During their discussion, Barnet indicated that his level of distress had lessened since Scott's last visit because he had more fully embraced Christian conceptions of sin and the role of God in his life, particularly the salvation that awaited himself and other sinners who accepted Christ. Barnet was also instrumental in establishing weekly meetings while the missionaries were away, although Barnet was soon supplanted by "one Reed, a chief whose name is Cornstalk, and Old Crane, who is the king of all these small nations."[84] While it is unclear from the source precisely why Barnet ceased leading these meetings, one cannot help but wonder whether the decision "to conduct their societies in the Roman Catholick [sic] form, by confessing their sins, then praying for pardon" was a factor.[85] This transition may have reflected a move away from a more Presbyterian liturgy.

Barnet also seems to have worked to counter Indigenous critiques of the mission. James Hughs noted that Barnet continued to publicly support the mission in spite of a growing sentiment among some Wendats that Christian-ity should be rejected.[86] He also gathered about twenty of his friends at his home to have an extended conversation with Hughs about Christianity.[87] During Tenskwatawa's 1806 witch hunt, Barnet was in great distress about the proceedings, particularly after the Shawnee Prophet had appointed Barnet one of the executioners of the four condemned women, though "he had not consented to be one."[88] Whether this was a test of Barnet's convictions or a potential punishment Tenskwatawa imposed because of Barnet's spiritual preference is unclear, but either seems plausible.

If such actions were not enough to indicate Barnet's commitment to the mission, his choice to commit his son to the cause certainly did. In April 1804 he decided to bring his eldest son, John, to a Presbytery meeting in western Pennsylvania (no small travel feat) and leave him in the care of the mission-aries, where he "expressed an earnest desire that his child might enjoy the benefits of a religious education."[89] When Barnet visited his son a year later, he "was asked if he did not feel troubled to leave his little boy at such a dis-tance amongst strangers. He replied not half so much as he was troubled about his poor tribe of people who were destitute of the light of the Gospel and the precious privilege we enjoyed in this country."[90] He also hoped that John "would yet be a great man, and do much good among the poor Wendats in teaching them to be christians [sic]."[91]

John Barnet remained in Pittsburgh for nearly two years, where he learned to read and write in English, by all accounts very aptly. Eventually, John was compelled to return home in May 1806. His mother came with her husband and three others with a letter from Tarhe, asking that the Presbytery release the boy to her. Barnet had not gotten her consent, or that of the chiefs, before sending him. Tarhe thought that the boy likely had sufficient learning, and if he did not, he could continue at the school being built on the reservation. The Presbytery debated their duty to the father versus the wishes of the chiefs (with no mention of the mother's desire) and gave the boy up. They felt that "the critical situation of the mission, the bad effects a refusal might have on the mind of the chief, and the danger of thereby defeating the flattering prospect of the gospel being preached, and its happy influence felt by the benighted heathen, were considerations seriously affecting."[92]

One might wonder why the chiefs, particularly Tarhe, who seems to have supported the presence of the mission, would take this step. A likely reason was that the power of women, in this case particularly in terms of child-rearing, mattered in the Wendat world. Barnet had taken his son without his mother's input, a serious breach of Wendat custom. For Tarhe and the other leaders on the Sandusky, her rights and desires likely mattered more than the potential damage John's removal could do to the missionary relationship.[93]

The devotion of Barnet emerges most readily, though, during Badger's tenure at the mission. Barnet engaged with the mission in every conceivable way. He helped Badger and his family set up their tents. He hosted religious services in his home and assisted Badger during services. Barnet sought Badger's aid in caring for his sick child and helped the missionary's son cut the timber for the mission house.[94] In addition to his frequent services at the mission, Barnet functioned as a Christian leader in his own right. He renewed his own outreach to other Wendat people, and his influence began to extend beyond his family to "a number of . . . Indians frequently com[ing] to his house at the hours of family worship, to join with him in prayer."[95] Barnet became the bulwark of Wendat support for the mission, even to the point of assuaging missionary doubts. When the mission experienced its most intense criticism by traders and Wendats, Barnet approached Reverend Elisha McCurdy and "urged him to be patient and bear with the unreasonableness of the Indians, and not give up the mission on account of the difficulties attending it."[96]

During the short lifespan of the mission, Barnet became, for lack of a better term, the mission celebrity in the Protestant presses. Most of the letters and mission reports printed in various Christian magazines and newspapers during the period include extended discussions of Barnet and occasionally his family. Readers followed him through his moments of doubt, when he questioned whether he was worthy of salvation. They read about his concerns for his community and his hope that all Wendats would one day be saved. Barnet's piety was a particular locus of discussion. One especially powerful example of Barnet's piety occurred when Badger

> told one of the chiefs, and Barnet, and some others who were present, of the prayers of good people for them; what the society had done; of the cattle and hogs given for the support of the missionaries, &c. Barnet was so affected with the account that he got up and prayed for about fifteen minutes with great fervency; thanking God that he had so disposed the hearts of people to help them; and pleading that he would incline the congress to give them their living here; and that he would dispose the heart of all the Wendat people to send their children to school.[97]

Such sentiments, expressed in print to thousands of devout Christians through a number of periodicals, clearly had an influence on the numerous donations to the mission from across the eastern United States and the Ohio country.

The culmination of Barnet's spiritual journey came in August 1810 when he appeared before the Western Presbyterian Assembly and expressed a general disillusion with his earthly existence. He believed that "he must be saved, by free mercy, through Christ Jesus." Though he "expressed great fears of unfitness, viewing himself unworthy of the name of Christian,"[98] he wanted to be baptized. After long discussion with the assembled ministers, who were greatly impressed by Barnet's meekness and devotion to God, they deemed Barnet fit for baptism and provided him that sacred rite. The following January, he brought his wife and three children to Washington County, Pennsylvania, where his children (Joseph, Elisha, and Sarah) were baptized.[99] He also chose to leave Joseph with the Presbyterians, hoping "that he might hereafter be useful to his nation, in teaching them the good ways of God."[100]

In addition to his firm religious conviction, Barnet had almost completely abandoned hunting in favor of agriculture. He noted that he had "lost his disposition to hunt" and that "he finds his mind most comfortable when he is working in his field."[101] While other males had begun to gradually adopt white agricultural mores, none seem to have devoted themselves so completely to their crops as Barnet. Thus, Barnet had adopted not just the religious beliefs of the mission but also the farming ethic taught by the mission and endorsed by the Jeffersonian government.[102] If there were a "fully converted" Presbyterian Wendat, Barnet was the most outstanding example.

OTHER WENDAT ADVOCATES AND PRACTITIONERS

Despite the paucity of records about individual Wendats' engagement with Protestantism, some fleeting references to other converts emerge in the missionary record. One example was Long House, a man described by George Scott as "one of the chiefs of the Wyandots." Long House spent significant time with Scott, conversing through Northrop and expressing his thanks to Scott for "explain[ing] to them the scriptures, of which they were ignorant." He also indicated that his people "had great need of instruction."[103] While Scott took this communication as a man potentially seeking a new religion, Long House may simply have been kind, or interested in learning more about Christianity from an intellectual rather than religious perspective.

Another local individual who expressed interest in the mission, and eventually became a key supporter, was Elizabeth Whitaker. Whitaker and her late husband, both former captives, had established a general store at Lower Sandusky to provide for the Wendats, other Native people, and some nearby white and black settlers. Whitaker's home "has been a free lodging for all the missionaries who have visited them."[104] She consistently emerged as a willing participant during religious services, sometimes acting as an interpreter. In the process Whitaker seems to have grown more attentive to religion herself, along with her eldest daughter, and she proved an important ally of the missionary cause. Like Barnet, Whitaker also entrusted her son, James, to the Presbyterians.[105]

A further example appears in the 1805 report by James Hughs. According to Hughs, a man called Broken Legs, who had been a leading figure in the Wendat religious society that met between missionary visits, delivered a long exhortation on the importance of the mission. In response to the influence of Handsome Lake, particularly the activities of an unnamed Wendat woman in promoting his religion, Broken Legs called on the people to return to the true way that Hughs's sermon had just described. The alternative was "if we go on this way; God will stop us and take us away if we do not repent."[106] This prompted "a number" to form a circle and sing a hymn they had memorized.

Another individual mentioned specifically in the record was a woman Badger called "a Jew." Her appearance in the historical record increased after Badger treated her for sickness in May 1807. Her condition was so dire that Badger had to "attend on the Jew three or four times a day, and watch with her one night with Samuel our interpreter." After her recovery, she came to the mission to "get her hoe ground, and get some milk." She wept openly during service that day.[107] Other individuals appear in the record, but few are named. Following one meeting, a Wendat man named Taynbonca "addressed the assembly to consider at length in his own language upon the importance of this attending to the Gospel which was offered to them." He later gave Atkins a large cut of deer meat from a recent kill.[108]

More frequently, general references to groups of Wendats pepper the missionary record. Often, missionaries emphasized how attentive audiences were to their sermons. A typical example appears in George Scott's 1803 journal, where he noted after a sermon that "there was a solemn attention given during the discourse, and I thought some appeared feeling."[109] Of course, Scott's reading of his audience could be questionable and is certainly based on his particular perspective from the pulpit. As was often noted about the Wendats and most other Native people of this region, the audience may simply have been courteous in allowing the missionary to deliver his speech.

Attaching spiritual significance to these frequent displays of courtesy is difficult, both for modern observers and the missionaries themselves. Despite these difficulties, numbers of regular attendees during worship may also indicate degrees of interest in, or even adherence to, Presbyterianism. Generally, Wendats attended summer and fall meetings in greater numbers than in the winter or spring due to their residence near the mission in Lower Sandusky. In the winter months—the time of the hunt—few remained in town. Atkins, who was more diligent in his accounting of Wendat attendance than Badger and other missionaries, asserts that on many Sabbaths all who remained in the village in the winter—between five and thirty individuals— attended services. During the summer, attendance tended to be higher, with upward of one hundred in attendance.[110] Other vague outlines of Wendat engagement with Protestantism offer possibilities of spiritual adherence. Reports such as that of a group of Wendat hunters in winter camp on the Scioto engaged in Christian prayer, outside of the gaze of the missionary, are tantalizing but ultimately inconclusive.[111]

CONCLUSION

Despite the clear interest of some Wendats in the mission, and the missionary hope that the mission was beginning to take root, the Presbyterian mission foundered. In 1810 Badger left the Sandusky for good, citing fatigue among other factors. With his exit, the mission continued briefly under a series of short-term missionaries, with some signs of success. An 1811 missionary visit indicated that "the School was still in a promosing [sic] condition, that the farm has been pretty well attended to the last Season."[112] Ultimately, while Badger's exit was a blow, the major problem the mission faced was the onset of the War of 1812. The war disrupted Wendat society and lifestyles for several years, creating a form of civil war that pitted Wendats against each other. The last significant gasp of the Presbyterian missionaries on the Sandusky was a February 1811 petition to Congress, calling on the federal government to grant the request of Moses Byxbe of Delaware, Ohio, to erect a grist mill adjacent to the mission at Lower Sandusky, citing as a rationale the "great difficulty in procuring bread for the support of said mission, from the want of a mill near the missionary station."[113] The apprehension about a war between the United States and Great Britain absorbed so much attention, from Wendats and missionaries alike, that the school fell by the wayside. With the outbreak of war in the region, especially the fall of Detroit in August 1812, the Presbyterian mission dissolved.[114]

What can we make of the Wendat-missionary contact of the early 1800s? Clearly, the Wendats exerted a high degree of control over their engagement with the mission. While they could not dictate which missionaries decided to contact them in the first place, the decision to establish a permanent mission was ultimately made by the Wendats. The level of engagement with the established mission was left to individuals in the community. Some chose to participate in nonspiritual ways capitalizing on the missionaries' connection to American power structures, some chose to engage with Presbyterianism more directly, and still others chose to ignore or even oppose the mission. The mission on the Sandusky was based on voluntary participation, and the missionaries had no power to compel obedience. The continued presence of traditional practices, along with the flirtation of some Wendats with Handsome Lake's and Tenskwatawa's religions, demonstrates the flexibility of early 1800s Indian country in Ohio. The presence of Presbyterianism was one of several alternatives in the Wendat spiritual world, but an important one. While this situation changed after the War of 1812, the first decade of the nineteenth century represents an exploratory period for the Wendats, when multiple spiritual possibilities cohabitated the same ground, and often the same bodies.

But what lasting impact did the first Protestant mission to the Wendats have within the Wendat community? Ferreting out specific numbers of converts, or defining the "authenticity" of practitioners, is not possible. With so few individuals emerging from the record, and such slipshod numerical accounting, it is not possible to clearly identify the depths of Christian attachment among large segments of the Wendat community. It is clear, though, that Wendat people gained sustained exposure to Protestantism, with some developing ties to the mission. Another clear point is that Barnet was firmly attached to Protestant Christianity. When he died, the mission lost its most important convert. Badger noted in his memoir that Barnet "died in the fall of 1812, and from the best information I could get, he supported his christian [sic] character to the last." From Badger's perspective, Barnet was the only truly converted Wendat. Though some "were attentive to religious instruction, and were reformed in their habits," none but Barnet had shown "conclusive evidence of a change of heart."[115]

If the longest-standing missionary only claimed one "true convert," then was the mission a failure? Or were his standards different from those of the Wendats themselves, where elements of the mission program (whether they be material, spiritual, or simply regularly attending services) could plausibly be adopted and adapted without "truly" converting in the eyes of the Presbyterians? When considered in these terms, the mission had more impact on the Wendat people. The fact that Protestantism only grew stronger and more widespread among the Wendats after the war also lends support to the notion that the Presbyterian mission, while not accomplishing the goals of the missionaries, served to establish the early bedrock of Wendat Protestantism, which had a profound influence on large numbers of Wendat people.[116] Indeed, a new tradition had begun to take shape.

NOTES

This chapter is based on my PhD dissertation, "The Ohio Wyandots: Religion and Society on the Sandusky River, 1795–1843," University of California, Riverside, 2016. I would like to thank Rebecca Kugel, Thomas Peace, and Kathryn Magee Labelle, as well as the Wendat, Wyandot, and Wyandotte partners who generously reviewed the draft version of this essay. I would also like to thank the following organizations, all of whom contributed funds used toward the research for this essay: the American Philosophical Society, the Lilly Library at Indiana University, the Newberry Library, the Rupert and Jeanette Costo Endowment, and the University of California, Riverside History Department and Humanities Division.

    1. Clyde Holler, "Black Elk's Relationship to Christianity," *American Indian Quarterly* 8, no. 1 (Winter 1984): 37.

2. Much of the scholarly attention to early nineteenth-century Protestant missions has been on Indigenous peoples of the southeastern United States. Two outstanding examples are William G. McLoughlin, *Cherokees and Missionaries, 1789–1839* (New Haven, Conn.: Yale University Press, 1984), and Clara Sue Kidwell, *Choctaws and Missionaries in Mississippi, 1818–1918* (Norman: University of Oklahoma Press, 1995).

3. A number of studies have analyzed the detrimental effects missionary activities could have on Indigenous communities. One extensive example is George E. Tinker, *Missionary Conquest: The Gospel and Native American Cultural Genocide* (Minneapolis: Fortress Press, 1993).

4. Holler, "Black Elk," 39. Holler argues that Black Elk's conversion to Catholicism was not "capitulation, nor did it imply the substitution of one religion (a failed one) for another (a better one)—rather it meant . . . a kind of theological bi-culturalism." This notion of biculturalism has broad application to Indigenous peoples in a variety of mission contexts.

5. Allan Greer, "Conversion and Identity: Iroquois Christianity in Seventeenth-Century New France," in Kenneth Mills and Anthony Grafton, eds., *Conversion: Old Worlds and New* (Rochester: University of Rochester Press, 2003), 176.

6. A good example of numerous Indigenous scholars grappling with these notions is James Treat, ed., *Native and Christian: Indigenous Voices on Religious Identity in the United States and Canada* (New York: Routledge, 1996). In his discussion of Charles Eastman, for example, Treat asserts that while observers "would judge a native Christian identity as inauthentic or unorthodox," Eastman's personal navigation of seemingly disparate religious, cultural, and racial contradictions "arises from human freedom and personal choice, not from the predicable conflict of deterministic identity politics" (6).

It is also important to note that perceptions of "inauthenticity" potentially pervade all perceptions of Native American histories. As Ned Blackhawk so eloquently argued in his study of the Great Basin, "adaptation" has too often become coded as cultural demise. "When Native peoples adapt to foreign economies or utilize outside technologies, they are assumed to abandon their previous—that is, inferior—ways while in the process of losing parts of themselves; they lose the very things that according to others define them. Once adaptation becomes synonymous with assimilation, change over time—the commonplace definition of history—becomes a death knell. The more things change, the greater the loss." Ned Blackhawk, *Violence over the Land: Indians and Empires in the Early American West* (Cambridge, Mass.: Harvard University Press, 2006), 4.

7. Studies of missions and Christianity among Native Americans have begun exploring these complex legacies in recent years. For a few outstanding examples, see Linford Fisher, *The Indian Great Awakening: Religion and the Shaping of Native Cultures in Early America* (New York: Oxford University Press, 2012); Rachel Wheeler, *To Live upon Hope: Mohicans and Missionaries in the Eighteenth-Century Northeast* (Ithaca, N.Y.: Cornell University Press, 2008); David J. Silverman, *Faith and Boundaries: Colonists, Christianity, and Community among the Wampanoag*

Indians of Martha's Vineyard, 1600–1871 (New York: Cambridge University Press, 2007); Sergei Kan, *Memory Eternal: Tlingit Culture and Russian Orthodox Christianity through Two Centuries* (Seattle: University of Washington Press, 1999).

8. For example, missionary John Anderson noted that there was an American settlement "round by the head of Scioto . . . within thirty five Miles of upper Sandusky." John Anderson to Rebecca Anderson, August 24, 1808, Anderson Family Papers, Kansas State Historical Society (hereafter Anderson Papers), roll 1. For a general discussion of American expansion into Ohio, see R. Douglas Hurt, *The Ohio Frontier: Crucible of the Old Northwest, 1720–1830* (Bloomington: Indiana University Press, 1996).

9. This ties very closely to the American government's conception of the Indigenous role in society, though the civilization program and Jeffersonian policy targeted assimilation as the ultimate goal of federal Indian policy. For Jefferson's policies toward Native Americans, see especially Bernard Sheehan, *Seeds of Extinction: Jeffersonian Philanthropy and the American Indian* (New York: W. W. Norton, 1973); Anthony F. C. Wallace, *Jefferson and the Indians: The Tragic Fate of the First Americans* (Cambridge, Mass.: Harvard University Press, 1999); Robert M. Owens, *Mr. Jefferson's Hammer: William Henry Harrison and the Origins of American Indian Policy* (Norman: University of Oklahoma Press, 2011).

10. The conceptualization of the Great Lakes region as a "middle ground" comes from Richard White, *The Middle Ground: Indians, Empires, and Republics in the Great Lakes Region, 1650–1815* (New York: Cambridge University Press, 1991).

11. For overviews of Protestant missions to Native Americans in the American Early National period, see Robert F. Berkhofer, *Salvation and the Savage: An Analysis of Protestant Missions and American Indian Response, 1787–1862* (New York: Athenaeum, 1976 [1965]); Henry Warner Bowden, *American Indians and Christian Missions: Studies in Cultural Conflict* (Chicago: University of Chicago Press, 1981); C. L. Higham, *Noble, Wretched, and Redeemable: Protestant Missionaries to the Indians in Canada and the United States, 1820–1900* (Albuquerque: University of New Mexico Press, 2000). For an excellent study of the changes taking place in American Protestantism in this era, see Nathan O. Hatch, *The Democratization of American Christianity* (New Haven, Conn.: Yale University Press, 1989).

12. For a more detailed discussion of the Quaker-Wendat connection in this period, see Michael Leonard Cox, "The Ohio Wyandots: Religion and Society on the Sandusky River, 1795–1843" (PhD diss., University of California, Riverside, 2016), chap. 1. There were two non-Quaker Protestant missionary societies active in Ohio in the early 1800s. One was the Western Missionary Society (under the jurisdiction of the Synod of Pittsburgh), the other the Connecticut Missionary Society, a Congregationalist group. The Western Missionary Society ultimately spent more time and energy on missions to Native Americans, particularly after perceived early success with the Wendats. Most of the missionaries appear to have been linked to the Presbytery of Pittsburgh, a Western Missionary Society sponsor.

13. Badger was a Congregationalist by training and was employed by the Connecticut Missionary Society. However, due to the cooperation between mission

groups at this time, and Badger's subsequent decision to work for the Western Missionary Society, his early work is included here.

14. Joseph Badger, *A Memoir of Reverend Joseph Badger* (Hudson, Ohio: Sawyer, Ingersoll, 1851), 31.

15. "Extracts from the Rev. Thomas Hughs' Journals: Of His Tours to Detroit, and among the Indians," *Western Missionary Magazine,* April 1803, 95.

16. George Blue Jacket was the son of the noted Shawnee chief Blue Jacket. He had spent the previous year living with Hughs and working as a translator. Blue Jacket spoke Shawnee, Delaware, and English. For more information on George Blue Jacket and his family, see John Sugden, *Blue Jacket: Warrior of the Shawnees* (Lincoln: University of Nebraska Press, 2000).

17. One is tempted to speculate that "sickness" may have been a convenient excuse to avoid the meeting, though there is not concrete evidence to that effect.

18. "Extracts from the Rev. Thomas Hughs' Journals," 97. Italics are original.

19. For a detailed discussion of this period, see Cox, "Ohio Wyandots."

20. Badger proved to be the most important Presbyterian missionary to serve among the Sandusky Wendats. Badger, as mentioned previously, had preached before to the Wendats but had turned to other duties for several years, mostly in northeastern Ohio among recently arrived white settlers. Although a Congregationalist, he agreed to accept a two-month missionary tour under the auspices of the Western Missionary Society. Badger left the most important single published source of information about the mission in the form of his 1851 memoirs, which also include his journal. Badger was also a frequent correspondent to both the Western Missionary Society and to missionary magazines, as well as an infrequent correspondent with state and federal government officials.

21. Joseph Badger to Thomas Worthington, December 13, 1806, Thomas Worthington Papers, Ohio Historical Society (hereafter Worthington Papers), roll 4.

22. Joseph Badger to William Hull, July 30, 1805, in *Michigan Pioneer and Historical Collections* (hereafter *MPHC*) (Lansing: Michigan Pioneer and Historical Society, 1876–1929), vol. 40: 63. John Anderson, a fellow missionary, heard a similar account: "They have quit drinking spirits [&] liquors intirely at the Sandusky Towns, & resolved to call a minister. The Chiefs informed Mr. Badger that in years past the[y] were afraid to have a minister lest the people would use them ill when they got drunk. This difficulty being now removed they appear much in earnest about getting a minister & a schoolmaster." John Anderson to Rebecca Anderson, August 17, 1805, Anderson Papers, roll 1. The Western Missionary Society was highly enthusiastic to begin the mission but worried that financial difficulties could be problematic. See Edward George, ed., "Transcription of the Original Records of the Western Missionary Society" (bachelor's thesis, Western Theological Seminary, 1936), 5.

23. For his part, Governor Hull was quite pleased with the developments at Sandusky, telling Badger and the Wendats, "I rejoice that My Children at Sandusky have consented to receive a Minister of the Gospel to point out to them the way of eternal happiness and a school Master to teach & instruct their Children." William Hull to Joseph Badger, August 7, 1805, in *MPHC*, 40:66n.

24. Badger, *Memoir,* 146. The land in question was the subject of much intercourse between the missionaries and government officials, particularly as questions arose over ownership/building rights on the land. See Joseph Badger to William Hull, August 20, 1805, in *MPHC,* 40:67–68; Joseph Badger to Thomas Worthington, December 13, 1806, Worthington Papers, roll 4; *Records of the Synod of Pittsburgh, from Its First Organization, September 29, 1802, to October, 1832, Inclusive* (Pittsburgh: Luke Loomis, 1852), 30–35.

25. The term "mission family" refers to the missionary and all of those attached to the mission (laborers, schoolteachers, etc.).

26. There is a rich body of scholarly literature on the seventeenth-century Wendats, with a great deal of attention paid to Wendat-Catholic history and interactions. For some outstanding examples, see Bruce G. Trigger, *The Children of Aataentsic: A History of the Huron People to 1660* (Kingston: McGill–Queen's University Press, 1987 [1976]); Elisabeth Tooker, *An Ethnography of the Huron Indians, 1615–1649* (Syracuse, N.Y.: Syracuse University Press, 1991); Georges E. Sioui, *Huron-Wendat: The Heritage of the Circle,* trans. Jane Brierley (East Lansing: Michigan State University Press, 1999 [1994]); Erik R. Seeman, *The Huron-Wendat Feast of the Dead: Indian-European Encounters in Early North America* (Baltimore: Johns Hopkins University Press, 2011); Kathryn Magee Labelle, *Dispersed but Not Destroyed: A History of the Seventeenth-Century Wendat People* (Vancouver: University of British Columbia Press, 2013).

27. "Extracts from the Rev. Thomas Hughs' Journals," 93, 95.

28. Secretary of War to William Hull, July 12, 1806, National Archives and Records Administration (NARA), Records of the Secretary of War, Letter Sent, Indian Affairs (hereafter RoSW, LS, IA), M15, roll 2, vol. B; Secretary of War to William Hull, August 18, 1806, *MPHC,* 10: 66.

29. Elizabeth Whitaker to Solomon Sibley, September 4, 1807, Lower Sandusky File, Rutherford B. Hayes Presidential Library, Fremont, Ohio (hereafter LSF). The trader later recanted his accusation, stating that he had been "induced to implicate the character of the said Elizabeth only from the advice of my friends and with a view of defending myself against alligations [*sic*], made by the said Joseph Badger against me." "Hugh Pattinson's Statement," February 19, 1808, LSF.

30. Badger, *Memoir,* 166–67.

31. "Religious Intelligence," in *A New Series of the Evangelical Intelligencer; for 1809* (Philadelphia: William P. Farrand, 1809), 380. The same account was also published in "Extracts from the Report of the Board of Trustees of the Western Missionary Society to the Committee of Missions," *The Panoplist, and Missionary Magazine,* September 1809, 2, 4.

32. George, "Transcription," 11–12.

33. "Religious Intelligence," 381. For discussion of the cattle and other donations, see "Missionary Intelligence," in *The General Assembly's Missionary Magazine; or Evangelical Intelligencer: for 1807* (Philadelphia: William P. Farrand, 1807), vol. 3: 257; Badger, *Memoir,* 114–45; George, "Transcription," 6; *Records of the Synod of Pittsburgh,* 29, 38.

34. "Religious Intelligence," 382.

35. The only notable move the Presbyterians made to bridge the language barrier was a November 1808 proposal "to look out for a suitable young man to go and live with Barnet in order to learn the Wendat language and to assist him in farming." No results are mentioned. George, "Transcription," 13.

36. For example, John Anderson plainly declared: "I find it difficult to speak thro an interpreter." John Anderson to Rebecca Anderson, August 17, 1805, in Anderson Papers, roll 1.

37. All three of these individuals were former white captives.

38. "The Trustees of the Western Missionary Society Report, to the Standing Committee of Missions," *Evangelical Intelligencer,* May 1808, 2, 5. William Walker Sr. was a former captive who lived near Brownstown. He and his wife Catherine Walker, of mixed Wendat-European ancestry, as well as their children, became prominent figures in the missionary legacy of the Wendats.

39. Ibid. For more on the later activities of the Walker family, especially William Walker Jr., who became an important community leader in the nineteenth century, see James Joseph Buss, *Winning the West with Words: Language and Conquest in the Lower Great Lakes* (Norman: University of Oklahoma Press, 2011), 73–96; John P. Bowes, *Exiles and Pioneers: Eastern Indians in the Trans-Mississippi West* (New York: Cambridge University Press, 2007): 152–218. Cox, "Ohio Wyandots," includes a detailed examination of Isaac Walker, another son of William Walker Sr.

40. "The Trustees of the Western Missionary Society Report," 2, 5.

41. The most comprehensive examination of Handsome Lake's religion continues to be Anthony F. C. Wallace, *The Death and Rebirth of the Seneca* (New York: Vintage, 1972 [1969]). For a detailed, Haudenosaunee-centered analysis of the Code of Handsome Lake, see Barbara Alice Mann, *Iroquoian Women: The Gantowisas* (New York: Peter Lang, 2000), particularly chaps. 5–6.

42. See Wallace, *Death and Rebirth of the Seneca*, 239–337.

43. "A Journal of a Mission to Sandusky, Brownstown, and Their Vicinities, under the Direction of the Board of Trust of the Western Missionary Society, by George Scott, A.M. and Mr. John Bruce, Student; performed anno Domini 1804," *Western Missionary Magazine,* October 1804, 226.

44. John Anderson to Rebecca Anderson, August 17, 1805, Anderson Papers, roll 1.

45. "Religious Intelligence," 382–83.

46. For Tenskwatawa's life and movement, see R. David Edmunds, *The Shawnee Prophet* (Lincoln: University of Nebraska Press, 1983). For an outstanding regional overview of Indigenous nativism in this era, see Gregory Evans Dowd, *A Spirited Resistance: The North American Indian Struggle for Unity, 1745–1815* (Baltimore: Johns Hopkins University Press, 1992).

47. For an account of Tenskwatawa's spiritual journey, see Edmunds, *Shawnee Prophet,* 28–41.

48. It is important to note that it was not simply "young men" in attendance. Badger wrote, "all the chiefs from the upper town were at the village [Lower Sandusky], attending to the Shawanee prophet." Badger, *Memoir,* 145.

49. Ibid., 114, 145. Also see Alfred A. Cave, "The Failure of the Shawnee Prophet's Witch-Hunt," *Ethnohistory* 42, no. 3 (Summer 1995): 461.

50. Badger, *Memoir*, 147–48.

51. For discussion of the Wendat witch hunt and its motivations, see Cave, "Failure"; Edmunds, *Shawnee Prophet*, 46–47. In addition to Tenskwatawa, some Wendats also traveled to the Delaware along the White River in Indiana to solicit the services of a female witch finder in September 1805. See Lawrence Henry Gipson, ed., "The Moravian Indian Mission on White River, Diaries and Letters, May 5, 1799, to November 12, 1806," *Indiana Historical Society Collections* (Indianapolis: Indiana Historical Bureau, 1938), vol. 23: 382–83.

52. Badger, *Memoir*, 160.

53. "Wyandot Missions in 1806-7—Diary of Quintus F. Atkins," *Western Reserve and Northern Ohio Historical Society Tract No. 50*, (1879?), 111.

54. James Hughs, "Extract of a Letter from the Rev. James Hughes [*sic*], to the Chairman of the Committee of Missions," *General Assembly's Missionary Magazine, or Evangelical Intelligencer for 1805* (Philadelphia: William P. Farrand, 1806), 401. In some cases, references to the Warrior are specifically tied to Handsome Lake's religion, while in others they are more generally associated with traditional spirituality.

55. Ibid. The interpreter and two others who understood the Wendat language told Hughs that it was "the most sensible speech they had ever heard delivered by an Indian." Ibid., 402. There is no compelling evidence from the available information that Tarhe ever became an adherent to Protestantism, though he often took the opportunity to lend his support to their words. One challenge to this assertion comes from the recollections of Jacob B. Varnum, who worked at the U.S. trading house at Lower Sandusky. In his recollections, he stated that Tarhe was not only the best and most outstanding chief he has ever known; "what is still better, he was a professed christian [*sic*]." This seems very unlikely, as there is no mention of Tarhe's conversion in the missionary records. Doubtless, the missionaries would have expended reams of correspondence and publications trumpeting the conversion of such a venerable leader. See "Jacob B. Varnum's Recollections," LSF, 3.

56. Admittedly this is speculative and can certainly be read in other ways.

57. Hughs, "Extract of a Letter" (1805/6), 404.

58. Ibid.

59. "Wyandot Missions in 1806-7," 112.

60. Quintus F. Atkins, "A Continuation of Quintus F. Atkins Diary while on a Mission with the Rev. Mr. Joseph Badger to the Wiandot Tribe of Indians Inhabiting the Sandusky River," entry from February 12, 1807, unpublished, unpaginated Photostat, Lower Sandusky File, RBHPL.

61. Joseph Badger to Thomas Worthington, December 13, 1806, Worthington Papers, roll 4.

62. Atkins, "Diary," entries for May 26–30, 1807.

63. "An Extract of a Letter from the Rev. James Hughes," *General Assembly's Missionary Magazine*, February 1807, 3.

64. Badger, *Memoir*, 148.

65. Atkins, "Diary," entries for May–June 1807.

66. Badger, *Memoir*, 159–61, 163, 151.

67. John Anderson to Rebecca Anderson, August 17, 1805, Anderson Papers, roll 1. It should be noted that missionaries were not the sole source of healing, as the missionaries took note of instances of Indigenous healing practices. An excellent example is an account of the healing practices employed for a man named Long Legs. See "Wyandot Missions in 1806–7," 111.

68. Badger, *Memoir*, 105.

69. Joseph Badger to William Hull, July 30, 1805, *MPHC*, 40:63. Ultimately, little came of this proposal for the Wendats.

70. Badger, *Memoir*, 156.

71. Joseph Badger to Thomas Worthington, December 13, 1806, Worthington Papers, roll 4.

72. Badger also wrote to John Johnston, the Indian agent at Piqua, Ohio, reporting on the progress of constructing the school and appealing to Johnston to raise awareness and support for the enterprise. Johnston was so impressed that he wrote to Governor Hull, suggesting that the government might provide a few hundred dollars to support the mission. Hull would not commit to funding the mission, though he thought if the school bore fruit funds might be made available. He also sent several farming tools to support the mission. See Joseph Badger to John Johnston, December 21, 1806, and John Johnston to Secretary of War, February 7, 1807, Letters Received, Secretary of War, Main Series, M221, roll 9, NARA; Secretary of War to John Johnston, 11 February 1807, RoSW, LS, IA, M15, roll 2, vol. B, NARA; Badger, *Memoir*, 152.

73. George, "Transcription," 9–10.

74. Badger, *Memoir*, 163.

75. The missionaries acknowledged that children in Wendat society were "at the mother's disposal, [and] her superstition can prevent the father from sending them to school." See "Trustees of the Western Missionary Society Report," 2, 5. See also Badger, *Memoir*, 157–65. Though the records about the early mission school are scant, it does seem that some students responded well to the experience. One early Ohio traveler noted that "Mr. Badger was among us not long ago, and he gives a flattering account of the aptness of the Indian children, and their willingness and desire for learning, and states that they do not want for capacity." Reuben Gold Thwaites, ed., *Early Western Travels, 1748–1846* (Cleveland: Arthur H. Clark, 1904), vol. 4: 90n45.

76. "Religious Intelligence," 379–80.

77. Harvey [Hervey] Newcomb, *The Wyandot Chief; or the History of Barnet, a Converted Indian; and His Two Sons; with Some Account of the Wea Mission* (Boston: Massachusetts Sabbath School Society, 1835).

78. William G. McLoughlin, *Cherokees and Missionaries, 1789–1839* (New Haven, Conn.: Yale University Press, 1984); McLoughlin, *Cherokee Renascence in the New Republic* (Princeton, N.J.: Princeton University Press, 1992). Many other scholars have noted the same trend, particularly in the Southeast and Upper Midwest.

79. William Elsey Connelly, ed., *The Provisional Government of Nebraska Territory and the Journals of William Walker, Provisional Governor of Nebraska Territory* (Lincoln, Neb.: State Journal Company, 1899), 225n.

80. Information about John Barnet(t) and his mother can be found in "Missionary Intelligence," *General Assembly's Missionary Magazine,* June 1807, 3, 6.

81. Connelly, *Journals of William Walker,* 225n; "Extract from the Report of the Standing Committee of Missions, to the General Assembly," *The Christian's Magazine,* June 1, 1811.

82. It is important to note that the willingness of Barnet to play host to missionary meetings was a major public acknowledgment of his relationship to the missionaries and to Christianity. For Scott's tour, see "A Journal of a Tour on a Mission to the Indians on Sandusky River. Performed by the Rev. George Scott in the Year of our Lord 1803," *Western Missionary Magazine,* October 1803, 339–44, quotations on 340–41.

83. "Extract of a Letter from a Member of the Synod of Pittsburg, to a Minister of the Gospel, in Philadelphia: Dated August 8th, 1804," *General Assembly's Missionary Magazine,* January 1805, 4–6.

84. "Journal of a Mission to Sandusky," 227.

85. Such a conclusion seems logical in light of Scott's account of his spiritual discussions with Barnet. Scott "found he was effectually weaned from the Roman Catholick [*sic*] scheme, and under doubts concerning the prophet." Ibid.

86. Barnet informed Hughes that on Easter 1805, many of the Wendats held a feast rather than worship Jesus. Some had chosen to cast their rosary beads into the fire and give up praying. When asked if in such times of doubt he questioned his own faith, Barnet expressed an unshakable commitment to Christianity. He was also willing to undergo a Christian marriage if his wife was willing and might also become baptized. Hughs, "Extract of a Letter," 403.

87. Ibid., 404.

88. Badger, *Memoir,* 145.

89. "To the Editors of the Western Missionary Magazine," *Western Missionary Magazine,* June 1804, 76.

90. "Religious Intelligence," *General Assembly's Missionary Magazine,* January 1805, 21.

91. "Missionary Intelligence," *General Assembly's Missionary Magazine,* June 1807, 3, 6.

92. Ibid.

93. For the power and influence of Haudenosaunee women in all aspects of Indigenous life, see Mann, *Iroquoian Women.*

94. Badger, *Memoir,* 146–52.

95. "Trustees of the Western Missionary Society Report," 2, 5.

96. "Religious Intelligence," *New Series of the Evangelical Intelligencer,* 384.

97. "Missionary Proceedings in the Western Country," *General Assembly's Missionary Magazine, or Evangelical Intelligencer: For 1807* (Philadelphia: William P. Farrand, 1807), 262.

98. "Extract from the Report of the Standing Committee of Missions."

99. Barnet's wife appears to have been somewhat disinterested in Christianity.

100. Ibid. An excellent short summary of Barnet's story is contained in "A Letter from Rev. Joseph Badger to Rev. Dr. Holmes, Dated Austinburg, Ap. 20, 1810," *The Panoplist, and Missionary Magazine,* October 1810, 3, 5.

101. "Extract from the Report of the Standing Committee of Missions."

102. For the best discussion of Jefferson's policies, see Wallace, *Jefferson and the Indians.*

103. "A Journal of a Tour," 343.

104. Hughs, "Extract of a Letter" (1805/6), 404.

105. "Journal of a Mission to Sandusky," 233. Along with James Whitaker, the son of James Spicer, a Seneca adoptee that lived near the Wendats, also went. The Missionary Society even bore the cost of young Whitaker's education. "That in consideration of the important services rendered by Mrs. Whitaker to the missionary business, the Treasurer be directed to pay the Rev. George Scott sixty dollars and five cents, out of the Missionary fund, the sum due to him for the boarding, &c. of Mrs. Whitaker's son." *Records of the Synod of Pittsburgh,* 40.

106. Hughs, "Extract of a Letter" (1805/6), 403–4.

107. Badger, *Memoir,* 159–61.

108. Atkins, "Diary," entries from January 11 and February 19, 1807.

109. "A Journal of a Tour," 341.

110. Atkins, "Diary," entries for March–April 1807. See also Badger, *Memoir,* 97–98.

111. "Trustees of the Western Missionary Society report," 2, 5.

112. George, "Transcription," 14–15.

113. "Memorial of Western Missionary Society to Buy Public Land on Sandusky River," February 4, 1811, in *New American State Papers on Indian Affairs* (Wilmington, Del.: Scholarly Resources Inc., 1973), vol. 2: 563. Judge Byxbe already provided the mission with flour from his home in Delaware. See George, "Transcription," 14–15.

114. In October 1812 the Presbyterians did appoint a two-man committee "to visit the Wyandot Indians near Urbana (the location of their wartime evacuation) to inquire into their situation, and the prospect of rendering further Missionary service to them." Ibid., 16. A few brief visitations also occurred in 1818–19. Ibid., 37–44.

115. Badger, *Memoir,* 114–15.

116. See Cox, "Ohio Wyandots," for a detailed explication of later Wendat-Protestant history. In recent years the history of the nineteenth-century Wendats has begun to receive more scholarly attention, especially in relation to the Indian removal movement in the 1820s to 1840s. For example, see Buss, *Winning the West with Words,* 73–96; Bowes, *Exiles and Pioneers,* 152–218; Shannon Bontrager, "'From a Nation of Drunkards, We Have Become a Sober People': The Wyandot Experience in the Ohio Valley during the Early Republic," *Journal of the Early Republic* 32 (Winter 2012): 603–32; and *Northwest Ohio Quarterly* 75, no. 2 (2004), which includes

Christine Raber, "An Introduction," 107–21; Paul A. Westrick, "The Race to Assimilate: The Wyandot Indians in White Ohio," 123–48; Christopher S. Stowe, "'One Could not but Feel Melancholy': Ohio Remembers the Wyandot," 149–59; and Kevin Kern, "'It Is by Industry or Extinction That the Problem of Their Destiny Must Be Solved': The Wyandots and Removal to Kansas," 161–68.

CHAPTER 5

Economic Activity and Class Formation in Wendake, 1800–1950

Brian Gettler

During the nineteenth and twentieth centuries, visitors to Jeune-Lorette often remarked on the perceived lack of Indigeneity among the village's inhabitants. Visitors frequently pointed out that the residents' physical attributes and material life were largely indistinguishable from those of their non-Indigenous neighbors.[1] For example, in 1871 the author of a Canadian travelogue claimed that, in addition to there having

> been a considerable intermixture of white blood at Lorette . . . , all traces of the old savage life have disappeared. The people live in neat, well-made frame-houses, each with its garden or piece of cultivated land. Many of them are well-to-do farmers; others make a comfortable living by the manufacture of snow-shoes, canoes, basket-work, and Indian curiosities. The people all speak French. We attended divine service in the chapel; here the prayer was intoned in the old Huron language, but not a soul in the congregation, I was assured, understood a word.[2]

The author of these words was clearly disappointed at having failed to find an exotic population at Lorette. Although such expectations of cultural difference owed much to widespread stereotypes, they were also sustained by a conscious effort on the part of some village residents. Indeed, by this time some community members presented themselves as being wholly distinct from their non-Wendat neighbors in order to reinforce their political claims and to promote the sale of goods produced in the village.[3] Despite the "traditional" light in which Lorette's entrepreneurs cast the moccasins, snowshoes, and "curios" they sold to non-Indigenous consumers, this industry, like the society from which it grew, underwent extensive changes during the nineteenth and twentieth centuries that paralleled the general development of industry throughout North America. While this chapter will not question the "authenticity" of Wendat-manufactured goods, it will demonstrate how this industry's marketing strategy remained consciously rooted in appeals to tradition and difference, how this manufacturing sector developed, and how its development fundamentally altered the social structure of the reserve. It will also consider the rise of manufacturing in relation to other, older economic activities such as hunting and farming and the ways in which a relatively small group of Wendats leveraged large-scale snowshoe and moccasin production to ensure the education of their children, several of whom ultimately exercised liberal professions.

Lorette's economy was not defined by production alone, however.[4] In recent years, scholars have increasingly come to consider consumption as an important economic motor and an activity that reveals a great deal about social and cultural norms and political movements.[5] Such general observations hold true in the context of nineteenth- and twentieth-century Lorette, where consumption generated significant revenue while also providing an important site of political struggle and socioeconomic differentiation. While briefly referring to the political content of Wendat consumption, this chapter demonstrates the importance of industrial development within the village to consumers of all socioeconomic profiles.[6] Indeed, it will make the case that such activity needs to be considered alongside production in order to understand the development of the Wendats' nineteenth- and twentieth-century economy.

Drawing on preliminary results of a much larger study of the credit market in and around the village, this chapter makes a related argument by demonstrating the interconnectedness of finance, production, and consumption. Those families that owed their wealth to the manufacture and sale of moccasins and snowshoes and to the retail sector consolidated their earnings from these activities through financial markets as they lent to both Wendat and Canadien neighbors alike. The wealth amassed by the village's socioeconomic elite during the period owed as much to investment strategies as it did to manufacturing. These investment strategies, which allowed wealthy families to make significant profits by loaning money, were based in Quebec's

distinct notary-centered legal and financial system. While this system favored the socioeconomic elite from the early nineteenth century, its most
dramatic reformulation of social relations did not begin until the Indian Act
had restructured property on reserves across Canada. From the end of the
nineteenth century, Wendat moneyed elites gained significant leverage over
other community members thanks to the credit market. Lorette, then, experienced social and economic pressures similar to societies the world over, as
industrial capitalism played a central role in reshaping the community.

Governmental reports, travelogues, notarial documents (e.g., loan contracts and land sales), newspapers, analyses made by contemporary social
scientists, and the writings of several Wendat community members shed light
on patterns of production, consumption, and finance. Given the heterogeneous nature of these sources, this chapter paints a qualitative rather than
quantitative portrait of economic activity in Lorette. Whenever possible,
however, figures compiled from the documentary record are reported to provide descriptive depth and to better situate Lorette in the context of the
North American economy.

Similarly, though this chapter, through its focus on economic activities,
analyzes the formation of several distinct social classes, elites either generated
or played a central role in creating the vast majority of available sources.
Nonetheless, this study applies to the entire village since many of these activities involved less fortunate community members. Furthermore, although
class is central to the analysis that follows, the concept should not be understood in rigid terms since the chapter describes the process by which social
relations developed.[7] This process underscores both the particularities of the
local context and the resemblance of Lorette to other contemporaneous societies. In this sense, the chapter counteracts the historiography's tendency to
claim First Nations historical experience as absolutely unique, a tendency that
leads historians to reduce Indigenous peoples to "others" while tacitly accepting the irrelevance that larger scholarly currents often afford them.[8] Indeed, by
and large, Wendat economic history paralleled that of European societies and
those that resulted from European colonization of North America.

PRODUCTION

During the nineteenth and twentieth centuries, the large-scale manufacture
of "traditional" wares provided Lorette with its most visible economic activity, an activity that continues to be of great importance to the village today.

However, the Wendats also involved themselves in other productive economic ventures such as hunting, trapping, and agriculture. The development of these various productive activities from the late eighteenth century through the middle of the twentieth century demonstrates that as time passed this aspect of Lorette's economic life came to be dominated by the manufacture of moccasins and snowshoes. As this industry developed, so too did the social relations underpinning it. At the same time that the Quebec economy underwent industrialization and the increasing concentration of capital in the hands of a relatively small number of individuals and families, the Wendats experienced similar changes as fewer community members drew their livelihood from more or less independent economic activities such as hunting and farming and transitioned to wage work.

The Slow Decline of Hunting and Agriculture

As we saw in chapter 1, from their origins in Wendake Ehen, the Wendats practiced agriculture, hunting, fishing, and gathering for both subsistence and trade. While these activities remained critical well into the nineteenth century, both the context and the manner in which they were practiced had changed substantially by the second half of the eighteenth century. In chapter 3, for example, Thomas Peace demonstrated that as the village came to resemble neighboring non-Indigenous settlements, the Wendats incorporated market activity, alongside the traditional economic activities such as hunting and farming, to a greater extent than they had in the past.[9] Even if their economic importance during this period is unclear, both hunting and farming provided critical evidence for the community's early nineteenth-century claims to the seigneury of Sillery.[10] The accuracy of these descriptions, however, seems to have sometimes been consciously distorted in order to strengthen the Wendat case. This is particularly true in the context of claims that community members could no longer hunt due to encroachment, even if population pressures did necessarily change hunting practices. Through the petitions and testimony given to the House of Assembly of Lower Canada, begun by Sawatanen, the village chiefs asserted that confirming their ownership of Sillery would allow them to ensure the community's subsistence since their hunting and fishing economy was then disappearing as a result of non-Indigenous encroachment. In an 1819 petition to Lower Canada's Parliament, the Wendats claimed that as a result of their loss of title to Sillery, they had been "reduced to utter poverty." The petition's signatories further asserted that "in a country of which their ancestors once were masters, they have lost all the right even of hunting, and dare no longer enter the forest, where they are daily expelled with violence by the Proprietors, who consider them as malefactors, and treat them accordingly."[11] When he appeared before the committee five years later, Nicolas Vincent Tsawenhohi renewed the claim that hunting had become problematic: "Even the Canadian Peasantry take upon themselves to hunt and fish, and they destroy every thing; they spread Snares for wild Pigeons, and are ready to kill us when we pass over the end of their Lands in the Forest. They justify themselves by saying, they have Grants of those Lands, and that on their own Grounds they are Masters. Since these Canadiens have Lands to cultivate, let them cultivate them, and leave to us our rights of hunting and fishing."[12] In an 1829 petition to the secretary of state for the colonies, the chiefs echoed Tsawenhohi's words.[13]

It is quite possible that such claims were somewhat exaggerated. When the chiefs appeared before the House of Assembly in February 1819, for example, one of their number, Gabriel Vincent Wawondrohnin, was absent. He was, at that moment, "out hunting."[14] As discussed in chapter 3, censuses rarely took into account these absences, which were frequent and continued to be the norm at least into the 1830s, causing the chiefs to schedule their meetings outside of hunting season.[15] This practice most likely continued much longer as nearly every male band member participated in at least one of the two seasonal hunts (autumn or spring) well into the second half of the century.[16]

Despite this massive participation early in the nineteenth century, the number of Wendats who earned the majority of their income from hunting or trapping had decreased substantially by the century's end. Between 1871 and 1891 the percentage of men who declared hunting to be their primary occupation fell from 37.5 percent to 14 percent, largely as a result of slumping fur prices.[17] Although the fur market, following a series of hard years, rebounded beginning in 1889 and remained strong through the mid-1890s, hunting and trapping had definitively lost their hold on the Wendat economy.[18] Indeed, even during these years of relative abundance and high prices, the Indian agent associated with the village—which had officially become a reserve in the 1850s—reported that community members were "unable by these occupations to provide the necessaries of life for their families."[19]

In addition to the increasing importance of other activities, the creation of the provincial Parc des Laurentides along with the establishment of numerous fish and game clubs with exclusive hunting and fishing rights in the region seem to have been partly responsible for this change. In 1896 the Indian agent reported to his superiors in Ottawa that "nearly all the lakes where they were accustomed to fish freely have been put under license by the provincial government. The establishment of the National Park has deprived them of the liberty of hunting as they please, and if one should attempt to break the law he would render himself liable to be severely punished and to lose his ammunition and hunting outfit."[20] By 1900 several Wendats had appeared in court for their hunting and trapping activities in the Parc des Laurentides and the lands reserved for fish and game clubs. Although the courts initially declined to impose the fines and imprisonment within its power, they did so only on the condition that the Wendats would "not return."[21] Some Wendats continued to hunt there, however, even when the courts reversed their stance on charging fines.[22]

Most often, the Wendats combined their own personal and relatively small-scale hunting and trapping operations with paid employment guiding tourists on hunting and fishing excursions in the region north of Quebec City.[23] In this way, they combined several activities of diverse origins and influences, Indigenous and non-Indigenous alike, extending the "moditional economy" discussed in chapter 3.[24] By the late 1880s the Indian agent claimed that community members who served as guides obtained a higher standard of living than those who continued to support themselves primarily by hunting.[25] In his 1896 report Bastien wrote that a majority of Wendat men found employment as guides, making good wages in the process. "At certain seasons of the year, especially during winter, it is nothing unusual to see three-quarters of our men accompanying gentlemen. They then earn on average $1.25 a day, clear of all expenses."[26] This sector of the economy continued to supply work to a limited number of band members through the mid-1930s, when Wendat guides secured $3 a day both while working at the fish and game clubs and when independently guiding hunting and fishing parties.[27] These men generally left the village for the clubs in the spring or early summer, where they erected camps that housed them through the fall. At that point they returned to Lorette and, at least during the difficult years of the early 1930s, a grim labor market.[28]

Like hunting, agriculture slowly lost its ability to generate appreciable revenue; by the turn of the twentieth century it had ceased to be economically important altogether. In the case of farming, the chiefs again somewhat exaggerated the information they provided Lower Canada's legislators with respect to their claims to the seigneury of Sillery. When appearing before a committee of the House of Assembly in 1824, Grand Chief Nicolas Vincent Tsawenhohi asserted that as a result of insufficient land, only some community members could farm: "Such of the Indians as have Lands, plant Indian Corn, Sow Potatoes, and a little Corn, but the number is very small. The others live on the produce of Hunting and Fishing, because they have no Lands." Tsawenhohi further claimed that most young families on the reserve could not farm because they did not have money with which to acquire land.[29] Six years later, still in the context of claims to Sillery, Wendake's chiefs asserted that the community "understood neither the theory nor the practice" of agriculture, contradicting both Tsawenhohi's remarks and those made by outside observers since the conquest. The chiefs told the House of Assembly that if the community possessed cleared land in the vicinity of the village, "our Children at least might be brought up with some knowledge of agriculture."[30]

Although such claims to complete ignorance with respect to agriculture were clearly inaccurate, comments asserting farming's marginal status are corroborated by other sources. As early as 1836, an Indian Affairs official reported that while some Wendats gained a portion of their revenue from farming, "none of them derive the whole of their Support from Agriculture."[31] As discussed in chapter 3, this seems to be linked to both Lorette's small surface area and its relatively poor soil.[32] Despite these explanations for the diminishing importance of agriculture in the village, farming remained of secondary importance even on the band's far larger, more fertile, and only sparsely populated Quarante Arpents reserve. Through the middle of the nineteenth century, agriculture proved less important on this second reserve than another economically marginal activity: the harvesting of timber.[33] In many ways, it appears that Indian Affairs' approach to Indigenous agriculture—its preferred method of "civilizing" First Nations—actually impeded its development on Quarante Arpents.[34] Although the department occasionally made grants to the Wendats for the purchase of seed and farming implements, the Indian Act adopted in 1876 theoretically prevented community members from mortgaging the lands they occupied in the hopes of improving them.[35] During the late nineteenth century the Indian agent often complained to his superiors about precisely this difficulty. In 1895 he wrote: "On the Quarante Arpents Reserve there are only about a hundred acres under cultivation this year, and these were worked by six Huron families. These families are in a difficult position. Although the land is suitable for cultivation, these farmers, not being able to make the improvements required for careful and profitable cultivation, not being able either to borrow or mortgage, get very little return from their land and are obliged to turn to expedients and work at day labour to support their families."[36]

Indian Affairs later used these arguments to justify the surrender and sale of Quarante Arpents and Rocmont, a reserve situated at some distance from Lorette. Although several members of the Sioui family lived on the Quarante Arpents at the time, Wendat leaders, engaged in ongoing disagreements with this family, asserted that "neither [piece of land was] occupied nor worked by them."[37] In August 1904 the federal government sold these lands at auction,[38] placing the proceeds in the trust fund that Indian Affairs maintained for the Wendats. This sale put an end to even the rudimentary form of agriculture that some community members had practiced over the preceding century. Although agriculture had disappeared, gardening remained relatively widespread.[39] This would remain the case through mid-century, when an undergraduate sociology thesis reported that of the seventy-six Wendats and seventy-five individuals of non-Indigenous descent who worked on the reserve, none were employed in agriculture.[40]

The Socioeconomic Consequences of Changes in Traditional Manufacturing

As hunting and farming provided the community with decreasing revenue, Lorette's market-oriented manufacturing sector grew ever more important. Like hunting and farming, this sector propelled traditional Wendat practice and savoir faire into the capitalist economy. However, as with these other activities, the marketplace contributed to changing the way in which manufacturing (particularly of moccasins and snowshoes) took place. It also profoundly altered village society, as a handful of families who had already been active in manufacturing came to control this activity and others transitioned from relatively independent production or piecework to wage labor. This shift in economic activity, and the changes that the ever more important manufacturing sector underwent, help explain the village's wider socioeconomic development during the nineteenth and the first half of the twentieth centuries. Looking first at economic developments in the village and then at their social effects, this section argues that market-oriented manufacturing caused a process of class formation that paralleled similar trends throughout much of North America and Europe.

Long before their arrival on the north shore of the Saint Lawrence, the Wendats manufactured utilitarian goods for their own use and for trade with neighboring nations.[41] As we saw in chapter 3, some community members had begun producing goods for sale to the French military by the 1740s. Following the conquest of New France, however, this practice underwent significant change as external demand led to its increasing integration with the growing market economy at Quebec. According to a history written in the 1880s, from the late eighteenth century the Wendats at Lorette manufactured and sold large quantities of "snowshoes, cariboo mocassins and mittens for the English regiments tenanting the citadel of Quebec." Wendat success in this sector drew on both community members' traditional manufacturing knowledge and their experience in hunting, a combination that appealed to the regiment's "wealthy officers [who] every winter scoured the Laurentine range, north of the city, in quest of deer and cariboo, under the experienced guidance of Gros Louis, Siouï, Vincent, and other famous Huron Nimrods."[42] While Nicolas Vincent Tsawenhohi informed Lower Canada's political authorities that the Wendats manufactured a vast array of utilitarian and decorative goods, including "Mocassins, Snow Shoes, Sashes, Baskets, Indian Sleighs, Fur Caps, and Mittens, Collars of Porcupine Quills, Purses, Reticules, Bows, Arrows, Paddles, small Canoes and little Figures of Indians," he claimed that they only "occasionally" sold such items, and then only "at half the price for which they were formerly sold."[43] This testimony too should be read with skepticism. Indeed, just as in the case of hunting and agriculture, Tsawenhohi made these assertions of economic hardship in the mid-1820s in an apparent effort to bolster Wendat land claims. Whatever the case, by 1836 the commissary general reported to the governor general of British North America that the Wendats' "chief Employment consists in the Manufacture of Mocassins, Snow Shoes, &c. for the Quebec Market, and in hunting and fishing."[44]

As described in chapter 3, during early stages of large-scale commercialization this sector appears to have been organized along household lines, each family producing and selling goods individually. However, by the 1840s, if not before, Marguerite Vincent La8inonkié and her husband Paul Picard Honda8onhont, along with their nephew Philippe Vincent Téonouathasta and son François-Xavier "Paul" Picard Tahourenché, had begun the first large-scale manufacturing business in the community based on a putting-out system whereby Wendats produced goods in their homes.[45] During the 1840s the Picards conducted a profitable business with the British military and civilians alike.[46] Among their customers, the Picards counted members of the colony's ruling elite, including Lord and Lady Elgin (as discussed in chapter 6); the governor's brother and military secretary, Robert Bruce; and the British army's commander of Canada's eastern district, General Charles Stephen Gore.[47] This patronage was made possible by Lorette's proximity to Quebec, the Picards' high social standing, and their ability to receive these individuals in a style fitting their rank.[48] During the 1850s the Picards promoted and sold their goods profitably at industrial exhibitions in Quebec and Montreal and at the Exposition Universelle in Paris.[49] A mid-century visitor to Lorette claimed that Philippe Vincent and Paul Picard lived "in comfort,—nay, in luxury."[50] By the early 1870s, the period during which Philippe Vincent's son (also named Philippe) assumed responsibility for operations, the family proved able to ship 1,700 pairs of moccasins to a single customer.[51] While such sales did not involve astronomical sums of money (in this case, each pair of women's moccasins sold for ten cents, and men's moccasins cost the buyer thirteen cents per pair), the volume of this transaction and the acknowledgment that this particular commercial relationship was ongoing suggest that the size of this exchange was not unusual.[52]

Following the lead of the Picards and Vincents, the Bastien family also successfully managed to gain control of the manufacture of moccasins, snowshoes, and other "traditional" Amerindian goods. The firm that, by the 1920s, would be known as Bastien Brothers began operations in Lorette under Maurice Bastien in 1876.[53] At this early date, Bastien manufactured snowshoes alone. According to sociologist Léon Gérin, Bastien's son, Maurice Bastien Ahgnionlen "the second," had taken over the prospering business by the time of Gérin's visit to the Wendat village in the 1890s. In addition to snowshoes, the Bastiens manufactured moccasins and tanned hides.[54] Although the family's business would later develop to sell its products through international wholesalers, during the 1880s Caroline Bastien, Maurice Bastien Ahgnionlen's daughter, traveled to the United States herself to sell the company's wares.[55] The expansion of the Bastien family manufacturing business is perhaps best demonstrated by the massive increase in its estimated net capitalization between 1880 and 1930. From 1882, when the firm's capitalization lay between $500 and $1,000, it jumped to $5,000 to $10,000 in 1900 and, finally, to $10,000 to $20,000 in 1930.[56] It is important to note that this increase took place at the same time that the Bastiens shifted their production decisively toward moccasins, making snowshoes a relatively minor sideline.

By the mid-1880s François Groslouis Sassenio joined the Picard (now headed by Philippe Vincent) and Bastien families in the manufacture of moccasins and snowshoes.[57] During these years, the Wendats' missionary claimed that "the trade in moccasins and snow shoes has made great advances, and has contributed to the prosperity of the village."[58] However, by the end of the decade, Canadien competition in "Indian industries" had begun to adversely affect manufacturing in Wendake.[59] By the middle of the 1890s the Indian agent, who was also Maurice Bastien Jr.'s brother, reported that the industry's continued struggles, the result of a 50 percent drop in prices caused by a "depression in trade" and intense competition, forced some families to try a venture in the United States. "Fortunately, however, the demands of Ontario and the west raised the state of affairs; the village was threatened with a regular emigration. This disaster was prevented through the efforts of some courageous men, notably Maurice Bastien, Jr., who, to the detriment of his own business, with the sole object of assisting his compatriots, continued to give work to families in the village and to prevent their leaving the country."[60]

The Indian agent considered the prospects of a lasting revival in the industry grim. He felt that "half of it has now passed into the hands of speculators, who trade on the margin of abatement on these articles which, however, do not lose any of their quality or actual value."[61] During this period the most serious threat to the Wendat industry appears to have come from Canadian tanneries that, along with Bastien, dominated the supply of raw materials for moccasin and snowshoe production. By the turn of the century, Cloutier, a Canadien who had married a widow from the Sioui family, and Henry Ross, a merchant of Scottish origin who had recently acquired Philippe Vincent's business, constituted the Wendats' primary competition in tanning as well as snowshoe and moccasin manufacturing. However, Bastien owned by far the largest such operation in Lorette.[62]

At the very end of the 1890s the industry experienced a dramatic change of fortunes as a result of the demand for snowshoes and moccasins brought about by the Klondike gold rush. In 1898 the Indian agent at Lorette claimed that "there are manufactured in the Huron village no less than seven thousand pairs of snowshoes, and at least twelve thousand dozen pairs of moccasins, representing a general business of from $70,000 to $75,000."[63] Léon Gérin agreed, estimating that the Wendat industry used 10,000 to 15,000 hides each year in the production of approximately 140,000 pairs of moccasins and 7,000 pairs of snowshoes.[64] In comparison, one of the largest shoe manufacturers in the province, Ames-Holden of Montreal, produced two million pairs of shoes annually in 1921.[65] Thus, the roughly 150,000 pairs of moccasins that the agent claimed Lorette produced during the Klondike boom years would mean that the Wendats manufactured quantities of footwear that, although falling short of those produced by the province's largest firms during the late nineteenth century, were far from negligible. By this point, Bastien produced the largest quantity of snowshoes and moccasins (more than half of the total value, according to the Indian agent) while Philippe Vincent's company (the former Picard operation, purchased by Henry Ross following Vincent's December 1897 death) also manufactured a large amount.

While Wendat entrepreneurs apparently made large profits from their products, their employees earned significantly less income. Even if by the mid-nineteenth century manufacturing provided roughly forty-five families with their primary economic activity,[66] a frequent visitor to Lorette claimed that Wendat tanners employed by a local Canadien received "a very low rate of remuneration."[67] During the 1890s the women who produced moccasins for any one of the companies in Lorette earned between $0.25 and $0.30 for every dozen pairs they completed. Thus, according to Gérin, they were able to make between $0.30 and $0.50 per day when working entirely by hand or twice as much when employing a sewing machine. As a result of this difference in income, many Wendat women had invested in this technology by the turn of the twentieth century.[68] However, while the Klondike boom in moccasin and snowshoe production provided jobs and ensured the continued existence of "the mother industry of our village of Lorette," the Indian agent wrote that this upturn increased neither the workers' wages nor the owners' profits to any meaningful extent.[69] Despite this situation, wage workers in Lorette appear to have earned more than many of their Canadien neighbors. The wages earned by the companies' employees proved significant enough to entice neighboring Canadiens to join the Wendats in producing moccasins, although only two had acquired the skills needed to manufacture snowshoes. By the turn of the twentieth century, Gérin felt that a new factory system had supplanted the older putting-out model in the production of Wendat "artisanal" goods, in the process significantly altering the village's work environment.[70] In other words, a new, class-based hierarchy had replaced the older, less formal system of production.

In addition to moccasins and snowshoes but on a markedly smaller scale and with less economic impact, the Wendats also manufactured "fancy wares" for sale in the village, to wholesalers in urban areas, and to tourists in the northeastern United States and at the "watering holes" along the lower Saint Lawrence (e.g., Malbaie, Cacouna, and Rivière du Loup).[71] Although its recovery lagged behind that of Lorette's production and sale of moccasins and

snowshoes, the souvenir art industry also rebounded by the end of the nineteenth century. In the same year that the more industrial production reaped
the rewards of the Klondike, the Indian agent wrote that souvenir art manufacturing "was not so remunerative, and the opinion at the end of the season
was that it will be still less so this year. The squaws, who work in ash wood
and sweet hay, not having had time during the winter to prepare as large a
supply as usual, went to the watering places without much stock in hand."
While hard economic times negatively affected this industry, it also suffered
as a result of the US decision to revoke the immunity Indigenous peoples living
in Canada had from paying customs fees, in the process imposing a "ruinous
duty on these articles."[72] In spite of these obstacles, the Wendat labor that
had been eliminated by the massive post-Yukon decrease in snowshoe and
moccasin production contributed to the following year's threefold increase
in revenue from the sale of "fancy wares." According to the Indian agent, this
happy coincidence, along with the newly introduced production of canvas
canoes, saved Wendake's economy from what would have otherwise been a
devastating loss of revenue. "Had it not been for the introduction into the village of a new work, the making of canvas canoes, many families would have
found themselves in discouraging want."[73] Regardless, throughout the period
this industry supplied markedly less income than the production of moccasins
and snowshoes.

While manufacturing of "traditional" goods provided the majority of Lorette's residents with income during the nineteenth century, not all community members benefited from this development to the same extent. In this
way, the industry contributed to significant socioeconomic stratification, as the
revenue generated by manufacturing provided the members of the Bastien
and Picard/Vincent families with the means of securing their social status
through access to prestigious forms of education and white-collar jobs while
less privileged families proved, at least initially, unable to keep pace. For
example, Prosper Vincent Sawatanen, one of Philippe Vincent Téonouathasta's sons, became a Catholic priest in 1870 and had become a vicar by the turn
of the twentieth century.[74] Similarly, in 1876 the provincial Department of
Colonization and Mines hired Paul Picard, the son of François-Xavier Picard
Tahourenché, as a draftsman and surveyor, a position he held through at
least 1888.[75] Prior to beginning this work, Picard had clerked in the office of a
notary from 1865 and had himself undertaken the profession five years later.[76]
Both of Picard's sons achieved similar education and status. Pierre Albert
Picard Tsichiek8an, who served as both grand chief and Indian agent during

the period, occupied a position working for the cadastre service of Quebec's Ministry of Colonization, Mines, and Fisheries from 1921 to 1942.[77] His brother, Louis Philippe Ormond Picard Arôsen, pursued both a prestigious military career and white-collar work. After having served in the Canadian militia beginning in 1897 and doing a short tour of duty in South Africa immediately following the end of the Boer War, Picard, an "Explorer & Draughtsman," reenlisted in the military in September 1914 as a lieutenant, a rank he had initially achieved in 1898. During his wartime service in France with the Twelfth Battalion he was promoted to captain,[78] making him one of only a handful of commissioned Indigenous officers serving in the Canadian Expeditionary Force.[79]

While members of the Vincent and Picard families excelled in education and social standing, the Bastien family set the standard of Wendat upward social mobility from the end of the nineteenth century. Ludger Bastien, elected as the Conservative member of the Legislative Assembly for Quebec County from 1924 to 1927, provides perhaps the most striking example. Other members of the Bastien family similarly experienced dramatic, if less public, advancement. Whereas Joseph Bastien, Ludger's brother, held the high-level position of manager of the fur department at Holt and Renfrew, a department store in Quebec, another brother, Ernest, along with Ludger himself, ran several of the family's successful businesses.[80]

The family's socioeconomic position stemmed from the dominant position it occupied in Lorette's manufacturing industry from the late nineteenth through the middle of the twentieth centuries as well as from its judicious use of profits from manufacturing and of funds originating elsewhere. The single most important injection of capital into the Bastien activities came from a landmark 1923 court decision. This case originated in 1909, after Ludger and his brother Ernest Bastien erected a hydropowered tannery operated by their company, Bastien Brothers, along the Saint Charles River in Lorette. Since 1895 Lac Saint Charles, a short distance upriver from the reserve, was an important source for Quebec's drinking water. At that time, however, the city failed to make any compensation to the landowners whose access to water would be affected. In 1914, following Quebec's installation of a larger pipe that drew significantly more water, Ludger and Ernest Bastien sued the city of Quebec over the tannery's inability to function at full capacity due to diminished water flow at certain times of the year. In 1923 the privy council awarded them $175,000 in damages in addition to free water in perpetuity for the washing and soaking of hides.[81] This massive payment provided the company with needed capital reserves while also providing a tidy personal profit to the Bastiens. They invested this money in a series of commercial ventures, including at least four companies controlled by the family (Alexandre Bastien Limited, Bastien Silver Fox Breeders, Bastien Brothers, and Bastien, Gagnon et Cloutier).[82]

While these families dominated Lorette's elite through the mid-twentieth century, a small number of Wendats from other families held white-collar jobs from the 1930s. Paul Launière, for example, worked for the provincial government, while the Metropolitan Life Insurance Company in Quebec employed one of two Gros Louis sisters.[83] Lorette also produced a handful of professionals during the period, with Léon Gros Louis crowning Wendat professional progress by becoming Lorette's first medical doctor in 1952 following his graduation from Université Laval.[84] Despite this handful of cases, the Picards, Vincents, and Bastiens dominated skilled, white-collar, and commercial employment throughout the period, underlining the major changes to society in Lorette. During the twentieth century manufacturing in Lorette reflected economic conditions well beyond the village's limits even as it continued to provide jobs to a large number of Wendats and wealth to a much smaller part of the community. After floundering during the new century's first decade, the industry had returned to relative health by the eve of the First World War,[85] when an unnamed visitor to Lorette observed that Maurice Bastien "conducts a large factory for the manufacture of snowshoes, which are marketed throughout North America. He has two sons living in the village, one of whom conducts a large moccasin factory and the other a large and up-to-date tannery, where thousands of skins of East Indian elk and Canadian moose were seen in the various stages of tanning. These three plants employ practically the entire population of the village, men, women and children, who work by the piece and who apparently earn a good living, as most of them have comfortable frame houses."[86]

Despite this prosperity, non-Indigenous competitors continued to encroach on Lorette's signature industry. Bastien told the visitor that "others, learning the art from the Indians, have started similar factories." He went on to state that "the competition had forced prices down so that it was barely possible now for the Indians to make a living and that the profits of his factory were growing constantly smaller."[87] After the war, the village's manufacturing sector continued its growth. According to a journalist writing in 1920, Wendat footwear sold well throughout Canada and in parts of the United

States, noting that in Lorette "one hears of half a million pairs [of moccasins] spoken of with equanimity."[88] Another visitor to the village, the anthropologist C. Marius Barbeau, likewise noted manufacturing's success following the end of the war. "In the matter of local industries, Lorette is ahead of most Canadian villages; and the demand for the manufactured goods (moccasins, snowshoes, gloves, toys and curios, leather, baskets, etc) is heavier than the supply."[89]

Such prosperity came to a brutal end with the onset of the Great Depression. While the Bastiens continued to make tidy profits during the 1930s as a result of the effective monopoly their store exercised in the distribution of in-kind welfare on the reserve,[90] the workers the family employed in its manufacturing operations failed to share in this prosperity. Indeed, during the Depression, Bastien Brothers significantly reduced its workforce, leading to dramatic increases in state relief and to the federal government's recognition that Lorette held no job prospects.[91] According to a reserve resident, "a girl working periodically in a slippers factory" in Lorette in the mid-1930s could expect to earn "just a few dollars a week" while "remaining without work at frequent intervals."[92] By the 1930s, then, class lines had clearly been drawn, as wealthy families such as the Bastiens solidified their standing while less fortunate community members were unable to keep pace, a phenomenon that was only exacerbated by the Great Depression.

While the Depression caused great harm to moccasin manufacturing, by the middle of the 1940s the industry had rebounded substantially, even if by this time it employed a much smaller portion of the reserve's population than it had earlier in the century. Gaston Blanchet observed in 1945 that snowshoe making had disappeared and that the only industry that remained, the manufacturing of shoes and slippers, employed no more than a handful of community members.[93] Despite the industry's relatively small Indigenous workforce, Maurice E. Bastien took advantage of his role as Indian agent to keep business running by enlisting the help of Indian Affairs' Handicraft Section in procuring scarce materials (imported Italian and Czechoslovakian beads) during the Second World War.[94] According to Ottawa, this strategy worked as "the Indians engaged in handicraft work were able to sell their wares, which are in great demand, at high prices."[95] Bastien Brothers, still owned by members of the Bastien family, continued to be the primary manufacturer of moccasins, shoes, slippers, and other "souvenir articles for tourists" through mid-century.[96]

CONSUMPTION

Although productive activity profoundly influenced socioeconomic change in Lorette, it was not alone in doing so. Consumption, a sector of the economy in which every community member was necessarily active, also played a role in shaping the village's development. Despite the relative paucity of sources concerning consumption, when combined with the previous section's discussion of production, it is clear that these two economic activities were related. The retail sector, and consumption more generally, created and reinforced the emerging social divisions in the community.

As we have seen in earlier chapters, trade had deep roots in Wendat society. While still in Wendake Ehen, the Wendats traded corn, fishing nets, and wampum beads, among other items, to the neighboring Algonquins for fish and skins that they consumed. Following the arrival of the French, they traded with the newcomers for European manufactured goods such as glass beads, knives, blankets, and kettles alongside other imported goods such as tobacco.[97] After their move to the Saint Lawrence Valley, trade grew and supplied the Wendats with an ever-increasing portion of their tools and household and perishable goods. By the late eighteenth century, as their material culture came to resemble that of their Canadien neighbors, residents of Lorette purchased whatever goods they consumed yet did not produce at Quebec's market or from traveling merchants who regularly visited the village.[98]

Although the size and form of the on-reserve retail sector remains unclear, by the mid-nineteenth century the "large and flourishing [French] Village" of Lorette (today Loretteville) directly across the Saint Charles River from the Wendat village hosted "considerable paper, flour, lumber, and general business," including forty-one individual merchants specializing in the sale of food and other consumer goods for a total population of 2,200.[99] This included a general store established "close by the Huron village, though on the *habitant* side of the stream." According to a Canadian who often visited the reserve, this store sold "the gay printed cottons indispensable to the *belle sauvagesse* . . . , as well as the blue blankets and the white, of so much account in the wardrobe of the women as well as of the men." The store also stocked "assorted beads and silks and worsteds used in the embroidery of moccasons [*sic*], epaulettes" along with cognac, decorative lithographs, and "anything that could possibly be required by the most exacting *sauvage* or *sauvagesse*, from a strap of sleigh-bells to a red-framed looking-glass."[100] It is clear, then, that by mid-century residents of the Wendat village had access, if they could afford it, to a wide variety of consumer goods.

Several Wendats worked as merchants in and around the reserve throughout the period. Unfortunately, little is known about the specifics of many of these individuals' retail trade.[101] Initially, at least, merchants did not restrict themselves to retail alone, earning revenue elsewhere to complement their income from trade. Charles Picard, for example, combined his merchant business with other economic activities, occasionally earning income by maintaining roads in the neighborhood of the reserve.[102] Despite this initial competition, retail, like manufacturing, slowly came to be dominated by a single family—the Bastiens.

By the turn of the twentieth century, Antoine Oscar Bastien, Lorette's Indian agent and a member of the community, owned and operated a grocery store on the reserve that distributed state-funded, in-kind relief and extended consumer credit to a large number of reserve residents. This second practice led several community members to fall heavily into debt, particularly in years when the village's manufacturing sector experienced difficulties.[103] Although Indian Affairs eventually forced the closure of the store, citing the Indian Act's ban on trade between Indians and Indian agents, Antoine Bastien's nephew, Maurice E. Bastien, named Indian agent in 1931, also operated an on-reserve store. Run with his brother, the former Conservative member of Quebec's Legislative Assembly Ludger Bastien, the store allowed its wealthy owners to establish a virtual monopoly over state-issued relief vouchers because during the difficult years of the Great Depression, manufacturing work supplied the only hope of gainful employment to much of the reserve population.[104] Even if this situation condemned the two stores respectively run by Gustave Gros Louis and Paul Sioui to the margins of the village's economy during the 1930s, by the 1940s several Wendat merchants not belonging to the Bastien family, including Georges Picard, were active in the village.[105]

At the same time that the Bastiens' hold on retail in the village slipped, a new feeling of economic nationalism developed in Lorette. In 1946 the presence of Canadian competitors operating within the village led the band council to adopt a resolution barring all traveling salesmen from the reserve with the exception of those from Loretteville.[106] This move appears to have been at least partially inspired by the Wendat political activist and "grocer-barber" Jules Sioui, who, in addition to working to organize Indigenous peoples across Canada, also refused to serve French Canadians in his business for a time.[107] Although the resonance that Sioui's short-lived policy had in the community is unknown, it clearly demonstrates the political importance that some Wendats attached to consumption as a means of promoting the community's economic well-being.[108]

In addition to consumption's role in promoting a shared sense of community, it also served to mark divisions within the village. While less fortunate community members fell into debt attempting to provision their households, some of Lorette's better-heeled residents spent impressively on luxury items. According to a visitor, in the mid-1850s Paul Picard "paid two hundred and seventy-five dollars for a piano for his daughter." The same visitor reported, "Whenever I visited Philippe [Vincent], that stately man of the Hurons would usher me into a little parlor with a sofa in it and a carpet on the floor; he would produce brandy in a cut decanter, and cake upon a good porcelain plate, and would be merry in French and expansive on the subject of trade."[109]

Such ostentatious displays of wealth also took the form of collections of cultural and historical relics. By the 1880s, for example, Paul Picard owned several such objects including a manuscript French-Huron dictionary, a silver medal minted in 1840 bearing the image of Queen Victoria, another silver medal bearing the image of George III, three other medals respectively stamped "Dublin (1565 ou 1865)[,] New York, 1853, [and] Prince Albert 1851," and two wampum belts.[110] Along with the more common trappings of economic success, by the eve of the First World War Maurice Bastien had also collected several Wendat heirlooms. According to a visitor to the village, "Chief Bastien owns a large home, and he has a most interesting collection of wampum belts and relics from the early days. He was especially fond of several coins that had been handed to a Huron delegation by the king of England in 1825, on the occasion of an official visit to the mother country. He also had a priceless ancient war headdress and some bracelets and silverware collected by his ancestors."[111] Given the family's financial clout and that no Bastiens were among the chiefs who visited England in 1825, it seems probable that, in the same way that the Bastiens accumulated real estate on the reserve, Maurice Bastien purchased these relics from other, less fortunate community members who needed to raise funds.

FINANCE

The vast majority of nineteenth-century Quebec, including the area around Lorette, offered limited opportunities for investment. Banks and other

financial institutions such as *caisses populaires* or credit unions had yet to
open any branches in rural areas, whereas in cities these businesses focused
largely on corporate clients.[112] As a result, individuals seeking to invest often
contracted private loans through notaries, in the process earning interest on
capital that may have otherwise remained unproductive.[113] Since stock markets were only just emerging during the late nineteenth century, land and
mortgages provided many with their primary source of large-scale credit
while also constituting one of the most important means of investing throughout Canada.[114] Building on their late eighteenth-century activity in the off-
reserve real estate market described in chapter 3, the Wendats participated
actively in the land-based financial market, both as lenders and borrowers.
The activities of wealthy families in this real estate–based credit market
played a major role in the rise and continued prosperity of the same families
that experienced great success in productive economic activities and consumption.

Beginning in the mid-nineteenth century, two families, the Picards and
the Vincents, set the pattern for Wendat participation in the local credit market. The Bastiens would continue this pattern, although in somewhat altered
form, through the middle of the twentieth century. Philippe Vincent Téonu-
athasta and his wife (and later widow) Henriette Romain, along with François-
Xavier Picard Tahourenché, played the most important roles in establishing
financial practice in Lorette. While they lent to community members and
non-Wendats alike, one example of a long-standing credit relationship with
a non-Indigenous neighbor will suffice to demonstrate the operation and the
profitability of this early financial market. In December 1859 the mayor of the
municipality of Saint Ambroise, Joseph Savard, borrowed £100 Hfx ($400)
from Philippe Vincent. Savard agreed to repay the debt within four years at
6 percent annual interest.[115] Vincent appears to have made this loan only after
Savard had repaid two earlier loans totaling £50. In 1848 and again in 1850
Savard borrowed £50 from Vincent, both times at 6 percent annual interest.[116]
While Savard had proved unable to reimburse these earlier loans within the
time officially allotted him, the 6 percent annual interest that he paid over a
decade appears to have proved sufficient incentive to Vincent to reinvest
funds with him. Indeed, since it took until 1859 for Savard to repay the capital he had borrowed in 1848 and 1850 along with interest, Vincent made a
profit of £63 or 126 percent of the funds initially invested.[117] Furthermore, although the phenomenon has not yet been studied in the context of Quebec,
practice elsewhere suggests that notaries had a vested interest in contracting

safe loans because lenders might blame the notary who had introduced the parties to contract in the case of unpaid debt.[118] Alongside other cases, this evidence suggests that borrowers likely reimbursed loans more often than not.[119] Together, the impressive gains that lenders stood to make combined with the apparent probability that loans would be repaid helps explain the economic success of Lorette's wealthy families.

By the end of the century, both the market and the loans contracted in Lorette had changed significantly. From this point, loans most frequently involved community members alone while taking a strikingly different form. Rather than being agreements that stipulated the amount of capital and interest owed along with the date at which reimbursement was due and naming collateral that might be seized through legal proceedings in the event of default, loans made by wealthy Wendats to other community members began taking the form of sales guaranteeing the right of redemption (*ventes à faculté de réméré*). This contractual form allowed the vendor to repurchase the item sold within a particular period of time. The specifics of these agreements might differ, but as time passed they became increasingly codified, notably with respect to the requirement that the seller pay both capital and interest by a particular date in order to repurchase their property. This type of agreement was essentially equivalent to any other loan except that if the borrower failed to reimburse his or her debt, the lender was not required to turn to the legal system in order to seize property for payment since he or she was already the legal owner of what would have otherwise been collateral. The widespread use of this form of contract in Lorette apparently dates to the 1880s, when wealthy Wendat families used it to secure loans to less fortunate community members. Although loans between these two segments of the population predated this decade, these earlier agreements offered greater protection to those Wendats who failed to reimburse borrowed funds.[120] By the end of the nineteenth century, then, credit favored the wealthy even more than it had decades earlier.

More than any other family, the Bastiens made purchases with the right of redemption. Initially, the family explicitly tied this type of loan into its manufacturing business. In 1884 Hermine Bastien and her son, Wilfrid Picard, sold to Maurice Bastien Jr. by *faculté de réméré* a house and lot in Wendake for $38.50. According to the contract of sale, they could repurchase their home by furnishing $1.50's worth of work per week manufacturing moccasins and snowshoes to Bastien over a six-month period. During this period, Bastien agreed not to charge them rent as they continued to occupy the house. This agreement, then, required that the sellers effectively pay $46.50 to repurchase their home—that is, the capital plus $8 in interest (an amount equaling nearly 42 percent annual interest).[121] Although the outcome of this particular agreement is unknown, this example illustrates the manner in which the Bastiens made use of the right of redemption in order to consolidate their socioeconomic position within the community.

The Wendats appear to have adopted the right of redemption as a means of bypassing legislation that restricted the use of on-reserve property in order to secure credit. From 1876 to 1930, the Indian Act declared, "No person shall take any security or otherwise obtain any lien or charge, whether by mortgage, judgment or otherwise, upon real or personal property of any Indian or non-treaty Indian within Canada, except on real or personal property subject to taxation." As this clause applied to all "persons," it formally excluded Indigenous people from making use of lien in contracts among themselves.[122] Although the degree to which the federal government actually enforced the Indian Act is not always clear,[123] Indian Affairs actively discouraged "conditional" sales that featured reimbursement over an extended period of time, making clear its preference for one-time payments.[124] In 1930 Parliament altered the wording of the section to permit band members to make use of lien in agreements between themselves.[125]

Although it is difficult to establish a causal relationship between the Indian Act and the adoption of this contractual form, the changes brought about by legislation had clearly altered Lorette's real estate market by the 1910s.[126] Following visits to the reserve in 1911–12, 1914, and 1919, anthropologist C. Marius Barbeau reported, "According to many statements, real property on the reserve is reduced to about one third, or less, of its normal value, if compared with property situated in the immediate vicinity. As, on the reserve, the owner may sell only to another member of the band, and as there is very little demand for more property, the price of purchase is very low." Barbeau insisted, however, that depressed prices did not prevent on-reserve real estate sales due largely to local practices with respect to ownership and exchange. "The holder of a lot or a house on the reserve justifiably considers himself its absolute owner according to European notions, save that he cannot alienate it to an outsider. Nevertheless he has the right to sell it to another person within the band. Such inside transfers of property often take place."[127]

However, such transfers did not take place irrespective of economic status. Indeed, as Barbeau noted, "The well-to-do Bastien (Maurice) family have in that manner purchased and resold several lots formerly belonging to others."[128] Although Ludger Bastien explained to Barbeau that his family was obligated to provide credit to other community members since banks in the area refused to do so, both he and the anthropologist failed to point out the structural importance of these sales to the on-reserve credit market.[129] Indeed, rather than simply purchasing and selling real estate, the Bastiens, using the right of redemption, accumulated low-priced property in exchange for credit—property they then sold at a profit.

Although little specific evidence for this practice has been found in the years in which Barbeau visited the village, it is abundantly documented by the Bastiens' affairs of the late 1920s and 1930s. In 1928, for example, Moïse Gros Louis mortgaged his home to Ludger Bastien for $550 by way of a contract including the right of redemption. This agreement required Gros Louis to repurchase the house over five years by repaying the full $550 in installments of no less than $100 per year along with 6 percent interest, twice annually over the lifetime of the loan. In other words, Gros Louis agreed to pay Bastien $166 per year ($100 in principal and $33 in interest, twice yearly). The contract also stipulated that Gros Louis was to insure the house against fire to the value of the mortgage ($550), the policy for which was to be in Ludger Bastien's name. During the period covered by the contract, Gros Louis was to continue to occupy the house.[130] Sadly, given that the average annual household income in Lorette entered free fall during the mortgage's lifetime (in 1929 it dropped from nearly $500 to roughly $150 in 1933 before rebounding slightly to $200 in 1934), it seems likely that Gros Louis lost his home.[131] In fact, Bastien may have resold this same house to Elzéar Sioui in the early 1930s. In 1930 or 1931 Sioui purchased a house on the reserve from Bastien. Although the price is unknown, Sioui, apparently succumbing to economic difficulties, rapidly proved unable to pay the installments required by the contract of sale, and at the end of the decade, a Quebec newspaper reported that the little money paid did not even amount to the interest stipulated in the contract.[132] Because the home was located on the reserve, jurisdiction fell to Indian Affairs who, although working more slowly than the superior court (the standard legal channel providing for the seizure of property), allowed Bastien to recover the house in 1938.[133] Once again, then, the Bastien family managed to take advantage of the generally unfavorable economic context of the Great Depression in order to increase its own fortune.

CONCLUSION

Between the beginning of the nineteenth century and the years following the Second World War, Lorette's economy changed enormously. Having at first been based on hunting, agriculture, and, to a lesser degree, the sale of "traditional" Wendat items, the village's economy came to be dominated by industrial manufacturing and local credit networks. At the same time, the state augmented its presence and influence on local conditions while Lorette's entire population grew increasingly dependent on the market for income, thereby rendering consumption an ever more important factor in the economy. This sea change paralleled concurrent developments taking place across much of the globe as the forces of industrialization and capitalism combined to bring about the "great transformation," altering the balance between social and economic relations through the adoption of the self-regulating market as society's primary organizational agency.[134] In Lorette, as elsewhere, such changes were not solely economic as they also had consequences that remade the community's social structure.

Although much has been written on the effects of First Nations internal political struggles born of the imposition of alien forms of governance, historians have only begun to analyze the ways in which economic reorganization brought about social changes in these communities in ways that resembled those being experienced elsewhere.[135] Indeed, just as individuals and families might have diverging political interests, interests that could best be served by maintaining traditional chiefs in power or by replacing them with elected leaders, this chapter demonstrates that community members often had opposing economic interests. These differences are perhaps best illustrated through Lorette's emerging class structure. By the early to mid-nineteenth century, a handful of Wendat families (the Picards and the Vincents) had already begun to distinguish themselves with regard to other community members, earning relatively large sums of money from manufacturing and reinvesting them in loans to neighbors, both on- and off-reserve. By the end of the nineteenth century, these families had begun concentrating their economic activities in white-collar and professional work, leaving commerce to the Bastien family who, in addition to their predecessors' industrial and financial activities, earned considerable income from local consumption. The Bastiens' activities in manufacturing, retail, and the credit market, particularly from the post–World War I era, contributed both to their own acquisition of formal political power and to the acceleration of the socioeconomic differentiation already under way in the village.

This second process seems to have ultimately included the emergence of a small middle class on the reserve as a result of the Bastien family's decision to reduce its manufacturing workforce during the 1930s and 1940s; as work tanning hides and making moccasins disappeared, community members needed to find alternative ways of earning a living. Although Lorette was in many ways an exceptional community, its experience of class formation and economic change suggests the need to conduct similar analyses in the context of other First Nations. This, in turn, should contribute to a reclassification of the nineteenth and twentieth centuries as a critical period in the history of First Nations and their relationship to wider social phenomena rather than as an "era of irrelevance."[136]

NOTES

This chapter is based on my PhD dissertation, "Colonialism's Currency: A Political History of First Nations Money-Use in Quebec and Ontario, 1820–1950," Université du Québec à Montréal, 2011.

1. For a study of both questions of community identity and external representations at Lorette during the nineteenth century, see Véronique Rozon, "Un dialogue identitaire: les Hurons de Lorette et les autres au XIXe siècle" (Mémoire de maîtrise, Université du Québec à Montréal, 2005). For a comparative study of Quebec Wendat and Oklahoma Wyandotte identity in the twenty-first century, see Linda Sioui, "La réaffirmation de l'identité wendat / wyandotte à l'heure de la mondialisation" (Mémoire de maîtrise, Université Laval, 2011).

2. Charles Marshall, *The Canadian Dominion* (London: Longmans, Green, 1871), 18.

3. In 1819 and 1824, Grand Chief Nicolas Vincent Tsawenhohi spoke before Lower Canada's House of Assembly in Wendat as another community member (Louis Vincent Sawatanen in 1819 and Michel Sioui Tehatsiendahé in 1824) translated his words into French. Stéphanie Boutevin, "La place et les usages de l'écriture chez les Hurons et les Abénakis, 1780–1880" (PhD diss., Université du Québec à Montréal, 2011), 99–101. In 1834 Vincent and the other chiefs again addressed the House of Assembly through an interpreter (Vincent Ferrier Sasinioyon). Canada, *Appendix to the Journals of the House of Assembly of the Province of Lower Canada, From the 7th January to the 18th March 1834* (Quebec City: Frechette, 1834), n.p., Evidence, 27 January 1834.

4. The most complete analysis of Lorette's economy during the period is found in Denys Delâge, "La tradition de commerce chez les Hurons de Lorette-Wendake,"

Recherches amérindiennes au Québec (hereafter *RAQ*) 30, no. 3 (2000): 35–51. However, this otherwise path-breaking article focuses exclusively on production.

5. For two pivotal studies in the history of consumption, see Lizabeth Cohen, *A Consumers' Republic: The Politics of Mass Consumption in Postwar America* (New York: Knopf, 2003), and T. H. Breen, *The Marketplace of Revolution: How Consumer Politics Shaped American Independence* (New York: Oxford University Press, 2004). For recent historiographical reviews, see David Steigerwald, "All Hail the Republic of Choice: Consumer History as Contemporary Thought," *Journal of American History* 93, no. 2 (September 2006): 385–403; Meg Jacobs, "State of the Field: The Politics of Consumption," *Reviews in American History* 39, no. 3 (September 2011): 561–73.

6. For a more in-depth examination of the politics of consumption in Lorette, see Brian Gettler, "La consommation sous réserve: les agents indiens, la politique locale et les épiceries à Wendake aux XIXe et XXe siècles," *Bulletin d'histoire politique* 20, no. 3 (Spring 2012): 170–85.

7. This concept of class as a process is drawn from E. P. Thompson's canonical historical study of class formation in England. E. P. Thompson, *The Making of the English Working Class* (Toronto: Penguin, 1963). Although the concept of class has increasingly come under attack in recent years, largely from historians subscribing to postmodern (particularly Foucauldian) analysis, the present study makes use of the concept in the belief that it need be neither rigid in its formulation nor tainted by its role in ongoing disputes pitting discursive against materialistic analysis. For a detailed version of this argument, see Geoff Eley and Keith Nield, *The Future of Class in History: What's Left of the Social?* (Ann Arbor: University of Michigan Press, 2007).

8. Nicolas G. Rosenthal, "Beyond the New Indian History: Recent Trends in the Historiography on the Native Peoples of North America," *History Compass* 4, no. 5 (September 2006): 962–74.

9. It is important to note that market exchange differed substantially from earlier forms of trade practiced by the Wendats. Whereas trade in Wendake Ehen emphasized reciprocity, exchange relationships in Lorette increasingly aimed at profit. On trade among the Wendats prior to their move east from the Great Lakes and the changes this system underwent following the arrival of the French and Dutch, see Denys Delâge, *Le pays renversé: Amérindiens et Européens en Amérique du Nord-Est, 1600–1664* (Montreal: Boréal, 1991), 65–69, 90–172.

10. The Wendats have a long history of laying claim to the seigneury of Sillery, an area of land adjacent to Quebec that until the mid-nineteenth century continued to be governed by the quasi-feudal land tenure system first implemented by France in the Saint Lawrence Valley during the seventeenth century. On the history of this claim, see Michel Lavoie, *C'est ma seigneurie que je réclame: La lutte des Hurons de Lorette pour la seigneurie de Sillery, 1650–1900* (Montreal: Boréal, 2010).

11. "Petition from Nicolas Vincent Tsawanhonhi et al. to the Honorable the Knights, Citizens and Burgesses of the Province of Lower-Canada, in Provincial Parliament assembled," January 26, 1819, in *Eighth Report of the Committee of the House*

of Assembly on . . . the Settlement of the Crown Lands (Quebec City: Neilson and Cowan, 1824), iii. It should be noted that the government official charged with maintaining relations with the Wendats made similar claims regarding the community's economic difficulties. In 1819 the Indian superintendent at Quebec City claimed that although "peaceable and industrious," the Wendats were "very poor and subsist[ed] only by their industry." He further stated, "the Indians are no longer able to make the necessary repairs [to the church and parsonage house in Lorette] on accounts of their poverty." Ibid., 17–18.

12. Ibid., 20–21.

13. They claimed that "their fishing and hunting scarcely produce them enough for the support of the Hunters and Fishermen, because Settlements are now formed over a very great extent of their hunting and fishing grounds, they feel deeply the loss they have sustained, and ask for their lands again, as the only means of subsistence for their families." Second Enclosure in No. 4, Petition from Nicolas Vincent et al. to George Murray, November 2, 1829, in *Journals of the House of Assembly of the Province of Lower Canada, Session 1832–1833* (Quebec City: Neilson and Cowan, 1833), appendix O.O.

14. "Petition from Nicolas Vincent Tsawanhonhi," 12.

15. For example, in July 1830 Wendake's chiefs sent a letter to the military secretary stating that they had "met in Council as soon as it was possible for us to assemble after the great hunt, for the purpose of deliberating on your letter of the 9th of April last." Enclosure in No. 6, Nicolas Vincent et al. to J. B. Glegg, July 9, 1830, in *Journals of the House of Assembly,* appendix O.O.

16. Jocelyn Tehatarongnantase Paul, "Le territoire de chasse des Hurons de Lorette," *RAQ* 30, no. 3 (2000) : 8.

17. Ibid. This percentage actually grew between 1871 and 1881, when it stood at 42 percent. However, fur prices dropped substantially during the 1880s.

18. Antoine O. Bastien, "Report on the Jeune-Lorette Agency," August 26, 1889, in *Indian Affairs Annual Report (IAAR), 1889,* part 1, 36; Bastien, "Report on the Jeune-Lorette Agency," August 29, 1891, in *IAAR, 1891,* 31; Bastien, "Report on the Jeune-Lorette Agency," August 24, 1892, in *IAAR, 1892,* 32; Bastien, "Report on the Jeune-Lorette Agency," September 6, 1893, in *IAAR, 1893,* 34; Bastien, "Report on the Jeune-Lorette Agency," August 31, 1894, in *IAAR, 1894,* 30. The successive departments responsible for Indian Affairs published these reports as stand-alone documents each year between the 1860s and 1990. For an easily accessible collection of these reports, see the Library and Archives Canada (LAC) website: http://www.bac-lac.gc.ca/eng /discover/aboriginal-heritage/first-nations/indian-affairs-annual-reports/Pages /introduction.aspx (accessed December 16, 2015).

19. Bastien, "Report on the Jeune-Lorette Agency," August 15, 1895, in *IAAR, 1895,* 31.

20. Bastien, "Report on the Jeune-Lorette Agency," July 16, 1896, in *IAAR, 1896,* 42.

21. Bastien, "Report on the Jeune-Lorette Agency," August 10, 1900, in *IAAR, 1900,* 51. See also Paul, "Le territoire de chasse," 9.

22. For example, in early May 1917 Daniel Groslouis and his son Théophile were arrested by a game warden from the Sportsman Protective Association near the Petit Batiscan Club. As a result, he was brought before the court in Quebec City and charged with hunting during the closed season. He requested the Huron-Wendat band council's aid. Although the grand chief accompanied Groslouis, he lost his case and was fined $16.30. June 18 and 21, 1917, Pierre Albert Picard Tsichiek8an, *Journal personnel, 1916–1920*, 52–53 (hereafter cited as Picard Journal), Archives du Conseil de la Nation huronne-wendat (ACNHW), F-1-79.

23. Bastien, "Report on the Jeune-Lorette Agency," August 26, 1888, in *IAAR, 1888*, 28.

24. By referring to Indigenous economies as "moditional," Lutz explains that in the context of colonialism, Indigenous peoples pursued neither purely capitalistic nor purely traditional economic activity. Instead, they continually modified their traditional economy to meet their cultural needs while simultaneously seeking to profit from the capitalistic colonial market. However, his analysis focuses solely on "productive" activities such as wage labor, hunting, and fishing, leaving aside the important economic spheres of finance and consumption. John Sutton Lutz, *Makúk: A New History of Aboriginal-White Relations* (Vancouver: University of British Columbia Press, 2008).

25. "Some of our best hunters were hired to serve as guides to American sportsmen, and their condition was materially improved thereby." Bastien, "Report on the Jeune-Lorette Agency," August 26, 1889, in *IAAR, 1889*, part 1, 36.

26. Bastien, "Report on the Jeune-Lorette Agency," July 16, 1896, in *IAAR, 1896*, 42. In 1901 Gérin reported that Wendat guides, in particular Daniel and Xavier Groslouis, earned the same amount per day ($1.25) in addition to provisions, tobacco, and whisky. Léon Gérin, "Le Huron de Lorette. À quels égards il est resté sauvage," in Denis Vaugeois, ed., *Les Hurons de Lorette* (Quebec City: Les éditions du Septentrion, 1996), 31.

27. In his MA thesis, Georges Boiteau notes that Emery Sioui was employed at Club Laurentides around 1925 and that Harry Groslouis worked at the Triton Club between 1926 and 1935. Georges Boiteau, "Les chasseurs hurons de Lorette" (MA thesis, Université Laval, 1954), 167. For information on wages, see "Quebec Indian Sells His Wares to U.S. Tourists," *Omnibuster,* vol. 2, no. 5, July 1934, n.p., ACNHW, P2-S3-B2, File B-2-19.

28. In June 1919, Pierre Albert Picard wrote: "Telesphore Picard, sous Chef, part pour les clubs bâtir des camps." June 16, 1919, Picard Journal. According to Agent Picard, Moïse Gros Louis, a band member who had requested departmental relief, "is a game warden and spent all last summer at his work up to the late fall. He is going back in the early spring." [Pierre Albert Picard] to the Secretary, Department of Indian Affairs, January 3, 1931, Bibliothèque et Archives nationales du Québec à Québec (BAnQ-Q), P883, S5, File 13.

29. "Petition from Nicolas Vincent Tsawanhonhi," 19, 21.

30. Vincent et al. to Glegg, July 9, 1830 (n. 15).

31. D. C. Napier, "Return of Indians under the Protection of the Indian Department of Lower Canada," December 12, 1836, in *Copies or Extracts of Correspondence since 1st April 1835 between the Secretary of State for the Colonies and the Governors of the British North American Provinces: Respecting the Indians in those Provinces* (London: House of Commons, 1839), 54.

32. Unfortunately, no evidence has been found indicating that the Wendats continued holding the appreciable amount of off-reserve land they had owned during the late eighteenth century. Furthermore, comments dismissing Wendat agriculture as marginal suggest that much of this land had been liquidated by the late nineteenth century, if not before. At the turn of the twentieth century, a study of daily life in Lorette described the community's natural resource base in the following negative terms: its soil "though generally deep, is sandy and rather poor. The land has been partly cleared of woods, but agriculture has not developed over it to any great extent. Along the upper course of the river St. Charles, back of Lorette, no farms are to be seen, but, instead, an after-growth of scrubby spruces and the summer villas of some professional men of Quebec." Léon Gérin, "The Hurons of Lorette," in *Report on the Ethnological Survey of Canada* (London: British Association for the Advancement of Science, 1900), 550–51.

33. According to a former Indian Affairs employee, writing to explain the lack of wide-scale agricultural activity among the Wendats, the band took its stewardship of its timber resources very seriously: "As fire-wood is a primary consideration with the Indians, the Hurons wish to save the little they possess for their descendants, [they] consequently do not clear much land." "Appendix 14: Extracts of Evidence of Mr. Robert McNab, formerly of the Indian Department, (having reference to the Tribes in Canada East)," in "Report on the Affairs of the Indians in Canada," Appendix T, *Journals of the Legislative Assembly of the Province of Canada, Sessional Papers* (Montreal: Rollo Campbell, 1847). For more on timber harvesting on Quarante Arpents, see Brian Gettler, "Colonialism's Currency: A Political History of First Nations Money-Use in Quebec and Ontario, 1820–1950" (PhD diss., Université du Québec à Montréal, 2011), 197–203.

34. Indian Affairs policy impeded agriculture in Indigenous communities throughout Canada during the late nineteenth and early twentieth centuries, particularly in the Prairie provinces. On this phenomenon see Sarah Carter, *Lost Harvests: Prairie Indian Reserve Farmers and Government Policy* (Montreal: McGill–Queen's University Press, 1993).

35. For example, in 1872 the federal government provided $75 in such assistance to the Wendats. List of Grants from Lower Canada Indian Fund, n.d. [1872], LAC, RG10, vol. 1861, file 201, reel C-11103.

36. Bastien, "Report on the Jeune-Lorette Agency," August 15, 1895, in *IAAR, 1895,* 32. The agent made essentially the same assertion in his reports over the following years. Bastien, "Report on the Jeune-Lorette Agency," July 16, 1896, in *IAAR, 1896,* 42; Bastien, "Report on the Jeune-Lorette Agency," July 28, 1897, in *IAAR, 1897,* 44; and Bastien, "Report on the Jeune-Lorette Agency," July 22, 1898, in *IAAR, 1898,* 44.

37. Community members did, however, "derive some revenue from it, the cut of pine and spruce over its area being leased out every year to lumbermen, and the proceeds usually paid to the 'band' in the form of allowances." Gérin, "Hurons of Lorette," 559. On aspects of the conflict between the Sioui family and other Wendats, see Gettler, "Colonialism's Currency," 223–24, 230–31.

38. For a description of the sale, see *IAAR, 1905*, xxxiv.

39. In the 1910s an outside observer reported, "There is no farming on this reserve, but most of the families have small gardens, and some keep cows and chickens." Frederick H. Abbott, *The Administration of Indian Affairs in Canada: Report of an Investigation Made in 1914 under the Direction of the Board of Indian Commissioners* (Washington, D.C.: self-published, 1915), 72.

40. Gaston Blanchet, "Étude de la communauté de Lorette" (bachelor's [licence], Université Laval, 1945), 64.

41. For example, the Wendats manufactured moccasins and snowshoes for their own daily use. Elisabeth Tooker, *An Ethnography of the Huron Indians, 1615–1649* (Syracuse, N.Y.: Syracuse University Press, 1991), 20, 23. The Wendats traded produce and manufactured goods such as corn flour, nets, and rope to their neighbors prior to the arrival of Europeans. Delâge, *Le pays renversé*, 65–69.

42. "Nimrod" means skillful hunter and has its origins in the Bible, being the name of Noah's great-grandson known for his hunting prowess. J. M. LeMoine, *Historical Notes on the Environs of Quebec* (Montreal: Burland Lithographic, 1880), 19.

43. "Petition from Nicolas Vincent Tsawanhonhi," 22.

44. R. J. Routh to the Earl of Gosford, April 28, 1836, in *Copies or Extracts of Correspondence,* 39. The Indian Affairs agent in Quebec echoed this comment later the same year when he wrote: "At Lorette, their principal means are in making & embrodering [sic] with camel hair and porcupine quills, shoes, mitts, [?] and many other articles; in making snow-shoes, hunting to a small extent and some in cultivating vegetable gardens & small tracts of land." Louis Juchereau Duchesnay, "Answers to Queries," November 19, 1836, RG10, vol. 92, 37645-51, reel C-11468, LAC.

45. Delâge, "La tradition de commerce," 46.

46. The Picards sold the army snowshoes manufactured by their employees. "Paid for the government snowshoes on 28 April 1842 by Commissary Millikin." François-Xavier (Paul) Picard Tahourenché, *Journal (1837–1875),* April 28, 1842, ACNHW. The entry for July 17, 1845, in the same journal refers to "Mr. Millikin Commissaire Général." For an example of sales made by François-Xavier Picard, see François-Xavier Picard, Vente de l'été 1846, November 1, 1846[?], BAnQ-Q, P883, S2, File 7. Translations of French archival documents are by the author.

47. [Paul Picard?], List of debts owed to Paul Picard and Philippe Vincent, March 29, 1849[?], BAnQ-Q, P883, S1, File 1.

48. Among Quebec's elite, François-Xavier Picard was known for his hospitality. As a result, he frequently received prestigious residents of the city in his home. "Received the visit of Lord and Lady Elgin, Colonel Bruce, his lady, Capt. Hamilton, another gentleman, Lord & Lady Warncliff, Lady Hamilton, and Lady Bruce at my home, 24 June 1852, the day of St. Jean Baptiste." Tahourenché, *Journal,* June 24, 1852.

49. The industrial exhibitions at Quebec and Montreal were held in 1850 and the Paris exhibition took place in 1855. Ibid., n.d. [September 1851]; Thomas Sterry Hunt, *Le Canada et l'Exposition universelle de 1855* (Toronto, 1856), 204–6.

50. The author mistakenly refers to Paul Picard as "Paul Vincent, a cousin of Philippe mentioned above." "A Nook of the North," *Atlantic Monthly*, March 1861, n.p., http://archive.org/stream/canadianwildstel34173gut/pg34173.txt (accessed December 7, 2012).

51. Philippe Vincent Téonouathasta died in 1870. Delâge, "La tradition de commerce," 46.

52. The ongoing nature of the relationship was made clear by the acknowledgment that another item sold by the Picards (men's overcoats) cost the same as the previous year. François-Xavier Picard to [?], February 15, 1872, BAnQ-Q, P883, S2, File 7.

53. The brochure contains an error when it states that Maurice Bastien was "the Only Manufacturer in Indian Lorette in 1826." It should instead read "1926," the year in which it was printed. Bastien Brothers, "The Call of Indian Lorette," n.d. [1926], ACNHW, E-4-66.

54. Gérin, "Le Huron de Lorette," 34–35.

55. Maurice Bastien to L. W. Vankoughnet, July 11, 1880, RG10, vol. 2116, file 22,010, reel C-11161, LAC. Until the very end of the nineteenth century, this practice had the added benefit of allowing the Bastiens to avoid paying import duties as a result of Caroline's Indian status.

56. Julie-Rachel Savard, "L'apport des Hurons-Wendat au développement de l'industrie du cuir dans le secteur de Loretteville aux XIXe et XXe siècles," *Globe: Revue internationale d'études québécoises* 8, no. 1 (2005): 75. These figures are taken from a book of commercial ratings periodically published between 1878 and 1930. Unfortunately, the firm's post-1930 capitalization is unknown.

57. Guillaume Giroux, "Annual Report on the Agency at Lorette," n.d., in *IAAR, 1884*, 35–36.

58. Guillaume Giroux, "Annual Report on the Lorette Agency," August 20, 1883, in *IAAR, 1883*, 28.

59. In his 1888 annual report, the Indian agent wrote: "Trade, which until lately was prosperous, has now considerably decreased, and the Indians are consequently not in such good circumstances. The competition entered into by the whites in Indian industries has been the cause, to a certain extent, of this state of things." Bastien, "Report on the Jeune-Lorette Agency," August 26, 1888, in *IAAR, 1888*, 28. Thomas Sioui, an inveterate political opponent of Bastien, echoed this sentiment: "for several years the Whites have given themselves over to the manufacture of all of these articles and have entirely removed this industry from the Indians who have thus lost their means of earning a living." Petition from Thomas Tsioui et al. to Lord Stanley de Preston, Governor General of Canada, August 26, 1889, RG10, vol. 6825, file 495-8-1, pt. 1, reel C-8545, LAC.

60. Of course, this report may have been overly flattering with regard to Maurice Bastien Ahgnionlen, given that he was the agent's brother. Bastien, "Report on the Jeune-Lorette Agency," August 15, 1895, in *IAAR, 1895*, 31–32.

61. Ibid. See also Bastien, "Report on the Jeune-Lorette Agency," July 16, 1896, in *IAAR, 1896*, 42.

62. During the 1890s three tanneries operated either within Lorette or in its immediate vicinity. Two of them were owned by Euro-Canadians (Ross and Cloutier) and the third by Maurice Bastien Ahgnionlen. Gérin, "Le Huron de Lorette," 33–35.

63. Bastien, "Report on the Jeune-Lorette Agency," July 22, 1898, in *IAAR, 1898*, 45.

64. Gérin, "Le Huron de Lorette," 36–37.

65. John Dickinson and Brian Young, *A Short History of Quebec*, 4th ed. (Montreal: McGill–Queen's University Press, 2008), 214–15.

66. *The Canada Directory for 1857–58* (Montreal: John Lovell, 1857), 289.

67. The visitor further pointed out that this remuneration was "quite disproportioned, indeed, to the fancy prices always paid by strangers for the articles turned out by their hands." "A Nook of the North."

68. Gérin, "Le Huron de Lorette," 34.

69. Bastien explains this by pointing out "the considerable rise in the value of leather and raw skins; for example, the raw skins which formerly were worth from $4 to $5 per 100 lbs. have risen to from $9 to $10." Bastien, "Report on the Jeune-Lorette Agency," July 22, 1898, in *IAAR, 1898*, 45.

70. "The collective workshop under the supervision of a non-family member has taken the place of the old familial workshop." Gérin, "Le Huron de Lorette," 37.

71. Ibid., 32.

72. Bastien, "Report on the Jeune-Lorette Agency," July 22, 1898, in *IAAR, 1898*, 45.

73. Bastien, "Report on the Jeune-Lorette Agency," July 15, 1899, in *IAAR, 1899*, 50.

74. Gérin, "Le Huron de Lorette," 55.

75. According to his application for life insurance, Picard had been employed by Quebec as "Government Employee Draughtsman" since 1876. Paul Picard, "Application for a Policy, Union Mutual Life Insurance Company," April 26, 1888, BAnQ-Q, P883, S3, File 7.

76. Brevet de Paul Picard à Philippe Huot, November 8, 1865, Notary Louis Panet, BAnQ-Q, CN301, S208, no. 14,856; Titre clerical de Prosper Vincent, May 20, 1870, Notary Paul Picard, BAnQ-Q, CN301, S368, no. 1.

77. Pierre-Albert Picard to J. E. Perrault, Ministre de la Colonisation, des Mines & des Pêcheries, March 23, 1921, ACNHW, P2-S3-A13, File B-2-16.

78. "Officers' Declaration Paper, Canadian Overseas Expeditionary Force: Captain Picard, Louis Phil. Ormond," October 31, 1918, RG150, accession 1992–93/166, box 7809-33, LAC. Picard began his military career as a private in the Eighty-Seventh Battalion of the Canadian militia in 1897 before becoming a lieutenant the following year. He again enlisted in April 1902 and served a short stint in South Africa before being honorably discharged in July of the same year. "Canadian Mounted Rifles, Attestation Paper, No. 383," April 16, 1902; W. E. L. Coleman, "Record of Service: Private Picard, Ormond," October 28, 1940, RG38, A-1-a, vol. 84, reel T-2082, LAC.

79. According to Indian Affairs, eight Indigenous commissioned officers were serving in 1916. *IAAR*, 1916, xxxvi.

80. Joseph Bastien, "Éleveurs, lisez-moi ça," *La revue des éleveurs de renards* 1, no. 3 (December 1934): 29–30, ACNHW, file E-2-17.

81. On the lawsuit, see "La cité et les Bastien font la paix après des années de lutte," *L'action catholique*, June 30, 1923, n.p.; "L'Oeil au Conseil de Ville: L'affaire Bastien," *L'Oeil aux affaires de Québec*, July 6, 1923, 1, ACNHW, P2-S3-B2, File B-2-19.

82. Raphaël Ouimet, "Ludger Bastien," extract from *Biographies canadiennes-françaises* (Montreal, 1926), 98, ACNHW, C-4-36. Although little is known about these companies' long-term success, Ernest Bastien revived Bastien Silver Fox Breeders after the Great Depression and experienced considerable success raising fur-bearing animals in the nearby village of Chateau d'Eau. [?] Potvin, "Une après-midi à Château-d'Eau," *Les pelleteries du Québec*, March 1947, 8–9, ACNHW, G-1-99.

83. Launière's post is unknown. M. E. Bastien to the Secretary, Department of Indian Affairs, June 18, 1938, RG10, vol. 7552, file 41,014-1, reel C-14817, LAC. One of Ovila Gros Louis's daughters, either Marguerite or Pauline, worked for the insurance company. W. J. F. Pratt to Mr. Sharpe, April 17, 1937, ACNHW, Fonds Marguerite Vincent, 8551-01.

84. Before taking the post with the Quebec government, Pierre Albert Picard Tsichiek8an worked as an engineer on several large construction projects in Quebec. For example, between summer and autumn 1917, Picard was employed by Quinlan and Robertson in Limoilou. 3 September 3 and November 4, 1917, Picard Journal. Speech by J. Arthur Vincent for Léon Gros-Louis, June 15, 1952, and Souscription en faveur de M. Léon Gros-Louis, n.d. [June 15, 1952], ACNHW, Fonds Marguerite Vincent, 8542-02.

85. In 1909 the Indian agent, Antoine Oscar Bastien, wrote: "In my last report I observed that the making of snow-shoes and moccasins, the chief industry of the Indians, was far from flourishing. I regret to say that this industry, instead of becoming vigorous again, has decreased more this year. The heads of families on the reserve are obliged in order to maintain their families to go off at a distance in order to earn money in the neighbouring towns." Bastien, "Report on the Jeune-Lorette Agency," June 14, 1909, in *IAAR, 1909*, 47.

86. Abbott, *Administration of Indian Affairs in Canada*, 71.

87. Ibid. Julie-Rachel Savard's study of the leather industry in the region demonstrates the impact of this competition on Lorette's manufacturing sector. Savard, "L'apport des Hurons-Wendat au développement de l'industrie du cuir."

88. Victoria Hayward, "Indian Lorette," *Quebec Daily Telegraph*, April 13, 1920, n.p.

89. C. M. Barbeau, "The Indian Reserve of Lorette (Quebec): A Report Concerning Its Proposed Disestablishment," [1920], Canadian Museum of History (CMH), Marius Barbeau Collection, B91, F3, 15.

90. On the state's role in the Bastien's Depression-era retailing profits, see Gettler, "La consommation sous réserve."

91. In 1929 Indian Affairs did not provide any relief in Lorette, presumably because of prosperity due to manufacturing. By 1938 the federal government

provided $11,110.73, or $23.24 per reserve resident. Although a huge increase, this figure had in fact decreased from a peak of $13,742.82 ($28.75 per capita) in 1935. *IAAR*, 1929–1938. In 1937 Indian Affairs rejected Ovila Gros Louis's request for state support since "there exists no chance of being employed" in Lorette. W. J. F. Pratt to Mr. Sharpe, April 17, 1937, ACNHW, Fonds Marguerite Vincent, 8551-01.

92. Gaspard Picard to T. G. Murphy, September 1, 1934, ACNHW, Fonds Marguerite Vincent, 8551-01.

93. He writes: "the reserve's only industry, which employs approximately 100 workers, very few of whom are Indian, manufactures shoes and slippers." Blanchet, "Étude de la communauté de Lorette," 6–7.

94. M. E. Bastien to Indian Affairs Branch, March 25, 1944, and Kathleen Moodie to M. E. Bastien, April 17, 1944, RG10, vol. 7552, file 41,014-1, reel C-14817, LAC. Indian Affairs launched the handicraft program as a means of diminishing relief expenditure. Despite the maturity of Wendake's manufacturing sector, a segment of the village's population benefited from state funds when engaging in such work during wartime. Thus, between April 1 and 30, 1940, the Branch invested $450.29 in Wendake while selling the community's production at a loss (for $439.83). Unfortunately, from the archival record it is unclear whether Bastien or other Wendats benefited from these funds. Statement of Handicraft Trust Account #470, April 1–November 30, 1940, n.d. [December 11, 1940], RG10, vol. 7551, file 41,001-1, reel C-14817, LAC.

95. *IAAR*, 1947, 212.

96. Author's translation. Potvin, "Une après-midi à Château-d'Eau."

97. Tooker, *Ethnography of the Huron Indians*, 25–26.

98. One late eighteenth-century observer reported that Wendat men plucked all of their facial hair using tweezers they had made themselves from copper wire. As a result of this universal practice in the village, "all peddlers make sure to carry this commercial good in order to furnish them [Wendat men] with it." J. B. L. J. Billecocq, *Voyages chez différentes nations sauvages de l'Amérique septentrionale* (Paris: Prault l'aîné, imprimeur, and Fuchs, libraire, [1792?]), 278.

99. This number includes butchers, general storekeepers, provisions dealers, bakers, wheelwrights, cabinetmakers, shoemakers, saddle makers, and blacksmiths. *Canada Directory for 1857–58*, 289.

100. "A Nook of the North."

101. The first traces of Wendat merchant activity are limited to titles given in contracts. For example, during the mid-nineteenth century Charles Picard was described as being a merchant in the village of Saint Ambroise (Loretteville). Discharge by Edouard Dubeau to Pierre Noël and Charles Picard, November 18, 1858, Notary Louis Panet, BAnQ-Q, CN301, S208, no. 14,090. Adolphe Picard was also a merchant, though he was based in Lorette. Sale by Adolphe Picard to Francis Groslouis, June 30, 1875, Notary Paul Picard, BAnQ-Q, CN301, S368, no. 210.

102. In this instance, Picard earned £1.18.0 Hfx after expenses for twelve and one-half days' roadwork. "Receipt from Charles Picard to Félix Fortier, écuyer, for work completed on the road from the rivière aux Pins to the rivière Sainte-Anne," June 30, 1855, BAnQ-Q, E21, S64, SS5, SSS3, D903.

103. For example, four years after opening his store, Bastien reported to Indian Affairs headquarters staff, "Money has circulated more than usual, but the lack of work during the last few years placed a good many in distress, and forced them to run into debt for maintenance and provisions which they have not yet liquidated. I have observed that generally they have acted with strict economy in order to retrieve the past, and to be ready to face the possibilities of the future." Bastien, "Report on the Jeune-Lorette Agency," July 22, 1898, in *IAAR, 1898,* 45. However, the following year Bastien observed that difficult times had returned, spoiling the attempts of some to escape debt. "The enthusiasm of last year, which made these Indians imagine that their success would continue, particularly blinded their foresight, and this year, compared with last year, the making of snowshoes and moccasins was nearly nil." Bastien, "Report on the Jeune-Lorette Agency," July 15, 1899, in *IAAR, 1899,* 50.

104. On the Bastien family's involvement in on-reserve retail, see Gettler, "La consommation sous réserve."

105. For mention of Picard's business, see Minutes du conseil, May 9, 1941, in Bastien, *Livre de conseils tenus au village des Hurons, 1919–1949,* 102, ACNHW.

106. Minutes du conseil, 27 November 1946, in ibid.

107. In his 1945 sociological study of Lorette, Gaston Blanchet claimed that Jules Sioui, to whom he refers as "Ti-Jules," "in his ardor refused for a time to sell to French Canadians under the pretext that he did not sell to Whites. (He has the distinction of having established 'community retail' [la 'vente chez nous'])." However, Sioui eventually dropped this policy for economic reasons ("he earns his profit from Whites"). Blanchet, "Étude de la communauté de Lorette," 31. Sioui was by this time a relatively well-known activist throughout Canada. On his political activity, see Hugh Shewell, "Jules Sioui and Indian Political Radicalism in Canada, 1943–1944," *Journal of Canadian Studies*34, no. 3 (Autumn 1999): 211–42.

108. On the history of economic nationalism in the United States, which helps situate Wendat politico-economic activity in the larger North American context, see Dana Frank, *Buy American: The Untold Story of Economic Nationalism* (Boston: Beacon, 1999).

109. "A Nook of the North."

110. "Copie d'une convention de vente à réméré de Paul Picard à Cyrille Tessier," June 6, 1888, BAnQ-Q, P882, S2, file 3.

111. Abbott, *Administration of Indian Affairs in Canada,* 71.

112. On the history of banking in Canada, see E. P. Neufeld, *The Financial System of Canada: Its Growth and Development* (Toronto: Macmillan, 1972); R. T. Naylor, *The History of Canadian Business, 1867–1914: The Banks and Finance Capital,* vol. 1 (Toronto: James Lorimer, 1975).

113. This practice resembles that used in other countries, such as France and Mexico, with similar legal systems that afforded an important role to notaries. For studies that deal with this issue in other national contexts, see Philip T. Hoffman, Gilles Postel-Vinay, and Jean-Laurent Rosenthal, *Priceless Markets: The Political Economy of Credit in Paris, 1660–1870* (Chicago: University of Chicago Press, 2000);

Juliette Levy, "Notaries and Credit Markets in Nineteenth-Century Mexico," *Business History Review* 84, no. 3 (2010): 459–78.

114. On this particular issue, see Peter Baskerville, *A Silent Revolution? Gender and Wealth in English Canada, 1860–1930* (Montreal: McGill–Queen's University Press, 2008), especially chap. 5, "Stretching the Liberal State: Legal Regimes, Gender, and Mortgage Markets in Victoria and Hamilton, 1881–1921."

115. Obligation by Joseph Savard to Philippe Vincent, June 2, 1860, Notary Louis Panet, BAnQ-Q, CN301, S208, no. 14,284.

116. Quittance by Philippe Vincent to Joseph Savard, June 2, 1860, Notary Louis Panet, BAnQ-Q, CN301, S208, no. 14,285.

117. Both loans were contracted in December (1848 and 1850) and were probably repaid in December 1859, equaling a total of twenty-one years. At a rate of 6 percent, the annual interest on £50 would have yielded £1.10.0 per year for a total of £63. Unfortunately, in view of the wording of the discharge (*quittance*) signed before the notary, it is unclear when these loans were repaid. However, it is reasonable to assume that the repayment happened at the same time the new loan was contracted, since all of the documents involved were signed on the same day (June 2, 1860).

118. For a discussion of this phenomenon in the French context, see Hoffman et al., *Priceless Markets.*

119. Another case serves to strengthen this reading. In 1860 Jacques Alain, a farmer from Saint Ambroise, contracted a $600 debt from Paul Picard Honda8onhont to be repaid within three years at 8 percent annual interest. However, since Alain required five years and four months to repay the debt, Picard earned $256 in interest as opposed to the $144 he would have earned had the terms of the contract been respected. Transport by Joseph Gauvin to Paul Picard, November 24, 1860, Notary Philippe Huot, BAnQ-Q, CN301, S350, no. 2,992; Quittance by François-Xavier Picard to Jacques Alain, March 27, [1866], Notary Philippe Huot, BAnQ-Q, CN301, S350, no. 5,457.

120. For examples of earlier loans that did not include the right of redemption, see Obligation by Magdelaine Geneste et al. to Paul Picard, June 2, 1849, Notary Louis Panet, BAnQ-Q, CN301, S208, no. 11,472; Obligation by Maurice Bastien to Philippe Vincent, April 25, 1857, Notary Philippe Huot, BAnQ-Q, CN301, S350, no. 1,543; Obligation by Louis Picard to François-Xavier Picard, September 1, 1866, Notary Philippe Huot, BAnQ-Q, CN301, S350, no. 5,586.

121. Sale *à faculté de rémére* by Hermine Bastien and Wilfrid Picard to Maurice Bastien Jr., May 15, 1884, Notary Paul Picard, BAnQ-Q, CN301, S368, no. 501.

122. Canada, *Statutes,* "An Act to Amend and Consolidate the Laws Respecting Indians," April 12, 1876, 39 Victoria, c. 18, s. 66.

123. On the disconnect between legal theory as spelled out in the Indian Act and on-the-ground practice, see Gettler, "La consommation sous réserve."

124. In 1894 Duncan Campbell Scott, the acting deputy superintendent general and Indian Affairs chief clerk and accountant, instructed Antoine O. Bastien that "transfers of this nature should be discouraged by you, as they are conditional in

their terms." Scott described the department's position to Bastien by stating, "Of course, there can be no valid objection to exchanges made by Indians of their lands, when paid for in full." D. C. Scott to A. O. Bastien, October 20, 1894, RG10, vol. 2773, file 154,998, reel C-11276, LAC.

125. Canada, *Statutes*, "An Act to Amend the Indian Act," 1930, c. 25, s. 10.

126. While different in form (it did not require interest payments), the first sale with right of redemption found dates to 1866, ten years before the adoption of the Indian Act. Sale *à faculté de réméré* by Charles Groslouis to Scholastique Groslouis, February 20, 1866, Notary Louis Panet, BAnQ-Q, CN301, S208, no. 14,875.

127. Barbeau, "The Indian Reserve of Lorette (Quebec)," 9, 3.

128. Ibid., 3.

129. Ludger told Barbeau, "The bank does not want to deal with them. It is necessary for them to obtain money from their own. Herman, our father, and I are obligated to help these people by lending them $100 or $500." Barbeau, typed copy of field notes for "The Indian Reserve of Lorette (Quebec): A Report Concerning Its Proposed Disestablishment," August 7 and 21, 1919, CMH, Collection Marius Barbeau, B91, F3, 30. For Barbeau's remarks on the Bastiens' real estate purchases, see Barbeau, "The Indian Reserve of Lorette (Quebec)" (n. 90), 10.

130. Adélard L'Heureux, Contract of Sale from Moïse Gros Louis to Ludger Bastien, October 27, 1928, ACNHW, Fonds Marguerite Vincent, 8551-12.

131. Although the Indian agent's income figures should be regarded skeptically, this picture of a generalized drop in income corresponds to the massive increase in state welfare distributed in Lorette during the period. The household incomes are based on the census returns of 1929 and 1934, which respectively reported 270 and 235 Wendat men and women between the ages of 21 and 65. Each household is assumed to be made up of one male and one female earner. For the census figures, see *IAAR, 1929*, 64; *IAAR, 1934*, 48. For the Indian agent's estimate of reserve income, see *IAAR, 1929*, 90; *IAAR, 1930*, 74; *IAAR, 1931*, 46; *IAAR, 1932*, 44; *IAAR, 1933*, 41; *IAAR, 1934*, 64.

132. Sioui clearly struggled to maintain solvency during the Depression. In 1939, for example, he pleaded guilty to having abandoned two children, the first in 1936 and the second in 1938, at La Crèche, an orphanage in Quebec. "Abandoned 2 Infants: Huron Reserve Indian Admits Separate Offences," *Montreal Gazette*, March 16, 1939, 21.

133. "Fin d'un long litige à la réserve huronne," *L'Evénement*, April 21, 1938, n.p., ACNHW, P2-S3-B2, File B-2-19. Although Indian Affairs required the assistance of the Royal Canadian Mounted Police in recovering the property for Bastien, it should be noted that this was not an instance of court-ordered seizure of collateral for repayment of a debt. Rather, since Bastien had bought the property by right of redemption, it constituted the eviction of a tenant.

134. Karl Polanyi, *The Great Transformation* (Boston: Beacon, 1944).

135. For an influential study among many of political reorganization in the Canadian context, see Gerald F. Reid, *Kahnawà:ke: Factionalism, Traditionalism, and Nationalism in a Mohawk Community* (Lincoln: University of Nebraska Press, 2004). Despite Rolf Knight's well-known early study of Indigenous work in the context of

wider social and economic changes, this sort of analysis has remained marginal to the immense historiography on Indigenous Canada and the United States. For the major works in the field, see Rolf Knight, *Indians at Work: An Informal History of Native Indian Labour in British Columbia, 1858–1930* (Vancouver: New Star Books, [1978] 1996); Alice Littlefield and Martha C. Knack, eds., *Native Americans and Wage Labor: Ethnohistorical Perspectives* (Norman: University of Oklahoma Press, 1996); Brian Hosmer and Colleen O'Neill, eds., *Native Pathways: American Indian Culture and Economic Development in the Twentieth Century* (Boulder: University Press of Colorado, 2004); Lutz, *Makúk;* Daniel H. Usner Jr., *Indian Work: Language and Livelihood in Native American History* (Cambridge, Mass.: Harvard University Press, 2009); Mary Jane Logan McCallum, *Indigenous Women, Work and History, 1940–1980* (Winnipeg: University of Manitoba Press, 2014).

136. This phrase is from one of the most widely read works on Native history in Canada: J. R. Miller, *Skyscrapers Hide the Heavens: A History of Indian-White Relations* (Toronto: University of Toronto Press, 1989). Steven High uses this phrase as a jumping-off point for a historiographical analysis of Indigenous labor during the nineteenth and twentieth centuries. Steven High, "Native Wage Labour and Independent Production during the 'Era of Irrelevance,'" *Labour/Le Travail* 37 (Spring 1996): 243–64. Despite the large body of scholarship that has been published on the question before and since High's article appeared, little progress has been made toward integrating Indigenous experience during the period into larger national and transnational historical narratives. Alexandra Harmon, Colleen O'Neill, and Paul C. Rosier, "Interwoven Economic Histories: American Indians in a Capitalist America," *Journal of American History* 98, no. 3 (December 2011): 698–722.

CHAPTER 6

Wendat Arts of Diplomacy

NEGOTIATING CHANGE IN THE
NINETEENTH CENTURY

Annette de Stecher

W endat women's arts of the nineteenth century, exquisite moose hair–embroidered objects of birch bark and hide, were prized by European visitors and tourists. This production became a thriving commercial enterprise that assisted the community through difficult decades of change to prosperity in the mid-nineteenth century. Beyond these well-known souvenir wares, evidence shows that a small number of moose hair–embroidered bark objects carried another layer of meaning, as ceremonial arts production. In Wendat diplomatic traditions, these artworks were a part of strategic initiatives designed to negotiate the changing circumstances of European settler presence.

During Lord Elgin's years as governor general of Canada from 1847 to 1854, he and Lady Elgin received from the Wendat community at Wendake, or Lorette, as it was then known, two birch bark trays that appear to be examples of this ceremonial arts production. The trays were acquired in 2010 by Library and Archives Canada as part of a remarkable assemblage of documents and Indigenous material culture (see figs. 6.1 and 6.2). The history of mid-nineteenth-century Wendat-British relationships coheres around these objects and the people associated with them.[1] Their stories create a narrative of events that throws into sharp relief the conflicting interests

Fig. 6.1. Lady Elgin's tray, Wendat, 1847–52, birch bark, moose hair, cotton thread, h. 31 cm, w. 39 cm. Photo by Stéphane Laurin. Courtesy of the Canadian Museum of History, Elgin collection, 2008.118.9.

of the two communities and the opposing policies of Wendat and British leaders, offering new perspectives on Wendat diplomatic initiatives of the period.

During the mid-nineteenth century the British colonial government formed stronger policies of assimilation, and Indigenous land rights increasingly became an issue. After the War of 1812 and particularly after the Rebellions of 1837 and 1838, growing numbers of European settlers arrived in the Canadas. It was a time when colonial attitudes toward Indigenous nations shifted significantly. With British policy focused on harvesting natural resources and providing for the land needs of increasing waves of immigrants, Indigenous peoples, once valued as essential military allies in times of conflict, came to be seen as obstacles to be overcome through various means of control.

Fig. 6.2. Lord Elgin's tray, Wendat, 1847–52, birch bark, moose hair, cotton thread, h. 24.7 cm, w. 38.7 cm. Photo by Stéphane Laurin. Courtesy of the Canadian Museum of History, Elgin collection, 2008.118.10.

This was a challenging period for the Wendat community. Historically, however, Wendat policies valued diplomacy, with affiliations between nations facilitated through meetings between leaders and the presentation of gifts. To smooth the path between Wendat and settler communities, Wendat leaders continued these traditions in the mid-nineteenth century.[2] The Elgin trays may have been created as gifts presented in this context, to further Wendat policies and efforts to maintain Wendat-British relations in a time of tension.[3] Through study of the trays, the Elgin family documents that accompanied them, the mid-nineteenth century journals of Wendat chief François-Xavier Picard Tahourenché and Wendat leader Paul Picard Honda8onhont, as well as British administrative correspondence of the period, this chapter explores the story of the Vincent-Picard family of Wendake, the Scottish family of Lord Elgin, and the diplomatic context of the 1852 meetings between Chief François-Xavier Picard Tahourenché and Lord Elgin. The resulting narrative offers fresh understanding of the texture of social relations and everyday interactions between Wendat and settler communities, set within the movement of larger historical events.[4]

THE ELGIN TRAYS

The Elgin trays, like the Wendat visual arts produced for the souvenir market, were made of birch bark embroidered with dyed moose hair. The trays represent an art form that was the outcome of intercultural exchange between the women of Eastern Woodlands Indigenous communities and the missionary sisters of the Quebec convents. Missions such as the Ursuline convent of Quebec were established in the early seventeenth century and were attended by girls and women from Eastern Woodlands nations. The European technique of embroidery taught by the sisters, the Indigenous materials of moose hair and birch bark supplied by Indigenous students, and Indigenous techniques of making bark containers (which the students taught to the sisters) came together to create a truly syncretic visual arts tradition.

Wendat moose hair–embroidered birch bark souvenir wares had entered the commercial market by the late eighteenth century, while the Quebec convents produced this genre of souvenir work throughout the eighteenth century and into the early decades of the nineteenth century. In her description of the origins of convent production, Ruth Phillips states: "Prior to contact, Native people did not embroider directly on the surfaces of bark containers either with quills or moosehair, nor did they make the lidded boxes and other fancy wares that became typical of the eighteenth-century curio trade. The origin of these wares was a true contact zone event."[5] Although the nuns developed an expertise in the use of moose hair embroidered on bark, their cloistered life suggests that knowledge of this material and its use in visual arts were introduced to them by their Indigenous students.[6] Dyed moose hair had long been used by Indigenous women of the Eastern Woodlands to create designs using twined weaving techniques. Using this material for embroidery in place of silk or cotton may have been the idea of European nuns or of Indigenous women, or it may have been a technique worked out jointly, in the creative space of the convent atelier. The technique of embroidery stitches, however, so similar to the stitches used in the European tradition, probably came from the Quebec convent nuns.[7]

In the embroidery technique used in the Elgin trays, as in the earlier convent works, moose hair is threaded through a steel needle and then stitched through the bark with the ends of the moose hair appearing on the reverse. The elastic quality of birch bark means that the bark tightens around the moose hair, holding it in place. A second layer of bark backing is attached to cover the reverse and protect the moose hair ends. Of this very time-consuming work, Lady Simcoe, who in 1791 visited the Ursuline convent in Quebec, wrote: "[moose hair] is so short that it must be put through the needle for every stitch, which makes it tedious."[8]

The botanical motifs of the Elgin trays—sprays of lavender thistles, strawberries, and flowers—are highly detailed, using a number of different stitches. Graduated shadings of color in the leaves, creating three-dimensionality and realism, are achieved using short and long or brick stitches.[9] The base of the thistle motif gains texture from a crisscross of overstitch, layered over laid satin stitches. The berry stitch appears in blossoms such as the blue flower and is used to depict jewels in the coronet.[10] The vivid colors of the moose hair in the Elgin trays were the product of Indigenous knowledge, obtained from plant dyes. Blue, red, black, and ivory were favored colors in the eastern Great Lakes Indigenous palette, with green shades and browns appearing in nineteenth-century bark work.[11]

Where the Elgin trays differ from the Wendat souvenir artworks is in the choice of motifs. Commercial objects were almost exclusively worked with floral motifs or genre scenes of Indigenous men, women, and children engaged in activities of daily life. However, the central motifs of the Elgin trays are detailed, accurate representations of British heraldic symbols, juxtaposed with floral emblems that represent national identity or beliefs. In Lord Elgin's tray, each of the side panels has a border of small green leaves, while in the center panel the initials of his title, "E & K," Earl of Elgin and Kincardine, are placed under an earl's coronet, surrounded by a garland of lavender thistles, white flowers, and pink and white flowers. The coronet motif includes the heraldic elements: a golden circlet, rays of gold topped with a pearl, and leaves at the base, with a crimson cap enclosed in the circlet.[12]

In Lady Elgin's tray, each of the side panels has a border of large tree leaves, possibly maple, while in the center panel the initials, which appear to be M. L. E., are placed under an earl or countess's coronet.[13] These initials may stand for Mary Lambton Elgin, Lambton being Lady Elgin's maiden name. The heraldry in this tray is as exact as in the other, and the focal points of floral motifs, three strawberries, and strawberry flowers are represented with detailed realism.

Iconographic analysis of the trays supports the argument that their presentation was made in a diplomatic context. Heraldic devices such as those of the trays are a complex symbolic language with layers of meaning; they can refer to a family structure within a larger political system, and they can also refer to and identify a nation. In a similar way, the trays' floral motifs are Scottish and Wendat symbols; to place them in close arrangement suggests an artistic choice to convey intentions of harmonious relations. The thistle is the national flower of Scotland, a reference to the Scottish origin of Lord Elgin and possibly to the Ancient and Most Noble Order of the Thistle, of which Lord Elgin was a member, while the strawberry fruit and flowers are associated with traditional Wendat beliefs. The significance of the strawberry, brought to Earth-Island from the Sky World by Sky Woman, who was the source of human life on earth, in Wendat narratives and ritual lies in its "inherent power of physical and spiritual renewal."[14] The abundance of strawberry flowers on Lord Elgin's tray, arranged to alternate with thistles, suggests a statement of diplomatic connection between nations, while the three strawberries on Lady Elgin's tray, in different stages of ripeness, suggest the cycle of life and renewal. The choice of the thistle rather than an emblem of England, the nation that Lord Elgin represented politically, suggests that the trays carry nuanced meanings: a personal recognition of the Elgin family that also connects these two people to larger political systems.

WENDAT TRADITIONS OF DIPLOMACY

The Elgin trays, with their distinct iconography and context, take their place in a history of gift presentation between Wendat leaders and leaders of Indigenous and European communities that dates from the earliest years of contact. Georges Sioui states that "the focus of Amerindian diplomatic culture was on affiliation and peace," and Wendat traditions of gift giving, trade, and diplomacy formed a complex of social practices that reflected these values.[15] Gifts were signs of generosity and sharing of wealth, as well as a means of smoothing social tensions and creating bonds of trust. Trade was considered a reciprocal gift exchange, and the Wendats referred to their trading partners in other Indigenous nations in kinship terms. In his discussion of early-contact Wendat trade and diplomatic practices, Bruce Trigger suggests that these kinship relations were "probably linked through formal bonds of adoption," and the well-documented nineteenth-century honorary adoptions of European or Euro-Canadians may have followed from this tradition.[16]

The Wendat Nation developed the structure of their relations with leaders of European nations within this Indigenous framework, integrating European religious and government institutions. Records of earlier addresses and the gifts that accompanied them illustrate traditional Wendat protocols.

In 1651 Wendat chief Taiearonk made an address to the Ursuline sisters in Quebec after their convent and school had been destroyed by fire. He accompanied his speech with gifts of wampum, to console the sisters for their loss and encourage them to remain in Quebec. In 1665 a Wendat chief who presented a welcoming address to the Marquis de Tracy, the Viceroy of New France, marked this speech and the meeting with the gift of a moose hide.[17] The moose provided everything needed for survival; it was the source of food, shelter, clothing, medicine, and materials for creative expression.[18] In Indigenous epistemologies, the gift of moose hide may have held significance in providing the means to wellness in all areas of life, and in these circumstances it may have been a symbolic replacement of the nuns' lost worldly possessions and shelter.

Later ceremonies took a syncretic form that brought Wendat traditions together with European religious institutions. The Jesuit priests had founded a shrine in Jeune-Lorette not long after the community was established, the chapel of Notre-Dame-de-Lorette, and it became a well-known pilgrimage site. In 1696 the Jesuits obtained from the Vatican a plenary indulgence for the festival of the Annunciation. This meant that visitors to the shrine would receive a remission of temporal punishment due to sin, making the shrine an important pilgrimage site. The plenary indulgence was renewed in 1699 and 1711. By the early 1720s the reception of colonial dignitaries was an established practice; visitors of note were welcomed with a feast and formal oration, continuing Wendat diplomatic practices.[19] In February 1721 M. Begon, the powerful intendant (the head of state appointed by the French king) of New France, was welcomed to the community with a military reception, a feast, and a public speech. The pilgrimages, based in Catholic religious practices, ended after the British takeover of Quebec, but the honoring of colonial dignitaries by the community, in the manner of Wendat practices, continued.[20]

Lord and Lady Elgin's visit to Wendake was situated within this framework. The nineteenth century saw a regular calendar of diplomatic events, meetings between Wendat and British leaders and their communities based in Great Lakes traditions and protocols.[21] Representatives of the British military and government administration and their friends and families attended events in Wendake, and Wendat leaders made formal visits to leaders at official residences. The journal of Chief François-Xavier Picard Tahourenché describes ceremonies in which officers in the British army stationed in Quebec City were honored with a Wendat *nom de guerre*. These events, accompanied by a feast, were well attended by members of the Wendake community, the officers of the garrison and their wives, and other visitors.[22]

In addition to the ceremony of the *nom de guerre,* Wendat chiefs made a public oratory or address of welcome to dignitaries visiting the community. Delegations of chiefs also paid official visits to heads of state, such as Lord Elgin in 1852, Lord Dufferin in 1873, Edward VII in 1860, and the Count of Paris in 1891.[23] The honorary adoption of a chief, a ceremony held at Lorette, was a special honor given to members of the settler community who had assisted the Wendat Nation in important ways. In the adoption ceremony, the grand chief made a speech or address, which was often memorialized by the presentation of a particular form of gift: a bark document on which the chief's words were written in Wendat and French, and in some cases elaborated with moose hair–embroidered motifs.[24] A gift of wampum was sometimes also made.[25] In an honorary adoption, a chief's ceremonial attire was also presented. These gifts were objects created within the ceremonial arts tradition.

Several honorary adoptions were recorded by European artists, offering detailed images of ceremonial wear and gifts. A lithograph by Frederick John Meyer depicts the adoption of actor Edmund Kean in 1826. Kean, who was given the Wendat name Alanienouidet, wears his gift of chief's regalia and holds a bark scroll on which the adoption address is written (see fig. 6.3). Although the beginnings of the tradition of the bark presentation scroll cannot be dated, the Kean scroll is the earliest documented example.

A painting by Henry Daniel Thielcke, *The Presentation of a Newly Elected Chief of the Huron Tribe* (1839), records the honorary adoption of Judge Robert Symes Hosa8ati (the Peacemaker), who had assisted the Wendats during the cholera outbreak of 1834. He is shown surrounded by the Huron tribal council and members of the Wendat community.[26] Judge Symes wears the ceremonial chief's outfit he received as a gift, and, as in the image of Edmund Kean, he holds a bark scroll (see fig. 6.4). In chapter 3 of this book, Thomas Peace describes a photographic portrait of Andrew Stuart in Wendat chief's regalia, an image that possibly records his ceremonial adoption. Stuart's father had assisted the Wendats in connection with land claims, supporting our understanding of the purpose of honorary adoption as recognition by the Wendat Nation of members of the settler community. The moose hair–embroidered birch bark scroll certificate of adoption given to Swedish consul general Folke Cronholm in 1905 is an excellent example of this ceremonial arts tradition (See fig. 6.5).

Fig. 6.3. Frederick John Meyer, *Edmund Kean*, lithograph, 1827, h. 36 cm, w. 25.8 cm. R9266 Mikan no. 3030046. Courtesy of Library and Archives Canada/Peter Winkworth collection of Canadiana at the National Archives of Canada/e010933058.

The Elgin trays and the diplomatic bark scrolls, with their symbolic textual and imagistic language, played similar roles: memorializing meetings, diplomatic exchanges, and agreements between representatives of nations, adapting the mnemonic aspect of the wampum and the oral tradition to the Western tradition of writing. While traditional Indigenous diplomatic practices were through oral literacy and the oral tradition, the Indigenous choice to add written texts to the oral record may have been strategic, "to place themselves on the same level in the political field" as European power became more dominant.[27] The Wendat community had knowledge of written literacy through the teaching of the Jesuit missionaries from the early seventeenth

Fig. 6.4. Henry Daniel Thielcke, *Presentation of a Newly Elected Chief of the Huron Tribe, Canada*, 1839. Courtesy of the McCord Museum, M20009.

century and through the importance they themselves placed on obtaining European education—to the ends of furthering their own national interests, as I will discuss later in this chapter.

The content of speeches by Wendat chiefs would vary according to circumstances, but addresses to heads of state consistently included a statement of the historical relationship between the Wendats and the French or English Crown, referring to the active military support given by the Wendat Nation in the past and the continuity of this allegiance. In this way, Wendat leaders and community members asserted the authority of their nation, culture, and distinct political structure, conveying a sense of continuity and permanence. The larger effect of these events was to affirm the national identity of the Wendats in the public eye of the European community, when in numbers— at some points during the nineteenth century, fewer than three hundred people—they were few in proportion to the population of the settler

Fig. 6.5. Address from adoption ceremony on birch bark, presented to Swedish consul general Folke Cronhome, Wendat, 1905–1906, birch bark, moose hair, pen, h. 43 cm, w. 60 cm. Folke Cronholm collection, 1936.22.0017. Courtesy of Etnografiska Museet, Stockholm.

communities. These strategies had an effect similar to the initiatives discussed by Thomas Peace in chapter 3, which—in his words—gave the community "greater political power than their demographic weight would suggest."

In addition to the public importance of the ceremonies, the ceremonial scrolls acted on several registers in their role as gifts. As public documents they recorded a meeting between representatives of nations. As personal souvenirs they memorialized a visit. As physical objects, to their recipients they were mementos of an exotic country and people, embedded in European understandings of the wilderness (symbolized by the birch bark material, often embroidered with moose hair). However, interpreted within a Wendat context, the scrolls continued Great Lakes traditions of public gift as memory device.

As a syncretic practice, the scrolls and the ceremony that surrounded them brought together two methods for collective memorizing: the method of the oral tradition, which comprised mnemonics together with rituals of song and oratory; and the method of writing. They were connected to early contact ceremonies and gifts such as Taiearonk's presentation of wampum in 1651, where the wampum memorialized the words spoken in the addresses. This function continued in the Elgin trays. The bark scrolls, through text, memorialized diplomatic exchanges between representatives of nations, adapting the mnemonic aspect of the wampum and the oral tradition to the Western tradition of writing. The bark trays, through their iconography, memorialized the presence of Lord and Lady Elgin in Wendake and harmonious relations between Wendat and British leaders. In addition, they acted as a personal souvenir, reflecting all aspects of the ceremonial arts tradition.

LADY ELGIN AND MARGUERITE VINCENT LA8INONKÉ: PARALLELS IN COMMUNITY ACTIVISM AND PASSION FOR NEEDLEWORK

While formal diplomatic practices and symbolic meanings helped create affiliations between Wendat and British leaderships, there is a second layer of communication embodied in the Elgin trays: the women's art of needlework acting as a connection between Wendat and settler communities. Marguerite Vincent La8inonké, of the Vincent family of hereditary chiefs and mother of Chief François-Xavier Picard Tahourenché, shared an interest in needlework with Lady Elgin, who enjoyed political influence as the wife of the current governor general and the daughter of the Earl of Durham, a former governor general. Marguerite Vincent excelled in needlework, which in the British social structure of the period was regarded as an essential, defining accomplishment of well-born women, a "specifically feminine art form."[28] Lady Elgin herself took lessons in moose hair embroidery during her time in Quebec in 1838.[29] The trays, with their demonstrated virtuosity in a needlework tradition highly valued in European terms, were a distinct and unique gift. They would be treasured by Lady Elgin and possibly were intended to convey a message to Lord Elgin, expressing wishes of harmony and respectful communication between the Wendat Nation and the Crown. In addition to this shared interest, both Lady Elgin and Marguerite Vincent advocated for social betterment in their communities. Exploration of their actions in this area gives depth to our understanding of relations between the British and Wendat communities.

Marguerite Vincent's role in relations between Indigenous and English communities is clear from archival documents that preserve colonial communications, and Lady Elgin's influence in public affairs is represented in the oral tradition and archives of the Elgin family as well as her friendship with Harriet Martineau, a politically engaged feminist writer and friend of the Durham and Elgin families. Lady Elgin represents a period in British history at the dawning of the women's movement, marked not only by her influence in issues relating to women but also in her close friendship with Martineau. Together with Martineau, who advocated for Poor Law reform and the right of working-class women to education and improved working conditions, Lady Elgin originated the *Weekly Volume,* a series of inexpensive, popular books intended for working-class men and women.[30]

While Lady Elgin and Martineau were engaged in social issues and had a public voice through their publications, this was not the norm in British society in this period. Women's rights, including the right to have a voice in the public sphere, were just emerging. Marguerite Vincent came from a society with a different tradition of gender roles. The voice of Wendat women elders was respected, and women speaking publicly on issues that affected the community were part of Wendat social structure. In 1640 Marie de l'Incarnation recorded the public speech of a woman elder at a meeting of the Wendat Confederacy, in which the elder stated that the Jesuits were responsible for spreading disease in the communities.[31] In this same period, women elders refused to let young boys of the community be sent to the Jesuit school in Quebec.[32] Later on, in 1740–41, women elders of the Huron-Petun spoke in public meetings to veto decisions to move the community then at Detroit to Montreal, where they would be under Jesuit influence.[33]

Continuing this Wendat tradition, Marguerite Vincent was similarly politically active. In 1823 she made a public presentation to the governor general, Lord Dalhousie, to argue for the reinstatement of the gifts of cloth, "useful presents from his most grateful Majesty," that had traditionally been given to the Wendats as military allies of the French and then English Crowns. Described by Amelia Murray, a friend of Lord Elgin, as "extremely intelligent" and a speaker of "good Canadian French," Marguerite Vincent impressed Lord Dalhousie.[34] He referred to her as "Her Majesty" and recommended that her request be granted.[35]

Marguerite Vincent took a lead in other areas in her community. Well-known for her excellence in needlework, she won recognition as a teacher of moose hair embroidery, as a businesswoman, and as an artistic innovator.[36] She turned her needlework skills to business development and played a leading role in organizing and expanding the souvenir arts industry in response to the economic difficulties of the community. The production and sale of souvenir arts greatly expanded, with the Vincent home playing a central role in the commercial production of moose hair–embroidered souvenir works.

In addition, Marguerite Vincent is linked to the trays as a member of a family of hereditary chiefs noted for their diplomatic and political activism. Her house, today known as Tsawenhohi House, was the home of the Vincent hereditary chiefs. Here her son, Chief François-Xavier Picard Tahourenché, received Lord and Lady Elgin during their visits to the community, at meetings she herself may have attended. She was politically aware within a family of politically active hereditary grand chiefs. Her father, Dartmouth College–educated Louis Vincent Sawatanen, moved forward with Wendat land claims in 1791 and founded a school at Lorette in the early 1790s.[37] Her close relative Nicolas Vincent Tsawenhohi (1769–1844) was grand chief and a highly respected diplomat who devoted much of his life to a judicial battle to reestablish the Wendat Nation's land title.[38] In 1819, 1824, and 1829 he represented the Wendat Nation of Lorette concerning land claims to the Chamber of Assembly of Lower Canada, and in 1825 he visited George IV at the court in Windsor for further discussion of land claims.[39] Such was the Wendat tradition, carried on by members of the Vincent-Picard family, of political activism and diplomatic meetings with heads of state to further Wendat political aims.

Marguerite Vincent's story illustrates the role that Wendat women artists and their creative works played in this negotiation, at the center of commercial and diplomatic engagement between settler and Wendat communities. While creation of the trays has been attributed to Marguerite Vincent,[40] community knowledge of mid-nineteenth-century moose hair embroidery production brought forward through discussion with Mireille Siouï opens other possibilities: the artist who created the trays could have been one of the artist-needlewomen who produced works for the Vincent-Picard family souvenir enterprise.[41] This suggests the depth of the Wendat artistic community, both in participation in ceremonial arts creation and in traditional knowledge.

Lady Elgin seems to have held a position of similar influence, in relation to the respective achievements of her father, John George Lambton, Earl of Durham, and her husband as governor general. The efforts of these two men were linked, and in some ways she acted as bond between them. During his term as governor general (1838), her father was responsible for the Durham Report, the famous document advocating a move toward Canadian autonomy. Her husband's time as governor general (1847–54) saw implementation of many of the changes recommended in his father-in-law's report. Lord

Bruce, son of the current Lord Elgin, believes that Lady Elgin felt a particular responsibility to carry this as her personal charge from her father to her husband. Lord Bruce describes Lady Elgin as a highly educated woman of substance, with a clear sense of duty and responsibility, particularly with regard to Canada. Traveling with her father through Canada in 1838 had given her a sense of embodied connection. Moreover, through her association with Queen Victoria, she felt she carried a matrilineal responsibility to the queen, on whose behalf she believed they ruled.[42]

Lady Mary Lambton (the future Lady Elgin) kept a journal during her Canadian travels with her father. Her writing offers a rich description of British upper-class perceptions of the milieu of Canadian horses, scenery, architecture, Indigenous peoples, settler society, and customs. Read from the perspective of the Wendat community, the journal tells of increasing settler habitation, the forestry industry, the loss of land and animal habitat, and the loss of an economy based on hunting, which had been the successful source of livelihood for the community. From a visitor's perspective, Lady Mary's diary describes the impact of the lumber industry on the land near Quebec. She writes of a trip to Coves in Quebec "to see how the ships are laden with timber . . . the Coves beautiful but spoilt by all the timber floating and the dirty houses."[43] This is a firsthand account of the industrialization of the region, leading to the Wendat community's loss of territory and livelihood from hunting, thus necessitating their increased reliance on the souvenir arts and the expansion of this industry.

LORD ELGIN AND CHIEF FRANÇOIS-XAVIER PICARD TAHOURENCHÉ

Through their representation of Elgin family emblems and motifs of Wendat traditional beliefs, the trays symbolize a connection between nations and between the individual representatives of those nations, demonstrated by the meetings between Lord Elgin and Chief Tahourenché. The two men grew up with, and upheld, family traditions of service to their community, but they had opposite views on questions of Indigenous identity and sovereignty. Lord Elgin, like his wife, was fluent in French and made a deliberate choice to use French in correspondence during his time in Quebec, facilitating meetings with the Wendat community.[44]

Chief François-Xavier Picard Tahourenché continued the Vincent and Picard families' tradition of representing the Wendat Nation in public affairs, building political and diplomatic relations with dignitaries of the period, as well as connections with the business world and literary community. As a teacher, fluent in English and French, he taught Wendat children at the school in the community; as a surveyor and businessman, he helped maintain Wendat land rights and continued Wendat traditions of commerce, keeping business in the community. As a culture keeper, known for his knowledge of the rites and ceremonies of the Wendat Nation (which is cited as one of the many reasons for his election as grand chief in 1870), he shared his cultural knowledge with future generations.[45]

The two leaders met on both formal and informal occasions. On a formal political level, Chief François-Xavier Tahourenché made a visit at the head of a deputation to Quebec's Château Saint Louis in January 1852, where he delivered an oration to Lord Elgin; in June of the same year Lord and Lady Elgin were received in the Vincent-Picard family home.[46] This visit was informal but still in an official context. As the former home of Grand Chief Nicolas Vincent, the residence was a central meeting point for diplomacy and exchange. It was not only a place where Wendat souvenir arts were made and exhibited, but also a location where heads of state, ambassadors, and governor generals were formally received, including Lord and Lady Durham in 1838.[47] This long tradition of such receptions of colonial dignitaries dated from the late seventeenth century.[48]

TENSIONS BETWEEN WENDAT AND BRITISH
NATIONAL INTERESTS AND POLICIES

The period when the Elgin trays were made and received was a pivotal time in relations between the British colonial government and Indigenous communities. Between 1837 and 1854 a major shift took place in colonial policy toward Indigenous peoples of Upper and Lower Canada, the consequences of which are still felt today. There was a total reconsideration of place of Indigenous peoples in British North America from their position as necessary military allies whose abilities and support were essential to the stability of the British colony. The new demands of colonial expansion moved Indigenous peoples to a position as subjects whose docility, "civilization," and conversion to agricultural practices and European education became the priority.[49] This period was marked by tensions around many issues, such as the strain in French-English relations evidenced by the 1837 and 1838 rebellions and their aftermath as well as the achievement of "responsible government." During this

time the government moved toward policies of assimilation and emancipation, and the development of industrial schools, the forerunners of residential schools.[50] In this same period, educational and land rights strategies
initiated by Wendat chiefs in the late eighteenth century moved forward, as
community members worked to further Wendat interests and boundaries of
geography and culture. Thus Wendat and British interests were in opposition,
creating areas of conflict.

EDUCATION AS ASSIMILATION, EDUCATION
AS RESISTANCE

The problems that exist today in the tragic aftermath of residential schools
and the ongoing difficulties faced by many Indigenous nations were foreshad-
owed in the mid-nineteenth century. Changes in colonial policy moved toward
the goal of assimilation through education and the ending of Indigenous
status as military allies—and their recognition as nations. Exploration of the
development of these policies and the unfolding of Wendat initiatives that
pursued their interests makes clear the acumen of the chiefs in the late eighteenth and early nineteenth centuries in their long-term planning for their
community.

Letters written in 1837 between the Earl of Gosford, then governor general
of British North America, and the secretary of state for the colonies, Lord
Glenelg, explore the beginnings of British policy changes. The governor was
asked to put two questions to the chiefs of the Nations of the Canadas: first,
could the gifts given to these nations as military allies be commuted to
money; and second, could part of this money then be retained by the government to pay for schools to teach Native children? Gosford was instructed
that the chiefs' wishes were to be respected, and "any change of the present
System [of gifts] . . . should be made with the free Consent and Concurrence
of the Indians themselves, signified through their Chiefs." Behind these questions is the British government's desire to phase out the gifts, the Indian Department that administered them, and the role of Native nations as military
allies, "to relieve . . . the British Public, from all unnecessary Expenditure on
account of this Service."[51] In 1837, with the tension of the soon-to-arrive rebellions in the air, the government was still anxious to keep good relations
with Indigenous leaders, first, in case their military aid was required, and
second, for fear of an uprising of Native nations, of "great Discontent among
the Indians, and perhaps . . . Consequences of a very serious Nature."[52]

The chiefs of the Nations of the Canadas, who met with crown representatives at meetings specifically to discuss these two questions, were clear in their replies in favor of education and retaining the gifts. For example, Tekanasontie, grand chief of the village of Caughnawaga, said: "we are aware that our Children will reap great Benefit in receiving an Education." The chiefs stated, however, that they could not have the cost taken out of their gifts. Among other things, it was a question of being on equal footing with settler communities. As the chiefs of Saint Regis stated, "we hope in this respect to be put on a Footing with our Brethren the White Skins, who, we are informed, have their Children educated at the public Expense. If Schools are established amongst us on such a Footing, we will cheerfully send our Children to them."[53] The chiefs' reply demonstrates their awareness of the social situation in their communities, their acknowledgment of the value of education for their children, and their desire to be treated equally in the question of education, with the people of settler communities.

Unfortunately, the chiefs' replies regarding education were reported in such a way as to give a negative spin. L. J. Duchesnay, the superintendent of the Indian Department, wrote that it was impossible to gather children among those who live in the "Woods," or those who are not living in villages. He also states: "they never would willingly contribute in any way towards paying Part of the Expenses of a Schoolmaster and other Expenses attending a School."[54] This distortion of the chiefs' replies to questions regarding education is disturbing, especially in light of the subsequent history of residential schools.

After the rebellions, no longer needing Indigenous warriors as allies and no longer valuing their abilities in the field of battle, the government wanted to substitute agricultural tools for the traditional gifts of guns and ammunition to encourage settled farming. Guns were thought to encourage their "wild and savage state."[55] Indigenous peoples were expected to become farmers, to be like the waves of settlers arriving in great numbers in this period, all desiring land. The government moved Indigenous peoples from their status as essential military allies to a status where custodial care was required. The earlier respect for the chiefs' wishes was gone. During Lord Elgin's tenure, the move toward residential schools was initiated; in 1847 Indian Affairs consulted with Rev. Egerton Ryerson on setting up Indian industrial schools, based on a move toward assimilation and emancipation, to legally end the distinct status and identity of Indigenous peoples.

While Lord Elgin himself showed insight into the difficulties facing Indigenous peoples in their relations with colonial government, he supported

British government policies and worked to move them forward.[56] His writing on education was grounded in European beliefs in progress and cultural hierarchy of the period. However, he acknowledged the difficulties with the "Canadian system," which treated Indigenous peoples "partly as independent peoples and partly as infants under its guardianship," writing that it was likely "in the long run to prove as disastrous to them [Indigenous peoples] as that of the United States." This statement suggests that he took a critical view of British colonial policy. At the same time, he saw emancipation, which to Indigenous nations represented a loss of national identity and community, as a possible way out of this dilemma, showing the gap in understandings of Indigenous identity between Indigenous and European communities. Industrial schools, later called residential schools, were seen as a means to assimilation and were tied in colonial policy to emancipation. It was thought that after a period of education in an industrial school, an Indigenous person would be prepared to "start in independent life," apart from the "tribe of which he was a member."[57] This is an expression of Elgin's views on assimilation and the beginning of the idea of emancipation of later government policy, clearly at odds with Wendat identity and nationhood.

While the British government saw education as a means to assimilation, as French missionaries had earlier, Wendat communities followed educational strategies that furthered their community interests.[58] Seventeenth-century Wendat children went to Ursuline and Jesuit schools, possibly in accordance with Indigenous traditions of sending children to live with families in allied nations as a way of establishing and maintaining cordial relations, to further economic and political goals.[59] In the late eighteenth century this tradition continued. After the English takeover of Quebec in 1763, there was a dramatic shift in power and a diplomatic realignment; the chiefs of the Wendat community worked strategically to build relations with the British government. Students from Lorette, along with students from other Indigenous nations of the Saint Lawrence Valley (the nations of the Seven Fires), attended Moor's Indian Charity School and Dartmouth College, a Protestant school in New Hampshire. In a very different situation from the residential schools of the nineteenth and twentieth centuries, Indigenous students together with those from New England settler communities received a liberal arts education. Louis Vincent Sawatanen, from the Vincent family of Wendat chiefs, was one of these students. He graduated in 1781 as a teacher and interpreter, speaking French, Wendat, English, and Mohawk. He was the first member of an Indigenous community in the Canadas to receive a college degree. Assuring educational opportunities for their youth continued to be a priority among Wendat leaders. In 1791 the chiefs requested free tuition for Wendat students at the Séminaire de Québec, and such an agreement was kept among the records of the Vincent-Picard family of Wendat hereditary chiefs.[60]

Sending students to Dartmouth College was a strategic decision by the chiefs of the Saint Lawrence nations. The students' knowledge of English culture gave them an advantage in dealings with British political and legal systems. The new generation of leaders in their community were familiar with European society and taste, while also having grown up in a culture rich in Indigenous visual arts, with strong traditions of trade and diplomacy, with the importance of community and a sense of the Wendat Nation at the core. On Louis Vincent's return, he set up a school outside the influence of the Jesuit priests and moved forward with a legal process of land claims. As an outcome of this educational strategy, Wendat instructors had taught the community's children at a school in Wendake since at least 1794.[61] The school continued in the nineteenth century, a possible resistance to the industrial schools discussed by Lord Elgin in connection with emancipation.[62]

The value of this strategy was evident, as these students became future leaders in the community, with knowledge of settler culture as well as political and bureaucratic systems. They were well prepared to further Wendat interests. At the same time, knowledge of Wendat traditions and beliefs was highly valued; the work of members of the community who were keepers of wampum, language, songs, and traditions was respected by the community.[63]

The success of Wendat education policies in maintaining the unity of the community and sense of Indigenous identity is clearly seen through the writings of German academic Johann Georg Kohl and his record of the voice of Wendat students in their school and their assertion of their own Indigenous identity. He visited Lorette between 1854 and 1856, describing the Wendats as "educated and civilized." He visited the school there and spoke to the Wendat teacher and the children, recording their responses to his questions. Everything about the teacher and students went against Kohl's understanding of cultural identity, for instance, the "free and bold attitude" of the children.[64] He notes with surprise that the cultivated man who was the teacher identified himself as Wendat; in Kohl's words, he "acknowledged his savage origin, as do the children, when he questions them." Much like we saw with the adoptees addressed in the third chapter, he was surprised that Native people of mixed blood, as he describes the teacher and many of the children, identified with their Indigenous rather than European heritage. He writes of the appearance of the children, "some were as fair and rosy-cheeked as Europeans. Some however had the brown faces and harsh coal-black hair of the pure Iroquois." Similarly, he was shocked that they were "always able to tell from what race they were descended," by which he meant which nation. He reports that while most of the students identified themselves as Huron, there were students from Algonquin, Abenaki, Iroquois, and Amalekite (Maliseet and Mi'kmaq) communities.

Some Wendat children went on from the community school to attend the Ursuline school, the Petit Séminaire, and the Séminaire de Quebec. For example, Chief François-Xavier Picard Tahourenché attended the school at Lorette, studied classics at the Petit Séminaire in Quebec, and became a teacher and surveyor. He later used his professional training to help the Wendat community protect its lands. His son Paul Picard Tsawenhohi, with others in the community, followed the same path, studying at the Séminaire de Quebec and becoming the first notary or lawyer from the Wendat community. His sisters attended the Ursuline school.[65] At the same time, however, the community honored their culture keepers and the continuity of their traditional beliefs and customs.

The Vincent-Picard family histories illustrate the Wendat community's tradition of engaging with European institutions and building from these engagements to further the interests of their nation's identity and sovereignty. They demonstrate the differences between European perceptions of Indigenous communities in relation to education, and how the Wendats and other Indigenous nations of the Saint Lawrence viewed education. The Wendats saw the value of European education for their children and a simultaneous education in their own language, customs, and beliefs. This dual education suggests a strategy for cultural continuity, adapting to change as a means to not only survive but also prosper. Wendat resistance to assimilation, furthered through these strategies, continued into the twentieth century with successful resistance to government pressures of emancipation.[66]

LAND CLAIMS

Two statutes passed in 1850 illustrate further moves toward the assimilation of Indigenous peoples and how much British policy had changed between 1837 and the early 1850s. The first was the Act for the Better Protection of the Lands and Property of Indians in Lower Canada, which established a commissioner to hold Indigenous lands in trust for Indigenous peoples but with full power to do what the commissioner wished with that property. The second was the Act for the Better Protection of Indians in Upper Canada from Imposition. By this act no one could deal with Indigenous lands unless the Crown approved.[67] As the government represented its position, its main concern was to protect Indigenous peoples and their lands from abuse only until such time as they gave up their Indigenous identity and culture, to become what the government saw as assimilated, part of the dominant society. In fact, the government gave itself control over what happened to the land, although settlers and the lumber industry, the government's first interests, had been encroaching since the 1820s.[68] In 1857 the Civilization of Indian Tribes Act was passed, which expressly made assimilation its goal.[69]

From as early as the 1810s, Chief Tsawenhohi, Sawatanen's cousin, made several presentations to the Assembly of Lower Canada, mapping Wendat territories and arguing against settlers who denied the Wendats access to this territory.[70] By 1837 representatives of the Seven Fires Confederacy presented an address to Governor Gosford, describing the negative impact of settlers and the forestry industry on their territories: "Our ancestors used to make their living from the hunt, but that is impossible for us and it will be even more so for our children; the advance of European immigration has invaded our hunting territories, and has destroyed the immense forests with which these lands once were covered, and has made the wild animals vanish, that were the source of a good business for us, providing for all our needs in life. Now . . . this resource has been torn from us."[71] In 1843 Stanislas Bastien and others made a petition to Governor General Metcalfe concerning the loss of their hunting territory to colonization and the forestry industry, including in it their difficulties in finding alternative ways of supporting their families.[72] Importantly, Chief François-Xavier Picard Tahourenché, who presented the ceremonial address to Lord Elgin in 1852 to maintain smooth international relations, was also the surveyor whose efforts in monitoring the Department of Lands and Forests ensured that the nation's boundaries were accurately represented.[73]

This was the political context in which the Elgin trays were produced. It demonstrates the pressures of assimilation and loss of territory facing the Wendat community as well as the political acumen, forethought, and strategic planning of Wendat leadership. It supports the suggestion of a diplomatic role for the trays within the Great Lakes and Wendat tradition of bark scrolls and the Wendat tradition of creating connections with other nations to improve their relations and the success of political or trade negotiations.

CONCLUSION

The story of the Elgin trays illustrates the rich diplomatic history of the Wendat community and the political acumen of their leaders in their strategies to maintain a distinct identity as a nation. The narrative makes evident the conflicts between Wendat and British interests and brings into focus Wendat initiatives to resist assimilationist policies while at the same time maintaining close relations of trade and diplomatic exchange. The trays themselves demonstrate the adaptation of Wendat traditions to the shifting circumstances of European presence in a mode of communication that negotiated relations with colonial powers. Positioned at the center of a network of such political relations, the trays also cast fresh light on the roles of individuals in Wendat and settler communities, men and women such as Marguerite Vincent La8inonké, François-Xavier Picard Tahourenché, and Lord and Lady Elgin.

In this exploration of the trays' diplomatic meanings, we see connections between nineteenth-century chiefs such as Nicolas Vincent Tsawenhohi and François-Xavier Picard Tahourenché, and seventeenth- and eighteenth-century leaders such as Ochateguin, who negotiated military and trade relations with Champlain,[74] and Kondiaronk, the Wendat leader who was a key figure in negotiating the Peace of Montreal in 1701.[75] The Elgin trays, presented at a critical moment, their symbolic content a recognition of national and cultural identities, illustrate Wendat values of affiliation through diplomacy and the role of the gift in Wendat society as a means to do this.

NOTES

This chapter is based on my PhD dissertation, "Engaged Histories: Wendat Women's Souvenir Arts of Cultural Preservation and Entrepreneurial Invention," Carleton University, 2013.

1. Chris Gosden and Frances Larsen, "What Is a Museum?" in *Knowing Things: Exploring the Collections at the Pitt Rivers Museum, 1884–1945* (Oxford: Oxford University Press, 2007), 5.

2. Jonathan Lainey, *La "monnaie des sauvages"* (Quebec City: Les éditions du Septentrion, 2004), 29, 32, 33, 34, 39, 52, 62.

3. Marguerite Vincent Tehariolina, *La nation huronne* (Quebec City: Pelican, 1984), 321–39; L'abbé Lionel Saint-George Lindsay, *Notre-dame de la Jeune-Lorette* (Montreal: La cie de publication de la revue canadienne, 1900), 227, 238; Alain Beaulieu, "Les Hurons et la Conquête," *Recherches amérindiennes au Québec* (hereafter *RAQ*) 30, no. 3 (2000): 59–60.

4. Elizabeth Edwards, *Raw Histories* (Oxford: Berg, 2001), 2–3.

5. Ruth Phillips, *Trading Identities* (Montreal: McGill–Queen's University Press, 1998), 104.

6. Annette de Stecher, "Engaged Histories: Wendat Women's Souvenir Arts of Cultural Preservation and Entrepreneurial Invention" (PhD diss., Carleton University, 2013), 208.

7. Virginia N. Wade, *The Basic Stitches of Embroidery* (London: Victoria and Albert Museum, 1960), n.p.

8. Mrs. John Graves Simcoe, *The Diary of Mrs. John Graves Simcoe* (Toronto: William Briggs, 1911), 67.

9. Wade, *Basic Stitches of Embroidery*, n.p.

10. De Stecher, "Engaged Histories," 310.

11. Ruth Whitehead provides a detailed discussion of vegetable dyes in *Micmac Quillwork* (Halifax: Nova Scotia Museum, 1982), 66–71.

12. "Earl," *Encyclopedia Britannica*, 9th ed. (New York: Henry G. Allen, 1888), 595.

13. Ibid. The coronet of an earl and a countess are the same.

14. George Hamell, "Trading in Metaphors: The Magic of Beads," in *Proceedings of the 1982 Glass Trade Bead Conference* (Rochester, N.Y.: Rochester Museum and Science Center, 1983), 8–10.

15. Georges E. Sioui, *Huron-Wendat: The Heritage of the Circle* (Vancouver: University of British Columbia Press, 1999), 171.

16. Bruce Trigger, *The Children of Aataentsic* (Montreal: McGill–Queen's University Press, 1998 [1976]), 64.

17. Vincent Tehariolina, *La nation huronne*, 321–23.

18. François-Marc Gagnon, *The Codex Canadensis with the Writings of Louis Nicolas* (Montreal: McGill–Queen's University Press, 2011), 339.

19. Lindsay, *Notre-dame,* 30–33, 35; Père François-Xavier de Charlevoix de la Compagnie de Jésus, *Journal d'un voyage fait par ordre du roi dans l'Amérique Septentrionnale; Adresse a Madame la Duchesse de Lesdiguières* (Paris: Rollin Fils, 1744), vol. 3: 84.

20. Lindsay, *Notre-dame,* 236–37, 234.

21. François-Xavier Picard Tahourenché, *Journal de François-Xavier Picard Tahourenché,* Archives du Conseil de la Nation Huron-Wendat (hereafter ACNHW); Vincent Tehariolina, *La nation huronne*, 323–29.

22. Tahourenché, *Journal.*

23. Lindsay, *Notre-dame,* 236–39.

24. Vincent Tehariolina, *La nation huronne,* 328; scroll presented to Princess Louise and the Marquis of Lorne, 1883, British Museum, Am 1887.1208.19.

25. Vincent Tehariolina, *La nation huronne,* 326.

26. Lionel Saint-George Lindsay, "Notre-Dame de Lorette en La Nouvelle-France," in Alphonse Leclaire, ed., *La Revue canadienne,* vol. 2, no. 40 (1901): 335–36, 343–46, https://archive.org/details/p2revuecanadien40montuoft (accessed December 1, 2015).

27. Lainey, *La "monnaie,"* 81. Author's translation from the original French: "pour se placer à son niveau sur le plan politique."

28. Deborah Anna Logan, *The Hour and the Woman* (DeKalb: Northern Illinois University Press, 2002), 59.

29. Lady Mary Louisa Lambton, *Journal of Lady Mary Louisa Lambton*, Library and Archives Canada (LAC), 1938, Archival ref. no. R977-17-6-E, pgs. 81, 82, 83.

30. Linda H. Peterson, ed., *Autobiography: Harriet Martineau* (Peterborough: Broadview Press, 2007), 421.

31. Marie de l'Incarnation, *Word from New France: Selected Letters of Marie de l'Incarnation*, trans. and ed. Joyce Marshall (Toronto: Oxford University Press, 1967), 81–82.

32. Trigger, *Children of Aataentsic*, 523.

33. Richard White, *The Middle Ground* (Cambridge: Cambridge University Press, 1991), 194–95.

34. Amelia Murray, *Letters from the United States, Cuba, and Canada* (New York: Negro University Press, 1969), 79.

35. Correspondence, Bastien et al., Library and Archives Canada, archival ref. no. RG10, vol. 49: 30754–30757.

36. Jean Tanguay, "Marguerite Vincent La8inonkie, 'La femme habile aux travaux d'aiguille,'" *Rapport Supplementaire, 2007–29* (Ottawa: Historic Sites and Monuments Board of Canada, 2007), 2–4, 12–15.

37. Jean-Pierre Sawaya, "Les Amérindiens domiciliés et le protestantisme au XVIIIe siècle: Eleazar Wheelock et le Dartmouth College," *Historical Studies in Education/Revue d'histoire de l'éducation* (Fall 2010): 15.

38. Pierre Drouin and Margot Rankin, *Marguerite Vincent "La8inonkie,"* Formulaire de Demande-Personne, 2000-42 (Ottawa: Historic Sites and Monuments Board of Canada, 2000), 2154; for discussion of the Vincent family genealogy, see also chapter 3 of this book, and Jonathan Lainey and Thomas Peace, "Louis Vincent Sawatanen: premier bachelier autochtone canadien," in Gaston Deschênes et Denis Vaugeois, eds., *Vivre la Conquête: Des parcours individuels* (Quebec City: Les éditions du Septentrion, 2013), 204–14.

39. Jonathan Lainey, *La "monnaie,"* 148.

40. *Culture and Democracy: Lord and Lady Elgin in Canada, 1847–1854*, Exhibition, Rideau Hall, 2004.

41. Mireille Siouï, personal communication, Congres d'Études Wendat et Wyandot, June 14, 2012.

42. Lord Bruce and Henrietta Lidchi, Keeper of the Department of World Cultures, personal communication, National Museums of Scotland, October 29, 2009.

43. Lady Mary Louisa Lambton, *Journal*, 83.

44. Sydney Checkland, *The Elgins, 1766–1917* (Aberdeen: Aberdeen University Press, 1988), 120.

45. Jean-Pierre Sawaya, *François-Xavier Picard Tahourenché,* Formulaire de Demande-Personne, 2000-43 (Ottawa: Historic Sites and Monuments Board of Canada, 2000), 2179.

46. Picard Tahourenché, *Journal de Paul Picard*, January 13, June 24, 1852, ACNHW.

47. Jean-Pierre Sawaya, *Ignace-Nicolas Vincent Tsawenhohi*, formulaire de demande-personne, 2000-41 (Ottawa: Historic Sites and Monuments Board of Canada, 2000), 2115; Vincent Tehariolina, *La nation huronne*, 167.

48. Lindsay, *Notre-dame*, 234–36.

49. *Copies or Extracts of Correspondence since 1st April 1835, between the Secretary of State for the Colonies and the Governors of the British North American Provinces Respecting the Indians in Those Provinces* (London: House of Commons, 1839), 1–10.

50. Enfranchisement was a "policy tool for assimilation." Holding legal Indian status and being a standard Canadian citizen were seen by the Canadian government as incompatible. The policy of enfranchisement required that an Indigenous person give up their legal Indian status in order "to become a standard Canadian citizen." However, this would also mean they would have to give up legal recognition of their Indigenous identity. In consequence, they would lose any of the rights the Canadian government was obligated to fulfill for those who decided to retain their Indian status. Alan C. Cairns, "Aboriginal Peoples' Electoral Participation in the Canadian Community," *Electoral Insight* 4, no. 3 (November 2003): 2–3. http://publications.gc.ca/collections/Collection/SE2-1-5-3E.pdf (accessed December 1, 2015).

51. *Copies or Extracts*, 11, 40, 13. The role of the Indian Department, created in 1755 as a branch of the British military in North America, was to maintain good relations with Indigenous nations, secure their military allegiance to Britain, and administer the distribution of gifts to maintain this allegiance. The Indian Department remained a military responsibility until 1840 and the Act of Union, joining Upper and Lower Canada, when the governor general assumed oversight of the Indian Department.

52. Ibid., 1.

53. Ibid., 46, 42.

54. Ibid., 46.

55. Ibid., 37.

56. Theodore Walrond, ed., *Letters and Journals of James, Eighth Earl of Elgin*, 2nd ed. (London: John Murray, 1873), 158.

57. Ibid.

58. Trigger, *Children of Aataentsic*, 522–23.

59. Vincent Tehariolina, *La nation huronne*, 321–22; Trigger, *Children of Aataentsic*, 523–24.

60. Jonathan Lainey, "Le fonds Famille Picard: un patrimoine documentaire d'exception," *Revue de Bibliothèque du Québec* 2 (2010): 96, 98.

61. Sawaya, "Les Amérindiens domiciliés," 11–16.

62. Thaddeus Osgood, *The Canadian Visitor* (London: Hamilton and Adams, 1829), 24; Walrond, *Letters and Journals*, 158.

63. Sawaya, *François-Xavier Picard Tahourenché*, 2175–76.

64. Johann Georg Kohl, *Travels in Canada and through the States of New York and Pennsylvania*, trans. Mrs. Percy Sinnet (London: George Manwaring, 1861), 1:177–78.

65. Sawaya, *François-Xavier Picard Tahourenché*, 2175–76, citing the *Cahier* of Pierre-Albert Picard Tsichikwen, grandson of François-Xavier Picard.

66. Patrick Brunelle, "Les Hurons et l'émancipation," *RAQ*, 30, no. 3 (2000): 79–80. Emancipation was a term used by the Canadian government meaning the release of Indigenous peoples from their position as wards of the Canadian government to become full citizens. The Act for the Gradual Enfranchisement of Indians of 1869 was an attempt to "Canadianize" and assimilate Indigenous peoples into settler society, offering Indigenous men the same rights as other British subjects if they relinquished Indigenous status and rights.

67. The Royal Proclamation of October 7, 1763, made by George III at the end of the Seven Years' War, had actually begun the British move toward taking control of Indigenous territories. The proclamation forbade settlers from settling west of a line drawn along the Appalachian Mountains. While the proclamation appeared to have as its intention the desire to maintain good relations with Indigenous nations, in fact, it gave the British Crown a monopoly on land acquisitions from Indigenous peoples.

68. In 1824 Grand Chief Tsawenhohi made an address to the Lower Canada House of Assembly in which he asserted the Wendats' rights to their hunting territories and argued against the newly arrived settlers who denied them access. In 1843 a petition was presented to Governor General Sir Charles Metcalfe, outlining the difficulties faced by the Wendat community as a result of pressures of increased numbers of settlers and the forestry industry. Jean Tanguay, "Les règles d'alliance et l'occupation huronne du territoire," *RAQ* 30, no. 3 (2000): 28.

69. See An Act to Encourage the Gradual Civilization of the Indian Tribes . . . , June 10, 1857, available online at http://caid.ca/GraCivAct1857.pdf (accessed December 8, 2015). This was a precursor to the modern Indian Act.

70. Jocelyn Tehatarongnantase Paul, "Le territoire de chasse des hurons de Lorette," *RAQ* 30, no. 3 (2000): 12.

71. The Seven Fires was a confederation of Indigenous nations of the Saint Lawrence Valley, to which the Wendat Nation belonged. Other nations of the confederacy had also sent children to Dartmouth College. See Sawaya, "Les Amérindiens domiciliés"; The Seven Nations to Archibald, Earl of Gosford, Kahnawake, February 3, 1837, *Correspondence and Other Papers Relating to Canada, 1854–58* (Shannon: Irish University Press, 1969), 62.

72. Stanislas Bastien et al. to Charles Theophilus Metcalfe, November 15, 1843, LAC, RG10, vol. 598, 47026–47028.

73. Sawaya, *François-Xavier Picard Tahourenché*, 2176.

74. Samuel Champlain, *The Works of Samuel de Champlain in Six Volumes: Volume 2, 1608–1613*, ed. H. P. Biggar (Toronto: Champlain Society, 1925), 68, 105, 186.

75. Gilles Havard, *The Great Peace of Montreal of 1701* (Montreal: McGill–Queen's University Press, 2001), 170–73.

Concluding Voices

Kathryn Magee Labelle and Thomas Peace
In collaboration with Sallie Cotter Andrews (Wyandotte Nation
of Oklahoma), Darren English (Wyandot Nation of Kansas), Judith
Pidgeon-Kukowski (Wyandot Nation of Anderdon), Jonathan
Lainey (Nation huronne-wendat), John Nichols (Wyandot Nation of
Kansas), Beverlee Ann Pettit (Wyandotte Nation of Oklahoma),
and Linda Sioui (Nation huronne-wendat)

These six chapters have brought us *From Huronia to Wendakes,* tracing the themes of adversity, migration, and resilience that permeate Wendat history. The Wendats, despite their multiple relocations, maintained systems of power by preserving and expanding their political, cultural, and economic traditions to meet the needs of their contemporary circumstances.[1] Although operating within different time periods and geographies, the diverse Wendat identities that developed in each of these places remained connected to their predispersal culture. Most importantly, when taken together, the chapters in this book illustrate resilience in Wendat culture seldom associated with these communities after 1650. Far from becoming marginalized societies dependent on Indigenous and European neighbors, the Wendats developed a handful of unique strategies to maintain their position in new homelands.

Choosing to move toward strategic geographic locations was a foundational component to this process. By establishing themselves at the heart of North American trade and political networks, the Wendats blended the North American system of power in which they had lived for centuries with newly arrived European influences. Through contraction and expansion of Wendat society over the seventeenth and eighteenth centuries, the Wendats exhibited similar spatial practices everywhere they settled. On Gahoendoe Island the Wendats came together in an effort to hold onto Wendake Ehen as warfare and disease simultaneously threatened to rip the confederacy apart. This strategy was ultimately unsuccessful due to uncontrollable environmental factors, but its strategic significance is important to note. Wendat expansion into the Ohio Valley was similar. There the Wendats from Detroit maintained considerable authority over developing satellite communities. In both cases these tactics were employed in an effort to maintain influence over an expansive territory. The Wendats at Lorette took a comparable approach by maintaining and developing new long-distance relationships with neighboring Indigenous (and non-Indigenous) societies. These connections gave them a geographic prominence beyond what their numbers suggested they could sustain.

As a result of these geographic strategies, Wendats also preserved key cultural practices. Ancient traditions of material culture, council negotiations, and diplomatic roles were kept and employed regularly as the Wendats sought to move past starvation in the mid-seventeenth century and reestablish Wendake within the colonial borders of New France, British North America, the United States, and Canada. Even at times of significant change, such as the establishment of the Presbyterian mission at Sandusky, Catholic and predispersal spiritual practices continued. Similarly at Lorette, as Wendat village life became increasingly integrated into the colonial market economy, their ceremonial artistic rituals continued to dominate diplomatic practices. In the past scholars have seen these events as evidence of cultural erosion—a form of Canadian or American assimilation—but the evidence in this collection suggests they were rather a form of Wendat cultural conservation. Embedded within these significant developments in everyday Wendat, Wyandot, and Wyandotte life were cultural continuities that have not been adequately recognized.

Individuals played an important role in maintaining these systems of power. Wendats were not passive bystanders to an inevitable demise; instead, they responded creatively and often effectively to the obstacles they faced. Through their actions, Wendat individuals enabled their nations to thrive. At the turn of the nineteenth century, men such as Sawatanen at Lorette and Barnet at Sandusky brought new influences into their communities, while people such as Anguirot, André Otehiondi, and Nicolas Orontony extended

Wendat influence into new territories. Later, during the nineteenth century, people such as Marguerite Vincent La8inonké, Maurice Bastien, and François-Xavier Picard Tahourenché capitalized on the nascent mid-eighteenth-century development of Wendat craft production, expanding the influence of Wendat culture on an industrial scale.

Although most of these examples are men, this research simultaneously highlights the important role of women in Wendat society. As most of our chapters demonstrate, women's councils and female leadership remained integral to Wendat life throughout the seventeenth, eighteenth, and nineteenth centuries, guiding communal decisions and providing direction in times of crisis. Wendat women leaders continued to shape migration, economic ventures, and political alliances through creative strategizing. By highlighting these individuals and the important role of women within these communities, we hope to provide students of Wendat and North American history tangible examples of Wendat activism, thus reorienting the historiographical discourse away from a narrative of destruction and toward one that more accurately conveys these communities' complexity, vibrancy, and innovative spirits. Without denying the challenges and dark periods within Wendat history, this new historiographical narrative better reflects the continued presence and importance of present-day Wendat, Wyandot, and Wyandotte Nations on the North American sociopolitical landscape and the agency of their Wendat ancestors.

Although this book makes a number of important observations and offers new interpretations of Wendat history, the collection itself is far from complete. The nature of a project such as this—anchored as it is in doctoral-level research—lends itself to inevitable gaps and outstanding questions. There is a need for more direct comparisons, incorporating Wendat pasts into larger reflections on Indigenous and North American history. We would have liked to include more on the migrations and communities of western Wendats, especially in the late nineteenth and early twentieth centuries. The chapters on Lorette, for example, demonstrate important continuities that indicate that this was not a marginal nation. Far from migrating to Quebec as a society weakened by warfare and disease, the Wendats who settled on the banks of the Lada8anna River rebounded relatively quickly. Within a century, they had rebuilt their society and maintained a prominent place on the northeastern landscape, despite their small numbers. This in turn, as chapters 5 and 6 illustrate, enabled the Wendats to capitalize on their local position near the colonial administration at Quebec as well as more global economic and industrial developments. Did the western communities have similar experiences? More research needs to be done to adequately address this question. As a book focused on emerging scholarship, we can only include what has been accomplished, pointing toward subjects where future research is necessary.

Also worth noting is the fact that none of the authors grew up in Indigenous communities, nor are any of us Wendat. Thus, our suggestions and questions remain steeped in an outsider's epistemology. Although our research seemed "complete" in terms of academic responsibilities, we acknowledge that in many cases our dissertations were the results of isolated research and that official and more structured relationships with the modern Wendat, Wyandot, and Wyandotte Nations, with the hope of hearing their opinions and gaining their guidance, will inevitably strengthen the work. We also know that this kind of collaboration is critical in terms of conducting further research beyond our graduate studies. It is with this in mind that from the very inception of this manuscript, following a Wendat studies symposium at Wendake, we sought consultation with tribal historians, archivists, and elders.

The process of putting this book together began in late 2012 with an initial correspondence with the grand chiefs of the four modern Wendat communities. We asked these leaders if they would be willing to provide contact information for individuals within their nations that could comment on our research and provide reflective feedback to the work that had been completed and was to be included in the manuscript. We were unsure of what kind of reaction we would receive, being fully aware that for many Indigenous people, "research" is a loaded term with many centuries of negative and abusive practices on the part of non-Indigenous scholars.[2] Certainly many would follow Wendat scholar Georges Sioui in arguing that part of the decolonizing process is to have history written from a Wendat perspective and produced by tribal members.[3] This is the official stance of the Conseil de la Nation huronne-wendat at Wendake, Quebec. Having been the subjects of numerous histories dictated by colonialist historians and anthropologists, the council maintains that they would rather write their own history. As we identify in the introduction, in cases where tribal governments were unable to participate in our formal requests, we reached out to Wendat, Wyandot, and Wyandotte friends and colleagues to comment on the text. Their opinions, therefore, must be understood as unique and independent from the official political bodies associated with their nations, while their status as respected members of their communities still allowed them to provide important context and insight from within Wendat societies.

In order to make this feedback meaningful for the book, as well as respecting the time of our Wendat, Wyandot, and Wyandotte collaborators, we asked each author to submit a ten-page prospectus of the chapter they planned to contribute to the project. Together with a table of contents and brief outline of our goals, these mini-chapters were sent to our Wendat partners alongside five questions to guide their reviews of our work:

1. What are the strengths of the overall project?
2. What are the strengths of particular chapters?
3. How does the research of these emerging scholars contribute to the preservation and promotion of Wendat and Wyandot history?
4. What is your reaction to the types of research methodology and topics covered in this book?
5. Are there areas of research that are missing from this book? If so, what topics or themes would you like to see in future projects to address these gaps?

Members of the Wendat, Wyandot, and Wyandotte Nations responded at length, providing written reports that included encouragement, critiques, and suggestions for future research. Jonathan Lainey (Nation huronne-wendat) reviewed our process in the following way:

> The vast majority of our history is still written by non-Wendat scholars. The Wendat can hardly control the image of their past. How often do we see researchers working on Wendat subjects as if it was a simple passive object of research, like rocks or flowers? As a society, the Wendat are still alive and have something to say about their past, its interpretation by others and its implications today. In this project, at many different stages, some authors have generously consulted with community members, not to seek their approval on their results, but to seek their advice, help, and opinions. We can only warmly applaud such a methodological approach.

From these responses we then expanded each chapter to reflect both their comments and our own dissertation research. We found these perspectives invaluable and recognized that their expertise could give an important window into the "state of the field" if incorporated into the text. Consequently, they gave us permission to publish their opinions as part of this book. Below we have synthesized their comments, but you can read their direct feedback in full on the website *Active History*.[4] These Wendat, Wyandot, and Wyandotte responses are an important indication of the vast and varied experiences of both modern and historic Wendat peoples, while highlighting their commonalities as well.

Despite Lainey's positive framing of our project, each of the authors recognize that our process, as outlined here, is far from perfect. By the time this manuscript began to take shape, our dissertation work was in its final stages, if not already complete. As research produced within a university program, this work was deeply shaped by supervisors, committees, and the broader institutions in which we studied. Though we had some control over these processes and take full ownership over the final products, the degree to which we interacted with present-day Wendat, Wyandot, and Wyandotte peoples varied. Ideally we all would have liked to have created more collaborative, community-based projects from the earliest stages of our graduate work. This desire to move beyond our doctoral work was one of the motivations for creating this book. We believe that through the approach we have taken here we have been able to begin seeking meaningful relationships and best practices for future research.

• • •

The Wendat, Wyandot, and Wyandotte experts with whom we consulted responded to the manuscript in diverse ways. Some of the feedback focused on each chapter individually, while others took a more global approach. In the rest of this conclusion we have synthesized this feedback in order to highlight some of the important themes and contextual information that helped shape the manuscript as it developed.

In her comments, Judith Kukowski (Wyandot of Anderdon Nation) emphasized the continuity of a distinct Wendat, Wyandot, and Wyandotte identity. "To those who say we are assimilated," Kukowski states, "I say hogwash!" In drawing this out, she notes the continuing importance of clan, kinship, and the role of women in Wendat society. In her response to Kathryn Labelle's chapter, for example, Kukowski observed that in the past the Women's Elders Council and its continuing role in Wyandot society has not been given the attention it deserves for maintaining this identity. Pointing to another area where deeper understanding is needed, Kukowski called attention to the absence of Catholicism and discussion of the Anderdon Nation in Michael Cox's chapter on nineteenth-century Wyandot Christianity. From her perspective, these are important issues. In order for us to better understand them, there is a need for translation and "thorough study" of the Jesuit missionary Pierre Potier's writings. For her, Potier's writings are "the missing link in our Wendat history."[5]

Jonathan Lainey took a different tack by reflecting on our collective position not only as outsiders to Wendat communities but also working within a primarily anglophone historiographical environment. Lainey states, "The place of the Wendat in Canadian history has a direct impact on the weight of contemporary land claims. Historical interpretations that view the Wendat as poor, dependent refugees seeking help from the French rather than as an influential people who moved within their territory and kept a central place in a vast, strong, and ancient network of Native nations have present-day consequences. It is easy to guess, though, which scenario the government of Quebec would rather consider as the 'historical truth.'" For Lainey, the differences in our interpretations from those espoused by francophone scholars partially derive from our position living and working outside of Quebec. In addition to these comments, it is important for us to explicitly note that Lainey's influence in our collective work is substantial. As a longtime archivist at Library and Archives Canada, and now curator of First Peoples at the Canadian Museum of History, as well as a scholar with an important record of publication on Wendat history, Lainey has played a significant role in shaping the direction and source material used in many of our doctoral dissertations.

Linda Sioui (Nation huronne-wendat) highlighted the need to continue working against the historiographical and popular narrative of Wendat destruction, emphasizing that "this side of history has been perpetuated for way too long." For her, questions such as "How did Wendats negotiate their removal?" and "What criteria informed these decisions?" have never seriously been asked about this moment in Wendat history. Though the influence of global imperial pressures on the Wendats is important to acknowledge, Sioui emphasizes that this did not implicitly mean the destruction or assimilation of minority cultures. Developing from her work on Wendat and Wyandotte identity markers, she emphasized that many of the observations Peace, Gettler, and de Stecher made about the eighteenth- and nineteenth-century Wendats at Lorette continue in present-day Wendat society.

Sioui's comments also helped develop some of the more specific aspects of Gettler's and de Stecher's chapters. After reading Gettler's chapter, in which he stated that Wendat land known as the Quarante Arpents and Rocmont was largely uninhabited and surrendered to the state at the turn of the twentieth century, Sioui responded to this claim by pointing to her own family history with this place:

> Among other Siouis, my great-grandfather was there with his family. There are old pictures of houses and barns on the Quarante Arpents reserve, and my old aunt Antoinette (who passed away a few years ago) remembered part of her childhood there.
>
> Some Siouis, including my great-grandfather, went to the auction sale that day in the hope of repurchasing his two lots of land. He did so. He did first and second payment and it cannot be found anywhere in the archives what happened next. All we know is passed on by oral tradition in the family: my great-grandfather unbuilt his house, one plank at a time, and rebuilt it in Wendake. A couple of more Siouis had also purchased their land, but for unknown and undocumented reasons, had to move back to Wendake. The RG 10 collections [Indian Affairs Records at Library and Archives Canada] contain much correspondence and documentation on the Quarante Arpents, but some other evidences seem to be missing from the archives.
>
> The Minister of Justice at the time, Charles Fitzpatrick, was MP for the riding where the Quarante Arpents were located. Since Indians didn't vote back in those days, he wanted to "clear the land" of the Indians, have it surveyed and sold to potential voters. Again, see collection RG 10 and other archives at the Conseil de la Nation huronne-wendat for further information.

Likewise, in her reflections on Annette de Stecher's chapter, Sioui offered additional insight into moosehair embroidery: "The nuns taught embroidery with threads. The Huron girls, back in their village, used a substitute of moose hair (which hunters brought back) as a means of replacement. The techniques used were clearly taught by the nuns, but the moose hair came with the Huron-Wendat. They used whatever material they had in their home environment to create Victorian artwork, clearly influenced by the fashion of the times." In both cases, as with all of these commentaries, the authors took these comments into consideration as they put together the final drafts of their chapters.

For John Nichols (Wyandot Nation of Kansas) it was the geographic and chronological scope of the text that drew his attention. Nichols found the chapters "helpful in seeing some of the patterns which were not as visible to us before." From this foundation, Nichols provides an important perspective on aspects of his people's history that are not reflected directly in our book but resonate with important themes in some chapters. Nichols writes that the Wyandots of Kansas found themselves as a buffer between migrant and Plains tribes and the United States. "We found ways to control our own destinies and refused to simply be victims. Like our cousins we chose education as a tool to help us survive. We continued our tradition of mobility to continue linking our people. When the Territory of Kansas was established we found ourselves in the front lines of a war we did not ask for. 'Bleeding Kansas' and the struggle between free-state and pro-slave ideologies put us between the warring factions, geographically, culturally, and ideologically." From this place in between, Nichols suggests that Wyandot relationships with town companies and slavery took on forms similar to those developed in response to outside influence by eighteenth- and early nineteenth-century Wendat and Wyandot nations discussed in the book. "No matter who loses," Nichols wrote to us, "there would still be Wendat on the winning side who can look to the good of the people."

For Darren English (Wyandot Nation of Kansas) the chapters evoked a reflection on the nature of history and its production. Specifically, English wonders about the accuracy of the *Jesuit Relations*. What if we took their creation more seriously and questioned the intentions of their authors, the process through which they navigated Jesuit ecclesiastic structures and how they were employed and deployed by subsequent French and British imperial endeavors? Perhaps the original Jesuit letters were "intended as a campaign of disinformation" that—in their emphasis on Wendat dispersal and destruction—helped the Wendats safely rebuild their communities. Maybe, English suggests, "When they said that the Wendats were scattered to the winds there may have been more calculation involved."

Sallie Cotter Andrews (Wyandotte Nation of Oklahoma) provided her feedback chapter by chapter. In her comments about the first chapter she emphasized the necessity of telling the story of the survival of the Wendats in the mid-seventeenth century. Chapter 2 was similarly well received, especially in its emphasis on Wendat agency and the continuity of the clan system. She questions, though, some of Sturtevant's statements about the identity of the people at Sandusky and Detroit, particularly as it relates to the influence of the church and the divide between the Tionontate at Sandusky and Attignawantan at Detroit. For chapter 3, Andrews saw similarities with present-day issues in which "the Wyandotte Nation has 'land held in trust' for various gaming operations and economic development—in a way, exhibiting the same skill set that Sawatanen had in his day." It was influential Wyandotte families that were of most interest in chapter 4. Andrews points out that both Barnet and Northrop are common Wyandot family names and suggests greater genealogical investigation. Pointing to her own connections to the Presbyterian Church, Andrews indicates that the direction of Cox's research is an important avenue to continue pursuing. In chapter 5 her focus was on the similarities between Lorette and Western Wyandot communities. She points to the use of similar strategies regarding the adoption of settler economic practices and the political consequences that this has had for the Wyandots of Kansas and Oklahoma. In making her comments, she encouraged Gettler to reflect more deeply on the themes of strategic thinking emphasized in earlier chapters. Her reaction to chapter 6 was somewhat similar, though here she emphasized the importance and continuity of public performance and its impact relative to her own people's political position both in Indian Country and relative to her settler neighbors. In sum, for Andrews themes of education, standing up for territorial rights, and strategic use of the market permeate the book. "This is the same as today," she suggests. "[It] still works."

Beverlee Ann Pettit (Wyandotte Nation of Oklahoma) approached the manuscript from her position as a Wyandotte woman, storyteller, poet, historian, and editor, while also trying to view the text as an outsider. From this position, she emphasized an important theme in the book by illustrating how cultural, linguistic, social, and spiritual bonds have strengthened Wendat communities, allowing Wendat and Wyandot peoples to "live anywhere and still be part of the greater village." Her commentary also called us to account, suggesting that throughout the book we could have included more scholarship written by Wendat historians such as Georges Sioui. As a starting point for scholarship that draws Wendat, Wyandot, and Wyandotte histories together, however, Pettit sees the manuscript as a "book with promise" for fostering a broader discussion that will continue into the future.

· · ·

Though diverse in their commentaries, there were also important continuities between the responses. Most prominent was an emphasis on community, nation, and confederacy. Despite distance and national borders, our partners consistently reinforced the importance of these concepts to themselves and their ancestors, encouraging us to explore the nature of these relationships throughout our projects. Beverlee Ann Pettit explained: "I was full of emotion and found the information soothing and confirming to my soul in that I have long believed our people, villages, and communities were held together by culture, language, and deep social and spiritual bonds. All of which create 'invisible' boundary lines, unlike the lines drawn on a map for only a specific region."

Sallie Cotter Andrews made similar remarks as she read our work, asking, "I wonder if the mention of 'continued to describe themselves as part of the village' could be emphasized more, because Wendat means 'villager.' Community is everything to the Wendat people, and still is today." Linda Sioui, however, calls for a more careful use of language. Rather than using the word "community," Sioui believes that "nation" and "confederacy" are terms that better describe the relationships in Wendake. "The term 'community' (*communauté* in French) is too reductive. . . . Wendake is a community, but together, with the Wyandottes, we are the 'Confederacy.'" It is for this reason that we have avoided using the term "community" in our introduction and conclusion in favor of specific references to each nation, or, when writing more generally, we have used the generic term "nation" or "confederacy."

John Nichols found that the connections between each chapter clarified his understanding of the Wendat diaspora. Nichols states:

Many of the experiences and patterns discussed in this book are as demonstrable in Kansas as elsewhere. We were part of a Diaspora getting here and we struggled to survive as did our ancestors. We found ourselves being part of a "buffer zone" with the Permanent Indian Frontier. The same nations who had served as a defensive buffer in Detroit were our neighbors here. This time we were the buffer between other Emigrant (or Immigrant, depending on your viewpoint) Tribes and the Plains Tribes on the one side and the citizens of the United States on the other. We found ways to control our own destinies and refused to simply be victims. Like our cousins we chose education as a tool to help us survive. We continued our tradition of mobility to continue linking our people.

For Judith Kukowski, continuity and Wendat resilience were of central importance. She wrote: "Every society changes. The Wendats of today certainly express their culture differently than those of 1650 or even 1710. Yet throughout all the years of Iroquois persecution, and wars with foreign invading governments, and the years of famine, we have survived."

While community, nation, and confederacy were certainly major themes throughout the feedback, new directions in research and a desire to work with scholars to create meaningful, Wendat-guided projects were of equal importance. Similar to Jonathan Lainey's comments cited above, Darren English believes the work to be a "fresh perspective." Sioui agreed, though she emphasizes that it is also necessary for the Wendats to write their own history, as part of the decolonizing process:

> This book presents itself in a fresh and different light and attempts to provide insight into a Huron-Wendat and Wyandot perspective, since history didn't only happen from a colonial point of view. The Huron-Wendat and Wyandot contingents reshaped, adapted to their new environment with attempts to reestablish their cultural and political pattern. As I have stated in my own research, the pressures by the global economy on cultures does not necessarily lead to the disappearance or assimilation of minority cultures. I can only agree with those that state that there exists a much needed call to *reorient school curriculums and post-secondary lectures,* to bring to light, and in spite of major global influence, the resilience and adaptation capacity of the people whose history is being told. Further on, Andrew Sturtevant states that *colonialism had eroded the separate identity of the Wendats.* If this is the case, then decolonizing history would perhaps help us regain part of it. It is our people, first, that need to decolonize, and create our 'school of thought' (*école de pensée*). But this present manuscript will help pave the way to change, hopefully.

These comments are invaluable. Through this collaborative process, they have not only reshaped many of our original narratives but have also inspired future projects, results that have fostered relationships beyond the book and academia. Thus, the authors of this volume are indebted not only to the ancestors of the Wendat, Wyandot, and Wyandotte peoples (who are the subjects of our research) but their modern descendants as well. It is these communities, who exist today in both Canada and the United States, that continue to grapple with the legacies of the historical studies highlighted throughout this text.

Echoing what Chief English stated in her prologue, we have put this book together not with the expectation that it is perfect or a final word about Wendat history, but rather so that it will be "read by many; and may it inspire others to build upon a foundation of understanding and respect for the processes that lead to disruption and renewal in the lives of people." *From Huronia to Wendakes* builds on the work of Wendat, Wyandot, and Wyandotte historians and knowledge keepers and the extensive scholarship produced on their pre-1650 history, but in bringing together new research and Wendat, Wyandot, and Wyandotte perspectives, we collectively hope that this book marks an opportunity for new approaches to Wendat, Wyandot, and Wyandotte histories. In many ways, it is from this place that we seek to begin again and anew.

NOTES

1. Elizabeth Mancke, "Spaces of Power in the Early Modern Northeast," in Stephen Hornsby and John Reid, eds., *New England and the Maritime Provinces: Connections and Comparisons* (Montreal: McGill–Queen's University Press, 2005), 32. Both editors also develop this idea in their own work. See Thomas Peace, "Two Conquests: Aboriginal Experiences of the Fall of New France and Acadia" (PhD diss., York University, 2011), 11–18, and Kathryn Magee Labelle, *Dispersed but Not Destroyed: A History of the Seventeenth-Century Wendat People* (Vancouver: University of British Columbia Press, 2013), chap. 10.

2. Linda Tuhiwai Smith, *Decolonizing Methodologies: Research and Indigenous Peoples* (London: Zed Books, 1999).

3. Georges E. Sioui, *Pour une autohistoire amérindienne: Essai sur les fondements d'une morale sociale* (Sillery, Que.: Les Presses de l'Université Laval, 1989).

4. See http://activehistory.ca/from-huronia-to-wendakes-wendat-responses/.

5. Recently John Steckley has produced a book about the eighteenth-century Wyandot that draws extensively on this material. See John Steckley, *Eighteenth-Century Wyandot: A Clan-Based Society* (Waterloo, Ont.: Wilfrid Laurier University Press, 2014). See also Robert Toupin, *Les Écrits de Pierre Potier,* 2 vols. (Ottawa: Les Presses de l'Université d'Ottawa, 1996).

Further Reading

SECONDARY SOURCES ON THE WENDAT PEOPLE

Anderson, Karen. *Chain Her by One Foot: The Subjugation of Native Women in Seventeenth-Century New France*. New York: Routledge, 1991.

Beaulieu, Alain. "Les Hurons et la Conquête: Un nouvel éclairage sur le 'traité de Murray.'" *Recherches amérindiennes au Québec (RAQ)* 30, no. 3 (2000): 53–63.

Beaulieu, Alain, Stéphanie Béreau, and Jean Tanguay. *Les Wendats du Québec: Territoire, économie et identité, 1650–1930*. Quebec City: Les éditions GID, 2013.

Carpenter, Roger. *The Renewed, the Destroyed, the Remade: The Three Thought Worlds of the Iroquois and the Huron, 1609–1650*. East Lansing: Michigan State University Press, 2004.

Clarke, Peter Dooyentate. *Origin and Traditional History of the Wyandotts and Sketches of Other Indian Tribes of North America: True Traditional Stories of Tecumseh and His League in the Years 1811 and 1812*. Toronto: Hunter, Rose, 1870.

Clifton, James A. *Hurons of the West: Migrations and Adaptations of the Ontario Iroquoians, 1650–1704*. Ottawa: National Museum of Man, 1977.

———. "The Re-emergent Wyandot: A Study in Ethnogenesis on the Detroit River Borderland, 1747." In K. G. Pryke and L. L. Kulisek, eds., *Papers from the Western District Conference*. Windsor, Ont.: Essex County Historical Society and Western District Council, 1983, 1–15.

Delâge, Denys. *Le pays renversé: Amérindiens et Européens en Amérique du Nord-Est, 1600–1664*. Montreal: Boréal, 1991.

———. "La tradition de commerce chez les Hurons de Lorette-Wendake." *RAQ* 30, no. 3 (2000): 35–51.

Garrad, Charles, *Petun to Wyandot: The Ontario Petun from the Sixteenth Century*. Ottawa: University of Ottawa Press, 2014.

Gettler, Brian. "La consommation sous réserve: les agents indiens, la politique locale et les épiceries à Wendake aux XIXe et XXe siècles." *Bulletin d'histoire politique* 20, no. 3 (Spring 2012): 170–85.

Gérin, Léon. "The Hurons of Lorette." In *Report on the Ethnological Survey of Canada*. London: British Association for the Advancement of Science, 1900.

Goudreau, Serge. "Étienne Ondiaraété (1742–1830): Un chef huron du village de Lorette." *Mémoires de la Société généalogique canadienne-française* 54, no. 3 (Winter 2003): 269–88.

―――. "Les Hurons de Lorette au 18e siècle." *Mémoires de la Société généalogique canadienne-française* 63, no. 2 (Summer 2012): 125–47.

Hale, Horatio. "A Huron Historical Legend." *Magazine of American History,* December 1883, 475–83.

―――. "Four Huron Wampum Records: A Study of Aboriginal American History and Mneumonic Symbols." *Journal of Anthropological Institute,* February 1897, 254–97.

Heidenreich, Conrad. *Huronia: A History and Geography of the Huron Indians, 1600–1650.* Toronto: McClelland and Stewart, 1971.

Hunter, Andrew F. *Notes of Sites of Huron Villages in the Township of Medonte (Simcoe County).* Toronto: Ontario Archeological Report, 1901.

Labelle, Kathryn Magee. "History Repeats Itself: Huron Childrearing Attitudes, Eurocentricity, and the Importance of Indigenous Worldview." *Canadian Journal for Native Education* 31, no. 2 (2008): 4–14.

―――. "'They Are the Life of the Nation': Women and War in Nadowek Society." *Canadian Journal of Native Studies* 28, no. 1 (2008): 119–38.

―――. "'They Spoke Only in Sighs': The Loss of Leaders and Life in Wendake, 1632–1640." *Journal of Historical Biography* 6 (Spring 2010): 1–33.

―――. *Dispersed but Not Destroyed: A History of the Seventeenth-Century Wendat.* Vancouver: University of British Columbia Press, 2013.

Lainey, Jonathan. *La "monnaie des sauvages": Les colliers de wampum d'hier à aujourd'hui.* Quebec City: Les éditions du Septentrion, 2004.

―――. "Les colliers de porcelaine de l'époque coloniale à aujourd'hui." *RAQ* 35, no. 2 (2005): 61–73.

Lainey, Jonathan, and Thomas Peace. "Louis Vincent Sawantanan, premier bachelier autochtone canadien." In Gaston Deschênes and Denis Vaugeois, eds., *Vivre la Conquête: à travers plus de 25 parcours individuels.* Vol. 1. Quebec City: Les éditions du Septentrion, 2013. 204–14.

Lavoie, Michel. *"C'est ma seigneurie que je réclame": Le lutte des Hurons de Lorette pour la seigneurie de Sillery, 1658–1890.* Montreal: Boréal, 2009.

Lindsay, Lionel St. George. *Notre-Dame de la Jeune-Lorette.* Montreal: La cie de publication de la revue canadienne, 1900.

Lozier, Jean-François. "Les origines huronnes-wendates de Kanesatake." *RAQ* 44, nos. 2–3 (2014): 103–16.

Mithun, Marianne. "Untangling the Huron and the Iroquois." *International Journal of American Linguistics* 51, no. 4 (October 1985): 504–7.

Otterbein, Keith F. "Huron vs. Iroquois: A Case Study in Inter-Tribal Warfare." *Ethnohistory* 26, no. 2 (Spring 1979): 141–52.

Paul, Jocelyn Tehatarongnantase. "Le territoire de chasse des Hurons de Lorette." *RAQ* 30, no. 3 (2000): 5–20.

Peace, Thomas. "The Slow Process of Conquest: Huron-Wendat Responses to the Conquest of Quebec, 1697–1791." In Phillip Buckner and John G. Reid, eds., *Revisiting 1759: The Conquest of Canada in Historical Perspective.* Toronto: University of Toronto Press, 2012.

Podruchny, Carolyn, and Kathryn Magee Labelle. "Jean de Brébeuf and the Wendat Voices of Seventeenth-Century New France." In "Part of a special issue on Relazioni/Relations," edited by Tom Cohen and Germaine Warkentin, special issue of *Renaissance and Reformation/Renaissance et Réforme* 34, nos. 1–2 (Fall 2011–Winter 2012): 97–126.

Pomedli, Michael M. *Ethnophilosophical and Ethnolinguistic Perspectives on the Huron Indian Soul.* Lewiston, N.Y.: Edwin Mellen, 1991.

Poirier, Jean. *La Toponymie des Hurons-Wendats.* Québec: Commission de Toponymie du Québec, 2001.

Sawaya, Jean-Pierre. *La fédération des Sept Feux de la vallée du Saint-Laurent: XVIIe au XIXe siècle.* Quebec City: Les éditions du Septentrion, 1998.

———. *Alliances et dépendance: Comment la couronne britannique a obtenu la collaboration des Indiens de la vallée du Saint-Laurent entre 1760–1774.* Quebec City: Les éditions du Septentrion, 2002.

Seeman, Erik R. *The Huron-Wendat Feast of the Dead: Indian-European Encounters in Early North America.* Baltimore: Johns Hopkins University Press, 2011.

Sioui, Georges E. *Huron-Wendat: The Heritage of the Circle.* Vancouver: University of British Columbia Press, 1999.

Sioui, Linda. *La réaffirmation de l'identité wendate/wyandotte à l'heure de la mondialisation.* Wendake: Hannenorak, 2012.

Steckley, John. *Untold Tales: Three 17th Century Huron.* Ajax, Ont.: R. Kerton, 1981.

———. "How the Huron Became Wyandot: Onomastic Evidence." *Onamastica Canadiana* 70, no. 198 (1988): 59–72.

———. "Wendat Dialects and the Development of the Huron Alliance." *Northeast Anthropology* 54, no. 2 (1997): 23–36.

———. *Words of the Huron.* Waterloo: University of Wilfred Laurier Press, 2007.

———. "The 1747 Wyandot Elders Council." *Northeastern Anthropology* 75–76 (Spring–Fall 2008): 93–111.

———, ed. *The First French-Huron Dictionary, by Father Jean de Brébeuf and His Jesuit Brethren.* Lewiston, N.Y.: Edwin Mellen, 2010.

———. *The Eighteenth-Century Wyandot: A Clan-Based Study.* Waterloo: Wilfrid Laurier University Press, 2014.

Steckley, John, and Charles Garrad. "A Review of *The Re-emergent Wyandot.*" *Kewa: Newsletter of the London Chapter, Ontario Archaeological Society* 84, no. 7 (October 1984): 10–14.

Sturtevant, Andrew. "'Inseparable Companions' and Irreconcilable Enemies: The Hurons and Odawas of French Détroit, 1701–1738." *Ethnohistory* 60, no. 2 (2013): 219–43.

Tanguay, Jean. "Les règles d'alliance et l'occupation huronne du territoire." *RAQ* 30, no. 3 (2000): 21–34.

———. "Marguerite Vincent La8inonkie, 'La femme habile aux travaux d'aiguille.'" *Rapport Supplementaire, 2007–29.* Ottawa: Historic Sites and Monuments Board of Canada, 2007.

Tooker, Elizabeth. *An Ethnography of the Huron Indians, 1615–1649.* Washington, D.C.: U.S. Government Printing Office, 1964.

Trigger, Bruce. *The Children of Aataentsic: A History of the Huron People to 1660.* Montreal: McGill–Queen's University Press, 1976.

———. *The Huron: Farmers of the North.* New York: Holt, Rinehart and Winston, 1969.

———, ed. *Handbook of North American Indians.* 15 vols. Washington, D.C.: Smithsonian Institution, 1978.

Vachon, André. "L'affaire du Long-Sault: Valeur de la source huronne." *Revue de l'Université Laval* 18, no. 6 (February 1964): 495–515.

Vaugeois, Denis. *The Last French and Indian War: An Inquiry into a Safe-Conduct Issued in 1760 that Acquired the Value of a Treaty in 1990.* Translated by Käthe Roth. Montreal-Kingston: McGill–Queen's University Press, 2002.

———, ed. *Les Hurons de Lorette.* Quebec City: Les éditions du Septentrion, 1996.

Vincent Tehariolina, Marguerite. *La nation huronne.* Quebec City: Pelican, 1984.

Warrick, Gary. "European Infectious Disease and Depopulation of the Wendat-Tionontate (Huron-Petun)." *World Archeology* 35, no. 2 (October 2003): 258–75.

———. *A Population History of the Huron-Petun, A.D. 500–1650.* New York: Cambridge University Press, 2008.

Contributors

THE AUTHORS

Michael Leonard Cox is an assistant professor of history at San Diego Mesa College. His research addresses the intersections of religion, spirituality, culture, and social life in Indigenous communities. He completed his dissertation, "The Ohio Wyandots: Religion and Society on the Sandusky River, 1795–1843," in 2016 at the University of California, Riverside.

Annette de Stecher is an assistant professor of Native American Art in the Department of Art and Art History, Colorado University, Boulder. She received her doctorate in Aboriginal visual arts and culture from Carleton University in 2013. Her thesis, "Engaged Histories: Wendat Women's Souvenir Arts," explores the visual arts traditions of the Wendat First Nation of Wendake, Quebec. De Stecher was a Research Fellow at the Canadian Museum of Civilization (now the Canadian Museum of History) and a Social Sciences and Humanities Research Council (SSHRC) postdoctoral fellow at Université Laval. She has published in the area of Wendat visual arts traditions and Indigenous museums and museology.

Brian Gettler is an assistant professor of Canadian history at the University of Toronto. He completed his dissertation, "Colonialism's Currency: A Political History of First Nations Money-Use in Quebec and Ontario, 1820–1950," at the Université du Québec à Montréal in 2011. His research interests include the influence of the law on everyday life in First Nations communities, Indigenous urban history, the economy in nineteenth-century Quebec, and state formation in post-Conquest Canada.

Kathryn Magee Labelle is an assistant professor in Aboriginal Canadian history at the University of Saskatchewan and an adopted member of the Wyandot Nation of Kansas. Labelle earned her PhD in 2011. She is the author of

Dispersed but Not Destroyed: A History of the Seventeenth-Century Wendat Peoples, as well as articles on Wendat child-rearing, warfare, ceremonies, and women.

Thomas Peace is an assistant professor of Canadian history at Huron University College. He earned his PhD from York University in 2011, with a dissertation titled "Two Conquests: Aboriginal Experiences of the Fall of New France and Acadia." Between 2011 and 2013 he was a Social Sciences Humanities Research Council postdoctoral fellow in the Native American Studies Program at Dartmouth College, and in 2014 he held a Harrison McCain Visiting Professorship at Acadia University. He is also a founding editor of ActiveHistory.ca.

Andrew Sturtevant is an assistant professor of history at the University of Wisconsin–Eau Claire, having received his PhD from the College of William and Mary in 2011. His dissertation, "Jealous Neighbors: Rivalry and Alliance among the Native Communities of Detroit, 1701–1766," explores how the relationships between the discrete Native peoples living at the post, including the Wendats, shaped the colonial experience there. His article "'Inseparable Companions' and Irreconcilable Enemies: The Hurons and Odawas of French Détroit, 1701–1738" appeared in the journal *Ethnohistory* in 2013.

WENDAT CONFEDERACY MEMBERS

Sallie Cotter Andrews (Tewatronyahkwa ["Lifting the Sky"]—Deer Clan) is a citizen of the Wyandotte Nation (Oklahoma). She is one of the Wyandotte Nation's historians and faithkeepers, and while her entire life she has known she was a Wyandotte, for the past twenty-five years she has actively served the tribe in the area of history and now in the traditional longhouse. In her private life, Sallie is a wife, mother, and grandmother of two boys, and in her professional life she works part-time as the historic preservation manager for the city of Grapevine, Texas.

Darren English is a member of the Wyandot Nation of Kansas (WNK). He has been the acting coordinator of the WNK Cultural Committee since 1994 and is the current creator and manager of the WNK website. He is an artist and avid researcher of Wendat and Wyandot history. He lives in San Francisco.

Janith English (Atrondahwatee ["an important task is picked up"]) is privileged to have spent the past twenty years serving the Wyandot Nation of Kansas as Second and Principal Chief. Her career in behavioral health, managerial, and hospice nursing has led her toward a concern for the implications of multigenerational effects of trauma, grief, and diaspora.

Jonathan Lainey (Nation huronne-wendat) was born in Wendake and is a curator of First Peoples at the Canadian Museum of History. His principal research interests address the social, cultural, and political history of Indigenous peoples in Quebec and in Canada, as well as the study of material culture and its interpretation. He is the author of *La "monnaie des Sauvages": les colliers de wampum d'hier à aujourd'hui* and, with Marshall Joseph Becker, *The White Dog Sacrifice: A Post-1800 Rite with an Ornamental Use for Wampum*. Lainey has also published book chapters and articles on wampum belts and on Indigenous peoples in general.

John Nichols (Wyandot Nation of Kansas) has an MA in history with a concentration in Museum Studies from the University of Kansas. He is the archivist for the Wyandot Nation of Kansas and has spent the last twenty years working to rebuild the Nation's archives to help tell the Wyandot story. He has worked with the Wyandotte County Historical Society as well as the Nation to preserve and share the stories. He helped with the formation and draft for Freedom's Frontier National Heritage Area, the Enduring Struggle for Freedom. He is currently working on projects with Freedom's Frontier, the Franklin County, Kansas Historical Society, and the Black Jack Battlefield Trust to help share the history of First Nations' involvement in the US struggle against the expansion of slavery.

Beverlee Ann Pettit is a daughter of the Wyandotte Nation of Oklahoma, sister to the Longhouse Women, and granddaughter to the history of the Wendat Nation. She is a poet, storyteller, artist, freelance writer, musician, and seeker of wisdom without regard to the culture of man. She has worked in service of all tribes for twenty-three years in human resources for the Bureau of Indian Affairs and the Indian Health Service, as well as ten years to the service of tribal peoples in the private sector.

Judith Pidgeon-Kukowski (Kwendae'to' ["She knows the Great Voice"]— Deer Clan) (Wyandot of Anderdon Nation) is a retired bank teller, mother of

four, and grandmother of thirteen. She presently serves the Wyandot of Anderdon Nation as a genealogist and historian and member of the Council.
Her genealogy work began more than forty years ago and prior to her official
role with the Nation. Her goal is to return her grandmothers to their proper
place in the history of her people.

Linda Sioui (Nation huronne-wendat) was born in Montreal. Of Wendat
origin, she is interested in the culture and heritage issues of her people. She holds
a bachelor's degree in sociology from the University of Ottawa and a master's
degree in anthropology from Université Laval. In 1983 Linda worked at in-
dexing Quebec anthropologist Charles-Marius Barbeau's fieldnotes and visited the Wyandottes of Oklahoma the year after, for the Canadian Museum
of Civilization (now Canadian Museum of History). This first contact was
followed by other visits. Identity issues relating to the revitalization of the
ancestral language, as well as material culture, have been a constant interest.
She is presently working as a project analyst for the First Nations Education
Council, a regional organization based in Wendake, Quebec.

Index

Page references in *italics* indicate illustrations.